ALL · IN · ONE

Google Cloud Certified Associate Cloud Engineer

EXAM GUIDE

Jack Hyman

Mc Graw Hill

New York   Chicago   San Francisco
Athens   London   Madrid   Mexico City
Milan   New Delhi   Singapore   Sydney   Toronto

1 2 3 4 5 6 7 8 9   LCR   24 23 22 21 20

Library of Congress Control Number: 2020914758

ISBN   978-1-260-47345-2
MHID   1-260-47345-7

Sponsoring Editor Lisa McClain	**Technical Editor** Richard Foltak	**Production Supervisor** Lynn M. Messina
Editorial Supervisor Janet Walden	**Copy Editor** Bart Reed	**Composition** KnowledgeWorks Global Ltd
Project Manager Garima Poddar, KnowledgeWorks Global Ltd	**Proofreader** Rick Camp	**Illustration** KnowledgeWorks Global Ltd
Acquisitions Coordinator Emily Walters	**Indexer** Ted Laux	**Art Director, Cover** Jeff Weeks

Hola Ada
Was Here

:)

d Emily:
as I do.

ABOUT THE AUTHOR

Jack Hyman is the founder of HyerTek, a technology consulting and research services firm specializing in ERP, CRM, cloud computing, information security, and marketing automation solutions for the private sector and government agencies in North America. He is an enterprise technology expert with over 20 years of experience in digital and cloud transformation, collaborative computing, usability engineering, blockchain, and systems integration. During his extensive IT career, Jack has led US federal government agencies and global enterprises through multiyear technology transformation projects. Before founding HyerTek, Jack worked for Oracle and IBM. As an IT professional and educator since 2002, Jack has authored numerous publications, provided peer-review guidance for scholarly journals, and developed training courseware. He has earned technical certifications by vendors such as Google, Microsoft, IBM, and HubSpot. Since 2004, he has served as an adjunct faculty member at The George Washington University, The American University, and Trinity Washington University. Presently, he is an associate professor of Information Technology and Global Business with Blockchain Technology at the University of the Cumberlands and is an active member of both the ACM and IEEE communities. Hyman holds a PhD in Information Systems from Nova Southeastern University.

About the Technical Editor

Richard Foltak is VP, Head of Cloud for Dito (ditoweb.com, a Google Premier Partner). Richard focuses on enriching Dito clients' business value streams in embracing and optimizing leading cloud technologies within their practices. Richard holds a B.Eng and an MBA, along with numerous industry certifications, including those in infrastructure architecture, data engineering, data analytics, machine learning, DevOps, networking, cybersecurity, IT governance, and ITIL4. His professional background includes being Chief Architect at Deloitte Consulting, Distinguished Architect at Verizon Data, and Senior Tech Leader at Cisco Systems.

CONTENTS AT A GLANCE

CONTENTS

INTRODUCTION

Google Cloud Platform (GCP) is a globally recognized public cloud hosting platform. The platform provides services such as compute capacity, data storage, networking, monitoring and logging, and specialized applications. GCP can meet the demands of developers, engineers, and end users looking for a highly reliable, scalable, and affordable way to build, test, and deploy IT solutions. Businesses, organizations, and individuals looking for a wide range of cloud computing options can often launch complete functional systems in minutes. Users can also store virtually unlimited data and implement a robust network infrastructure to manage highly distributed technical needs. Any organization that selects GCP as its cloud platform of choice can choose services using a combination of tools, including a graphical user interface–based (GUI-based) web browser experience via Cloud Console, command-line tools such as Cloud SDK and Cloud Shell, and application programming interfaces (APIs) for handling resources within a cloud setting. The platform offers an array of technical options, including storage, industry-targeted applications, and computing options intended for virtualized consumption.

As a Certified Associate Cloud Engineer, you must understand how to deploy and manage applications as well as provision services in GCP. Google expects you to understand the way it structures its cloud platform, starting with user identity and access management. Also, the cloud engineer must articulate the required skills to deploy numerous infrastructure types, storage, networking, monitoring, and services.

About the Exam

The Associate Cloud Engineer exam contains 50 multiple-choice questions. You have two hours to complete the exam. Whether you are taking the exam in a testing center or using the online-proctored platform, the type of questions will be the same. The exam is intended for those individuals who create, deploy, and manage cloud infrastructures and resources using GCP. While Google states no prerequisite skills are necessary to take the exam, you should be very comfortable using the GCP environment in an administrative capacity for at least six months.

As a cloud engineer, you should be familiar with how to handle, with hands-on experience, each exam objective using the Cloud Console or command-line tools such as Cloud Shell and Cloud SDK. The exam itself does not ask you any direct definitions; all questions are written using a use-case approach. Google indicates that for the Associate Cloud Engineer certification, you should be familiar the following:

- Setting up a cloud solution environment
- Planning and configuring a cloud solution
- Deploying and implementing a cloud solution

- Ensuring successful operation of a cloud solution
- Configuring access and security

There are numerous other subtopics within these five critical areas, including storage, networking, and operations management.

Each area listed in the exam objectives is covered proportionally in a multiple-choice or multiple-select format. Google does not specify what it takes to earn a pass/fail grade but instead tells you at the end of the exam if you pass or fail. You can assume that to pass the exam, you need to earn at least 80 percent or better, like with other certification vendors.

You can take the exam at an official Google Cloud testing site convenient to you. Alternatively, you may complete the exam using the online-proctored environment, using the Webassessor platform by Kryterion. This vendor manages the exam process on behalf of Google.

Testing Site

If you choose to take the exam at a testing site, you must arrive 15–20 minutes before your scheduled time. You will be checked in by a test center professional who will validate your government-issued photo ID against your registration information. The testing center professionals will take all items from your possession, as you are not allowed to bring anything into the exam proctoring room. That includes food, beverage, and paper to write your thoughts down. You are not allowed to leave the testing room at any point, including going to the bathroom, as this is against the exam policy. Once you are seated at your workstation, the testing center professionals will monitor your performance during the two hours via testing center cameras and direct observation. After the exam, once you click Submit, you will be informed within a few minutes of your preliminary results: pass or fail. After you leave the testing center, you will receive official notification from the Google Cloud Platform testing administrator team within two to three business days.

Online Proctoring

If you choose to take the exam online versus at a testing site, you must complete several prerequisite activities before the day of the exam. Do not wait until ten minutes before the exam, as there is only a ten-minute window to log in and start; otherwise, the exam fee is forfeited. The Webassessor platform provides you with a link to a downloadable application called Sentinel when you register for the exam and choose online enrollment. The application must be placed on your computer and configured before the exam. Sentinel is used for validating biometrics and acts as the delivery tool for your exam. To take the exam, you need a working camera and microphone that are operable and on at all times during the exam. Make sure the equipment works properly and your Internet connection is stable. The testing platform is susceptible to any form of connectivity degradation. Also, make sure any connected device allows the proctor to monitor your facial expressions and hear your voice. Any alteration within the environment may cause the exam to end prematurely. Finally, make sure your workspace is free of any items, as you are not allowed to have anything around you during the exam. Also, your lighting must be adequate, as the proctors will disrupt you if they are unable to see you in the camera at all times.

EXAM TIP I cannot stress this enough: test your equipment and Internet connection *before the exam.*

On the day of the exam, log in to the Google Webassessor Portal. Approximately ten minutes before the exam starts, you will be able to initiate the credential validation process with your online proctor. They will ask you to show your government-issued ID. Once your ID is validated, the proctor will ask you to pick up your laptop or web camera to pan the room. This assures Kryterion and Google that there is no way for you to cheat, as your surroundings are free of distractions. The proctor will even ask you to show them the floor below your sitting area.

Once you get past the verification process, the exam will be loaded onto your screen. You will have two hours to complete it. If there is an issue where your eyes roam to an area unacceptable to the proctor, your signal is weak, or a disturbance warrants the attention of the proctor, your exam will be interrupted. You will need to reply to the proctor right away by responding to them in the chat box. Assuming all issues are resolved, the proctor will start the exam again. The proctor should issue back the time lost during the interruption.

After the exam, it takes about five minutes for your submission to be processed. Be patient! You will then find out your preliminary result of pass/fail. After two to three days, you will receive your official notification.

Retake Policy

Should you not pass the certification on your first attempt, you will need to wait approximately 14 days to register again. If you do not pass the exam a second time, you will need to wait an additional 60 days to register and complete your exam. After your third attempt, you are not allowed to retake the exam until one year has passed.

Registering for and then being able to take the exam quickly are two separate situations. Depending on the delivery method, you may need to wait for another two to three weeks to take the exam once registered. The wait time is especially true for online proctoring, as there are only so many testing slots available daily for active test takers. In summary, be prepared for the retake process to take a bit of time.

Special Accommodations

You need to contact Google Cloud Testing Support before registering for your exam if you have mobility or health issues that require special accommodations. They will then forward the request and approval to the appropriate party at the Kryterion testing center or have it on file when you are ready to take your exam. It will take some time to get confirmation—be it in the testing center or via online proctoring format—fully executed. Therefore, do not plan to register for an exam and assume approvals will be granted a few hours or even days later. You are asked to document your issue. Before making a request, make sure it can be substantiated as quickly as possible by a medical or educational institution professional. Google indicates that from the time of application to completion, it usually takes about two to three weeks to gain the necessary approvals.

Exam-Taking Strategies

As stated earlier, you are given two hours to complete 50 multiple-choice and multiple-select questions. You are presented with questions one at a time. Assuming you spend two minutes per item, you will have 20 minutes left to review and submit your exam. As part of the exam interface, there are various icons you may click so that you can review any question you were uncertain of or did not answer throughout the exam.

A reliable test-taking strategy is to read the question first, look at all the answers, and eliminate those possible answers that you know are not feasible. If you can reduce 50 percent of the choices, you should focus on answering that question before moving on. Assuming you are still uncertain of the response, it is strongly recommended that you pick the response that is the best fit. Once you select the answer, make sure you click the button to review the question later on before submission. Whatever you do, you are strongly encouraged not to spend too much time on a single question because a finite amount of time is available.

As you go through each question, you may be able to glean some hints for those questions you are uncertain about during your exam. It would be best if you marked these questions, too, as a way to reflect on them later before submitting the exam. At the very end of the exam, you will be presented with your entire answer submission sheet. If you have time, you should validate your responses one more time. Once you are sure you are done with the exam, click Submit.

Pace yourself, read each question thoroughly, and pay attention to the nuances of both the question and the response. One word or even a symbol can make the difference between a correct answer and an incorrect one.

About the Book

The *Google Cloud Certified Associate Cloud Engineer All-In-One Exam Guide* is designed to help you become better acclimated to GCP, not only for the exam but also as a GCP cloud practitioner. The goal is that after the exam is over, you can use this text as a technical reference as you work with clients and educate others on the features with GCP. Using this book should be one part of your exam preparation to pass your Associate Cloud Engineer certification exam. A combination of hands-on practice using GCP, real-world experience with the platform, and a review of Google's growing library of documentation to complement study objectives should also be used to prepare for the exam. The exam goes well beyond what is needed to pass; it guides you on how to lead technical operations as a cloud engineer in light of various business conditions.

The book has 11 chapters. Each chapter focuses on a specific topic within the exam. However, many of the exam objectives are not in chronological order against GCP's exam objectives outline. As you review each chapter, you are presented with clear objectives as to what will be covered to help you pass the exam. Once you complete the chapter and any supplemental exercises, you are provided a chapter review that includes the key themes addressed. Following the review is a series of questions, written with the actual exam in mind. The questions all employ a similar tone and style to help you become more familiar with what to expect on the exam. Finally, the book comes with two full-length sample exams, using the TotalTester platform. Each of the companion exams provides 50 questions, which is the number you will have on your actual Google Certified Associate Cloud Engineer exam. Unlike in the book, which has some definitions-based questions, the online TotalTester exam questions are crafted to provide you with a real exam experience.

Understanding the Naming Convention and Use Cases

A book such as this follows the instructional framework set forth by Google Cloud Platform. The book is written to help you understand as much of the technical documentation Google Cloud Platform has on its site, in an easy-to-follow manner across all topics. I have included many practical examples and hands-on exercises so that you can experience the required skills expected for a cloud engineer to know. That said, you need to be aware of a few key details at the onset of this text, before you go through each of the exercises.

I have deliberately created a day-in-the-life organization instead of using the standard naming terminology you would find in an official certification test. The reason for this is twofold. First, you need to become familiar with real use cases, as you are likely to see numerous scenario-based questions on the exam. Becoming familiar with the use-case model is critical to the success of your being able to answer the exam questions. Second, you will have a better understanding of how an enterprise platform such as Google Cloud Platform works. Random naming conventions often confuse a learner when trying to see the global picture.

In this text, I have created a fictitious organization called DynaLearning, whose domain is dynalearning.com. The organization is a provider of online learning and training solutions. Within the organization, the team has launched a new Google Cloud Platform project called eDynaLearn. This e-learning application suite contains a combination of resources hosted by GCP. Each of these resources has a unique naming convention. As you read each chapter, you will undoubtedly see the name dynalearning.com and eDynaLearn appear many times, along with a resource or capability specific to GCP as a cloud offering.

Google Product and Services Background

Like every cloud technology platform, things do change. A few significant changes have occurred in the GCP product line that have not necessarily made it to the exam just yet. The text is based on available guidelines and procedures provided by Google as of June 2020.

The most significant differences between this text, GCP, and the exam are the name of products and capacity limitations. I have aligned the book with the product's formal names in production today, not the legacy product branding. For example, in March 2020, Google rebranded Stackdriver to Google Operations Suite. Throughout the book, you will see references to Google Operations Suite unless we are explicitly talking about the Stackdriver APIs. The API names have not changed, though; the change is to the broad collection of monitoring and logging tools. On the exam, however, the Stackdriver name remains for now.

Similarly, you will not find a reference to a beta product. Please know, as of June 2020, what is published in this book is considered general availability based on documented standards available from Google Cloud Platform at cloud.google.com. Beta products are never covered on an exam, as indicated by Google.

A final note is that some of the service offerings have also evolved during the writing of this book. It was not until early May 2020, in part due to the COVID-19 pandemic, that Google Cloud began offering online exam proctoring with Kryterion, its exam hosting provider. As Google tries to make modifications to its online delivery system, what is in the text are the practices in place as of the summer of 2020. I strongly encourage you to keep abreast of the latest delivery methods on both the Kryterion and Google Cloud Platform websites, found at https://www.webassessor.com/googlecloud/ and https://cloud.google.com/certification.

Book Coverage

The book covers every exam objective by compartmentalizing the various topics in the respective chapters as a broad category. However, a few areas are covered in multiple chapters, given the extensive coverage GCP expects you to know for the exam. Each chapter is constructed with a concise introduction, the core topical coverage, a chapter review, and a series of questions about content from the chapter. Many questions are written using a tone similar to what you are likely to find on the actual exam. Each chapter has numerous integrated hands-on exercises. In several chapters, there is a dedicated end-of-chapter exercise to reinforce critical skills. Such skills covered in the exercises are likely to appear on the exam. The following is an overview of what is included in each chapter of this book.

Chapter 1: An Introduction to the Google Cloud Platform   The first chapter of the book introduces you to numerous fundamental concepts. First, you learn about the different types of cloud computing architectures and consumption models. You also learn what makes cloud computing different from an on-premises solution. The next section provides an overview of the Google Cloud Platform (GCP) and the various product offerings available in the enterprise cloud platform, including storage, networking, identity and access management, and monitoring. This chapter sets the stage for the remainder of the book by establishing key themes and definitions you should pay close attention to as you prepare for the Associate Cloud Engineer certification.

Chapter 2: Setup, Projects, and Billing   Chapter 2 begins by addressing different architectural design options in creating a GCP project, including the prerequisite design requirements that ensure access and billing are correctly assigned. Next, a brief review of identity and access management concepts is provided so that you can better organize and set up a project, including billing management. Once you are familiar with architecting a project in GCP, you must understand how to configure billing. If a project is not associated with a billing account, all users, including a cloud engineer, will not be able to utilize any resources within a project. Finally, the chapter ends with an overview of the Stackdriver API and its importance to logging and monitoring activity throughout a GCP project.

Chapter 3: Compute Engine   Google Compute Engine (GCE) is Google's Infrastructure as a Service (IaaS) offering. The chapter begins with a review of the different virtual machine instance environment types: individual, instance groups, managed instance groups, unmanaged instance groups, and preemptible instances. You learn how to select, configure, deploy, and manage each of these instance types. The discussion includes configuring solutions to be CPU, memory, and storage optimized. Topics addressed in the chapter include autohealing, autoscaling, sole-tenant nodes, health checks, images, and snapshots. You also learn how to fully manage the VM instances using a variety of GCP tools, including Cloud Console and the command-line tool offerings Cloud Shell and Cloud SDK. The end of the chapter focuses on management best practices.

Chapter 4: Kubernetes Engine   Google Kubernetes Engine is the compute option that includes cluster and container management. You learn about Kubernetes cluster basics, including the full lifecycle use of Nodes, Pods, and Services. Extensive coverage of Kubernetes terminology is provided at the beginning of the chapter as well. You also learn more about viewing cluster status and using image repositories. Throughout the chapter, you will learn how to support operational management requirements for GKE using the GCP Cloud Console, Cloud Shell, and Cloud SDK.

Chapter 5: App Engine   Google's PaaS option is App Engine. You learn about the standard and flexible App Engine options in the context of applications, services, versions, and instances. Later in the chapter, you learn about defining, configuring, and specifying application dependencies and files. Throughout the chapter, you learn how to manage App Engine features using both Cloud Console and command-line tools. Two areas of particular interest are traffic splitting management and autoscaling.

Chapter 6: Cloud Functions and Cloud Run   Continuing the extensive discussion of compute options in Chapters 3 through 5, Chapter 6 provides a review of Cloud Functions, Cloud Run, and Cloud Run for Anthos. Coverage of Cloud Functions includes a discussion on receiving events, evoking services, and returning results. You also learn about Cloud Functions integration with capabilities, including third-party APIs. Another topic covered is Cloud Functions and Cloud Pub/Sub for publishing and subscribing to Cloud Storage events. Also included is a detailed review of Cloud Storage events and how Cloud Functions support such events. The chapter explores how Cloud Run and Cloud Run for Anthos are utilized for serverless computing as well. A brief discussion on how to monitor and log data using Cloud Functions and Cloud Run alternatives is also provided at the end of the chapter.

Chapter 7: Storage and Database Management   Storage and databases are two of the most critical subjects for a cloud engineer to learn. In earlier chapters, storage is referenced numerous times in conjunction with the availability of Compute Engine, Kubernetes Engine, App Engine, Cloud Functions, and Cloud Run. You are introduced to the variety of storage system alternatives available in GCP. The chapter focuses on three key areas:

access, persistence, and data model options. Storage models you will learn about include cache, persistent, and archival storage relative to regional and multiregional support. There is extensive coverage on the use of persistent, nearline, coldline, and archival storage. As the chapter progresses, you learn how to deploy, configure, and load data into numerous storage options. Three storage classes are covered: objects, relational databases, and nonrelational databases. Storage options covered include Memcache, Cloud Storage, Cloud SQL, BigQuery, Datastore, Firestore, BigTable, and Dataproc. Additionally, the chapter ends with a review of data loading and movement topics, including data streaming from Cloud Pub/Sub.

Chapter 8: Networking   Earlier in the book, you are introduced to some of the key networking features. This chapter provides a comprehensive overview of all the networking services a cloud engineer should be familiar with in deploying GCP cloud capabilities. The chapter covers networking capabilities such as IP addresses, network types, CIDR blocks, Virtual Private Clouds (VPCs), virtual private networks (VPNs), Cloud DNS and routing management, and peering. Using the definitions as a framework for success, you will learn how to configure network-specific features in GCP, including VPC types, firewall rules, VPN options, and load balancers. The end of the chapter addresses the configuration of Cloud DNS.

Chapter 9: Deployment Management   Google Cloud Marketplace is where you would be able to access preconfigured solutions and services for your GCP environment. The chapter addresses Marketplace offerings, including how to browse, filter, deploy, and remove applications from Cloud Marketplace. The second half of the chapter covers Deployment Manager, with specific emphasis on template automation and deployment of applications. As part of Deployment Manager, you learn how to provision and configure resources using both Cloud Console and the command-line tools available in GCP.

Chapter 10: Access and Security   This chapter focuses on identity management, access controls, and data protection using various methods, including establishing identities, roles, and groups. You also become familiar with identity and access management naming practices, which are used for virtual machine instances, for service accounts, and across projects. A section of the chapter covers how to configure service accounts under various conditions. The end of the chapter provides insights into auditing access for projects.

Chapter 11: Operations and Pricing   The last chapter in the book covers a range of capabilities offered in the Google Operations Suite, formerly known as Stackdriver. Features covered include alert management, logging, tracing, and debugging. While the service offering is called Google Operations Suite, the products throughout the chapter follow the current Google naming convention, using API names with the Stackdriver extension. The Stackdriver platform allows for a cloud engineer to efficiently monitor services across their GCP environment. The final topic covered in the book is the Pricing Calculator. It is an essential tool in estimating the pricing for GCP resources.

Objective Map

The objective map included in Appendix A has been constructed to help you cross-reference the official exam objectives from Google with the relevant coverage in the book. Official Exam Objectives have been provided exactly as Google has presented them, with the corresponding chapter and section title references in the book that cover those objectives.

Supplementary Online Exam Tool

Using this book alone is just one step in preparing for the Associate Cloud Engineer certification exam. McGraw Hill includes a digital practice exam preparation solution, featuring the TotalTester exam software, which allows you to generate a complete practice exam or to generate quizzes by chapter or exam domain. See Appendix B for more information.

ACKNOWLEDGMENTS

Writing a book is an extraordinary effort that requires not just the author, but the help of many talented experts. It was a privilege to work with so many exceptional individuals during this project.

I am very grateful to Lisa McClain, sponsoring editor at McGraw Hill, and Carole Jelen, VP of Waterside Productions. Carole and Lisa provided me this opportunity to take their idea and create a rich learning experience for a well-respected brand and its technology platform. Throughout the entire authoring process, both of them made sure I had every resource available to get to the finish line on time. Their patience, wisdom, and guidance have shaped so much of the final product, one that would be vastly different if I had completed the effort solo.

As an author, you are only as good as the technical experts you surround yourself with. The McGraw Hill team provided me a best-in-class technical editor, Richard Foltak. As an author, you naturally assume you have captured everything the reader needs to know, which makes sense. Rich's advice and sound judgment made this project a much stronger effort by offering the team solid examples and content refinements to help you, the reader.

Thank you to Emily Walters, the editorial coordinator for this project. You made the entire process to production seem easy, although I know there were many moving parts and questions from me. To Janet Walden and Bart Reed from the McGraw Hill editorial team, thank you for making sure the text was clear and accurate. Finally, thank you to the production team at KnowledgeWorks Global Ltd, especially Garima Poddar. I appreciate your efforts in taking the written word and making it come to life in book format.

It is truly an honor and a great fortune to be among a group of highly respected professionals in the IT and education communities. To those of you who I have had the honor of working and collaborating with or serving professionally, thank you for all you have taught and instilled in me over the past two decades. I am especially appreciative of the faculty leadership at the University of the Cumberlands and The George Washington University for allowing me to share my passion for education and love of technology with learners worldwide over the years.

No project of this magnitude is ever complete without a personal cheerleading squad. My family and friends have been my biggest champions, but during this project, they outdid themselves. The most important three people within the group are my wife, Debbie, and my children, Jeremy and Emily. Thank you for allowing me to take on this labor of love and see it through to the very end. This project would not be complete without you. I love the three of you to pieces.

An Introduction to the Google Cloud Platform

In this chapter you will learn to

- Describe the different cloud computing business architectures
- Describe the different cloud computing consumption models (pricing)
- Understand the difference between data center computing and cloud computing
- Become familiar with key features found in the Google Cloud Platform

Cloud computing allows for the consumption of IT resources in an on-demand capacity. A cloud provider offers IT resources that an organization would typically need to purchase for the data center. The provider offers a range of services, including storage, compute capacity, networking, analytic packages, processing capacity, application development, machine learning, artificial intelligence, security, and managed operations. Instead of having to make significant capital IT investments every few years, an organization could make computing an operational expense.

Cloud computing enables forward-looking organizations the ability to improve flexibility, support cost reduction, and focus on the competitive advantage. As you read this chapter, you will see there are numerous benefits to cloud computing, depending on the consumption model and the type of cloud computing environment that an organization decides to embrace. Benefits include the following:

- Resources can be purchased and consumed on an as-needed basis. Utilization can increase or decrease on demand.

- Capital expenditures are convertible to operational expenses. Cloud customers can focus on innovation without the expense of complex infrastructure investments.

- End-user productivity increases are noticeable because of centralizing software management.

- Infrastructure, performance, reliability, and security are consistent across the organization; therefore, integration is more affordable over time.

The next few sections go over the type of cloud environments and services delivered within each model. Afterward, we explore the key features of the Google Cloud Platform (GCP).

Cloud Architectures

As shown in Figure 1-1, cloud architecture consists of nine components: applications, data, runtime, middleware, operating systems (OSs), virtualization, servers, storage, and network, depending on the need of the organization. In the cloud computing environment, it is relatively easy to scale as demand increases based on capacity controls. In the data center environment, also known as *on-premises*, an organization would have to manage all of these functions on its own. It is very difficult to scale quickly and affordably, based on user demand at a moment's notice. By moving to the cloud, organizations can bypass the concern of having to deal with planning for operational challenges and focus on innovation in their IT processes.

When organizations plan out their cloud architectures, they must think through their design using a three-layered approach: infrastructure, platform, and software. Each one of these layers is defined as part of the cloud service architecture model, described in Table 1-1 and explained in the following sections.

SaaS

Software as a Service (SaaS) is the software layer of the cloud architecture model. Instead of software being downloaded to a person's desktop and stored on a hard drive, the software is exposed using a web browser. Accessing the software requires an active Internet connection. Examples of SaaS applications include Gmail, G Suite, and YouTube.

Users of SaaS software never have to worry about development, maintenance, support, or backups because the software vendor updates the applications on a rolling basis.

Figure 1-1 Comparison of cloud architectures

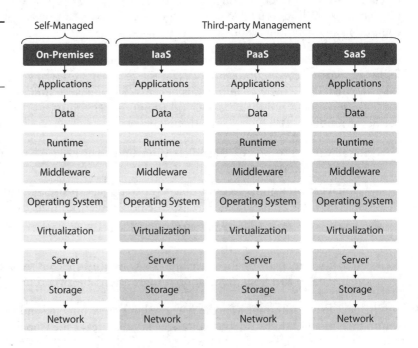

Cloud Architecture	Description
SaaS (Software as a Service)	Makes software available exclusively through the Internet
PaaS (Platform as a Service)	Offers the ability to develop and deploy applications in the cloud
IaaS (Infrastructure as a Service)	Provides extreme flexibility to scale and deploy environments using automation

Table 1-1 Cloud Architecture Models

Outages rarely occur, but when they do happen, users are notified well in advance. There is a downside, however, to using cloud-based software through a provider. Most software vendors charge a recurring fee, unlike the on-premises model, which follows a perpetual licensing structure. Application performance is also dependent on the stability of your Internet hosting provider.

PaaS

Platform as a Service, also known as PaaS, appeals to developers more than any other user group. Developers like to spend time coding, testing, and deploying applications for their organizations. In the data center environment, though, the responsibility of the developer is also to manage infrastructure, security, and operating system support activities. By moving to the cloud, the developer no longer needs to focus on those operational responsibilities.

In the Google Cloud Platform, PaaS features are available in Google App Engine in addition to the managed infrastructure. Additional application programming interfaces (APIs) and specialized tools enable developers to create network management, monitoring, and version control capabilities using the platform.

IaaS

Instead of having to physically own the storage, networking capacity, servers, and operating system components to run their IT facilities, many organizations outsource these functions. This architecture topology is known as Infrastructure as a Service (IaaS). IaaS providers offer the deployment and management capacity of preconfigured and virtualized hardware to organizations that require compute power. Prior to IaaS, many of these organizations used to install and maintain their own hardware and software applications within the data center. However, due to the labor-intensive nature of running an IT infrastructure, it is often more advantageous to outsource this function to an experienced vendor. Companies such as Google create affordable IaaS packages that cover end-to-end solutions for a business.

Public, Private, and Hybrid Cloud

Cloud services can be delivered in one of three ways. The first delivery method is the *public cloud,* where data is stored in an infrastructure that is shared by many organizations. No single organization can take ownership of the infrastructure—they all simply share the computing resources offered by the cloud computing provider for security and operational reasons. The organization is unlikely to know where its data physically resides. The data and applications for the organization are likely hosted in multiple data centers around the world. Commercial applications such as iTunes, Netflix, Twitter, Dropbox, Office 365, and Gmail are all examples of public cloud applications.

Private cloud applications are similar to those in public clouds. The key difference is resource allocation. By definition, with a *private cloud*, the organization has exclusive rights to the infrastructure capacity that the data resides on within the hosting provider's domain. While the servers are not hosted in the organization's data center, the infrastructure that the organization is paying for is dedicated to a given businesses need and is not shared with anyone else. The environment is configurable for specific operational needs without any interference from other third-party application resources. Organizations that have very specific security needs or require their data be tightly controlled are more apt to use private cloud infrastructures. Financial institutions and government agencies are examples of use cases for private cloud.

Hybrid cloud allows an organization to combine data center and public cloud computing features. If an organization requires the use of available applications distributed via public cloud, yet its sensitive data and custom applications require maintenance in a dedicated hosting environment, a hybrid cloud environment is desirable. Many global enterprises are adopting the hybrid model because it combines the best of both infrastructure options. Hybrid infrastructures offer high-level security alternatives at a fraction of the cost of data centers without organizations losing any business functionality. Enterprise architects prefer hybrid cloud solutions because they provide the best combination of tools and resources to achieve business-specific outcomes.

Comparison of Data Centers vs. Cloud Consumption

The difference between running a data center and supporting a cloud computing environment may seem slight, but there are in fact significant differences. The onus of responsibility falls on the hosting provider in a cloud consumption model to ensure the environment remains stable, provides disaster recovery, and complies with necessary regulatory controls for all of its clients, not just a single entity. Even if an organization co-locates its environment across several cloud data centers, the provider is responsible for ensuring operational continuity. The customer's responsibility is generally limited to handling the virtual machine instances by completing activities such as patch and security management. When an organization is held accountable for managing its own data center, all infrastructure and operational responsibility falls on the organization that owns the applications and data.

 NOTE The location of Google Cloud regions is dynamic, with new locations being established often. Be sure to check https://cloud.google.com/about/locations for the latest information.

Rent vs. Own

Data centers house expensive hardware, including server clusters, networking equipment, and disk arrays. The companies that own this equipment must purchase these items for an extended period of time. Either the organizations make a lump-sum acquisition or agree to a long-term lease to operate such equipment. Owning equipment is ideal when compute capacity is predictable over an extended period of time.

Making a significant capital acquisition of IT hardware is not ideal when capacity and workloads fluctuate significantly based on user demand. For example, suppose a company purchases 50 servers. At any given time, 30 of those servers might remain idle. However, for two busy weeks during the year (for example, the holiday season), a capacity spike might require extra server usage. Does it make sense for the organization to deploy excess capital for equipment that it barely uses? The answer is often "no."

There are alternatives to meeting user demand during these short incremental periods. A public cloud offering provides such an alternative to meet the compute capacity demand during peak periods. The short-term incremental cost might be higher; however, the total cost of operations is often significantly less. Why? The organization is not responsible for purchasing or leasing the equipment under capital expenditure terms. All acquisitions are on-demand, or under the terms of operational expenditure conditions.

Pay As You Go

Similar to the on-demand model is the "pay-as-you-go" model, where you pay for what you use as you use it. When you are using virtualized resources within a cloud environment, you are consuming networking capacity and bandwidth. The organization pays for how much capacity it uses. Capacity is measurable by CPU utilization, memory allocation, or storage capacity.

Cloud engineers should understand the pricing model of the selected hosting provider. It is possible to accumulate a substantial invoice for compute capacity due to unexpected spikes in compute utilization. Most applications are more cost-efficient running in the public cloud; however, there are some instances where data- or memory-intensive applications cost less running in an on-premises setting. Therefore, careful monitoring of utilization metrics is an integral part of the IT administrator's role when migrating to the cloud.

 NOTE Although production environments require a cloud environment to be running at all times, organizations that deploy development and test environments can shut their virtual machine instances on and off to reduce expenses. Unnecessary uptime of cloud resources often drives up cloud expenses. To reduce your overall spend, make sure to turn off cloud resources in a development or test environment if they are not in use.

Resource Allocation

Cloud hosting providers create their data centers with the ability scale at a moment's notice. Because cloud hosting providers know their customers' usage patterns through the use of analytics, it is fairly easy to predict the capacity demands if additional hardware or software is required for one or more customer instances.

Whether the cloud infrastructure is enterprise class or meant for a small business, it is easy to shift resources quickly to meet business demands based on systemwide utilization and capacity. Pooled resources can be shifted from one domain to another in the event increased demand is required at a moment's notice. In an on-premises data center environment, architectural planning, design, and implementation are required to make any systematic changes. Such changes could take weeks if not months before a system is provisioned to meet the demands of what can be accomplished with a shared public cloud instance.

Specialized Services

Every cloud provider offers unique services with its platform. Such services are developer-driven, tailored to the creation of specific business domains. Each provider offers these enterprise-class services with a price premium attached to the offering. Capabilities might range from integrating large datasets using machine learning and artificial intelligence to augmented reality, enterprise search, or mobile compute capabilities specific to a business domain. These offerings enable the cloud provider to attract a broader audience of enterprise and small-business clients that otherwise might not be able to create capabilities at such a scale and capacity. Specialized services also offer vendors, partners, and providers alike an opportunity to generate an increased margin on a low-profit product.

Google Cloud Platform Core Features

Cloud providers such as Google offer a range of services to deploy computing, storage, networking, identity and security management, development, and custom development features. Some organizations migrate their data centers to a cloud environment, while others build out their IT infrastructure from scratch. Every organization has a different set of requirements.

Most cloud providers help organizations identify their business and technical requirements by associating needs to one of five broad categories:

- Compute resources
- Networking infrastructure
- Storage and databases
- Identity and security
- Management and developer solutions

Cloud customers typically require services across one or more of these categories. These categories are not exclusive to public cloud alone. They are also applicable to private and hybrid environments.

Compute Resources

Compute resources are made available through both infrastructure-independent and application-based deployments.

Google Compute Engine and Virtual Machines

Google Compute Engine (GCE), the Google IaaS offering, allows users to create virtualized environments, called virtual machines (VMs), instead of having to manage traditional hardware and software in a server environment. A virtual machine is an OS-based environment installed on a hosted environment that imitates dedicated hardware. The virtual machine often has specific end-user applications installed within the virtualized environment.

Similar to a traditional client–server environment, provisioning a virtualized environment to meet the needs of an end user's security is reasonably consistent. Management features of a VM are similar to those of a standard PC or server-based computer. The user controls who has access to the system, when it can be on and off, and what features/ functions are available within the compute environment.

GCP offers many enterprise-class features, such as load balancing, high availability, and autoscaling, as part of the Compute Engine. These features are useful as they ensure operational continuity as well as minimized cost by only running workload resources that are currently in use at a given point in time.

Kubernetes Clusters

There are times when an organization is looking to bundle the applications it runs in a single environment. That means if one instance of an application fails, the redundant instance of the application operates. Similarly, like-kind applications can operate using the same infrastructure capabilities, such as operating system, CPU, and memory capacity. Instead of the organization handling each environment independently, a managed container is often the way an organization handles distributed application management. Managed containers are a function within the Google Kubernetes Engine (GKE). The GKE provides a managed environment for adequately managing all aspects of containerized applications using Google infrastructure, specifically the Google Compute instances, grouped to form a cluster. While the hosting provider manages the infrastructure's health, the organization is still responsible for managing the applications' health. It is up to the IT staff to ensure the applications remain healthy should they fail over to a secondary cluster. Figure 1-2 illustrates the difference between an on-premises deployment and a hypothetical deployment of a virtual machine and managed Kubernetes container using GCE.

Serverless Computing

Virtual machines and Kubernetes clusters require configuration and administration to some degree by the organization's IT staff. There are instances where an organization may want to free IT from controlling system ownership responsibilities. Google Cloud Platform offers three options: Google App Engine (GAE), Cloud Functions, and Cloud Run. App Engine is GCP's PaaS offering. GAE is ideal when an organization is running a system for an extended period and is looking for a hands-off approach.

An example might be a website, a transactional system, or a custom business application. These are typically low-touch applications. Cloud Functions is intended for event-driven applications. Examples include message queues, cron jobs, discrete processes, and triggers that lead to a specific action. A serverless option is optimal when an event

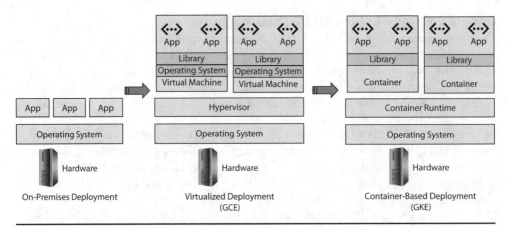

Figure 1-2 Deployment examples of Google Compute Engine solutions

response can operate by using a coded function or through a simple execution query on a virtualized machine or cluster. Cloud Run is a fully managed platform that takes a Docker container image and runs it as a stateless, autoscaling service.

Networking Infrastructure

Google Cloud Platform offers a robust infrastructure for organizations to develop virtual networking operations. Networking capabilities are available for all GCP offerings. You should familiarize yourself with the following six core networking services within the GCP:

- **Virtual private cloud**   A VPC network is similar to a physical network, except that it is virtualized in GCP. With GCP, a VPC will consist of regional virtual subnetworks across one or more data center. The subnets are connected to the global wide area network. Each VPC is isolated. Whether you have a Compute Engine VM instance, a Kubernetes Engine cluster, or implement App Engine, each of these instances rely on a VPC network for connectivity. Public Internet is not required so long as the organization's internal network is connected to the GCP via Cloud Interconnect, a secure way to route traffic without requiring a public Internet infrastructure.

- **Cloud Load Balancing**   Allows for the even distribution of workloads across the GCP infrastructure. There are several load-balancing features within GCP to support scaling and IP-less management. GCP can load-balance HTTP, HTTPS, TCP/SSL, and UDP bound traffic.

- **Cloud Armor**   GCP's built-in load-balancing security service for HTTP-bound traffic. Cloud Armor is a variation of a web application firewall. Cloud Armor restricts access based on IP address. It also offers protection from SQL injection and scripting attacks, blocks activity using geolocation targets, and applies rules at the network and application layers.

- **Cloud CDN**   GCP's content delivery network solution. CDN enables users to request content from anywhere around the world and experience consistent performance at a given endpoint. Since the content is cached through a distributed global network, there are often few issues with latency.
- **Cloud Interconnect**   Enables an organization to connect its networking infrastructure to the GCP through extended reach.
- **Cloud DNS**   GCP's domain name service. The DNS enables the mapping of a domain name to an IP address.

Storage and Databases

Depending on the business requirement, the type of storage an organization must use is different for a cloud deployment. Cloud computing environments require either file, object, block, or cache storage. Each of the storage types is defined here:

- *File storage*, also called file-level or file-based storage, organizes data inside structured folders. The folders may maintain a hierarchical design within the structure.
- *Object storage* is a data storage approach that allows for items to be broken out into distinct units, or objects in isolation. Objects have relevant metadata and a custom identifier.
- *Block storage* is a data storage approach that breaks up data into smaller increments, known as blocks. Each block has a unique reference identifier.
- *Caches* are in-memory data stores that allow fast access to data. Cache access is measurable in sub-milliseconds. Any delays in access to data results in latency, which is a reduction in transfer from one location to another.

Now that you understand the fundamental options that cloud storage is measured in across all industry platforms, the type of storage utilized in GCP is easier to understand. GCP offers several storage options, depending on the business requirement. Attach storage consists of either persistent disks or solid-state disks, two types of storage that can be connected to your system. Blob storage is cloud storage available in virtually unlimited quantity that is cheap, object-based, and scalable. Table 1-2 describes each cloud storage offering available in GCP.

The database also constitutes another form of cloud storage management. Google provides its users with five database options among three database classes (relational, non-relational, and in-memory):

- A *relational database management system* (RDBMS) is the most common type of database in use for businesses today. Instances of data in tables have one or more relationships between each other. Applications based on enterprise resource planning (ERP) and customer relationship management (CRM) commonly use RDBMS systems.

Type of Cloud Storage on GCP	Description	Attach or Blob
Zonal standard persistent disk and zonal SSD persistent disk	Efficient, reliable block storage	Attach
Regional persistent disk and regional SSD persistent disk	Regional block storage replicated in two zones	Attach
Local SSD	High-performance, transient, local block storage	Attach
Cloud Storage Buckets	Affordable object storage	Blob
Filestore	High-performance file storage for Google Cloud users	Attach

Table 1-2   Types of Cloud Storage Available in Google Cloud Platform

- A *non-relational database* does not incorporate a table/key relationship, a common feature with an RDBMS. A common non-relational database in use is the NoSQL database within large enterprise organizations handling big data use cases.
- An *in-memory database,* also a non-relational database, relies on data storage within the CPU or RAM, in contrast to a relational database, which stores all information on a disk. In-memory databases aim for quick response time, given the purpose of these databases is in line with big data analytics.
- A data warehouse is a system used for reporting and data analysis. Data warehouses are central repositories that bring together one or more sources of relational or non-relational data as an integrated collection from disparate locations.

Table 1-3 provides an overview of the different GCP database offerings.

Type	Database	Purpose	Use Case
In-memory	Cloud Memorystore	Web, mobile application, gaming, big data	Cache, game state, user state sessions
Relational	Cloud SQL	MySQL, PostgreSQL SQL Server	Content management systems, e-commerce
	Cloud Spanner	RDBMS+scale, HA-global	Transactional, AdTech, MarTech, FinTech
Non-relational	Cloud Datastore	Hiearchical data, Mobile web	User profiling, gaming
	Cloud Firestore	Next generation document data storage	Real-time mobile, web, and IoT apps
	Bigtable	Heavy read/write events, big data	AdTech, FinTech, IoT
Warehouse	BigQuery	Enterprise data warehouse	Data analytics, dashboards

Table 1-3   GCP Database Options

EXAM TIP   Make sure you review Chapter 7 to fully appreciate the different storage and database options. There are many options that can be utilized in GCP. Several questions may come up during the exam asking you to select the best architectural approach in Google Compute Engine for storage.

Identity and Security

As an Associate Cloud Engineer, you should familiarize yourself with identity and access management (IAM) concepts such as the difference between users, roles, and profiles. Another concept you must become familiar with is the authentication and authorization process of resources, specifically in the context of the Compute Engine and virtual machines. A responsibility of the Associate Cloud Engineer is to be able to administer IAM identities, roles, and permissions within the GCP console for projects and across an organization. The terminology you should familiarize yourself with throughout your studying as it relates to IAM is found in Table 1-4.

Management and Developer Solutions

Most cloud providers develop unique tools specific to their platform to help their customers develop applications, business processes, workflows, or business services. Services might include the ability to configure a server, support analytics translation, or provide industry-specific API functionality. Cost to use such features is generally tied to consumption. Here are some of the management and development services in the Google Cloud Platform:

- **Recommendations AI**   Add recommendations to websites to deliver contextually relevant data for the end user.
- **Translation**   Train a custom model using an individual's own dataset of sentence pairs.
- **Vision**   Three services consisting of search, detection, and classification. API allows for pre-trained models to label and classify images into predefined categories.

IAM Concept	Definition
Group	A method of applying a policy to a group of users.
Domain	Virtual group of all the Google accounts that have been created in an organization's G Suite domain (that is, Website.com).
Resource	The assignment of a specific role to a user.
Permission	What operations are allowable to a user, role, or group.
Roles	Sets of responsibilities or tasks assigned to a given identity.
User	Single person who is responsible for executing an action. Can be associated with one or more roles and identities.

Table 1-4   IAM Key Concepts

- **Natural language**   Train a custom model using a dataset of text documents and annotations.

- **Hosted third-party solutions**   Platforms include Apache, Mongo, and DataStax inside GCP.

- **Monitoring**   Google Cloud Operations Suite services collect metrics, logs, and event data from PaaS applications (GAE) and/or across the GCE environment. They also integrate data into analytics-ready reporting capabilities for active monitoring for best-in-class support.

Management and developer solutions are an affordable way for organizations of all sizes to integrate advanced computing features within their business. The organization may not have the technical or business domain expertise to develop such sophisticated tooling in-house. Google Cloud Platform is constantly adding more specialized services, including APIs and SDKs (software development kits) for public consumption, with an emphasis on big data, machine learning, and artificial intelligence capabilities. Google is also building industry-specific solutions for the healthcare, life sciences, and financial markets.

Chapter Review

In this chapter, you became familiar with the core cloud computing concepts. You should be able to differentiate between the three types of as-a-service models: Software as a Service (SaaS), Platform as a Service (PaaS), and Infrastructure as a Service (IaaS). After reviewing this chapter, you should also have a better understanding of the advantages and disadvantages of an organization moving their on-premises data center to the cloud.

Some organizations require specific security measures or have custom business applications that require a dedicated hosting environment. These organizations tend to embrace private or hybrid cloud computing architectures. Private cloud options are best when there is a need for an organization to have complete control of their outsourced technical infrastructure. Hybrid offerings provide organizations with partial control of the cloud infrastructure. Part of the hosted infrastructure is shared while a portion of the capacity is dedicated to the paying customer. Public cloud options are best for those who are willing to share the same server infrastructure as other organizations. Using a public cloud option does limit the ability to customize certain operating environment features such as security.

In this chapter, you learned the cost benefits of moving to the cloud over remaining in a data center environment. Businesses tend to base their financial modeling decisions on four considerations: pay-as-you-go purchasing, rent-versus-own procurement, resource allocation consumption, and special services opportunities. When you build a data center, you often make capital investments and pay for those solutions over time, referred to as capital expenditures. Cloud computing is synonymous with direct expenses attached to business operations, also known as operational expenditures. Since you do not own the data center, it is difficult to write off the IT investment over time; you are only paying for on-demand consumption. While cloud computing is often more affordable for most organizations, sometimes running IT operations in a data center can provide financial benefits.

This chapter also provided an overview of the Google Cloud Platform. There are five core areas you need to familiarize yourself with during your studying: compute resources, storage and databases, networking infrastructure, identity and security, and management and developer solutions. In this first chapter, you became familiar with crucial cloud concepts and terminology within the GCP. Throughout the rest of the text, we conduct a deep dive into each of these domain areas to help you succeed in passing the Google Cloud Associate Cloud Engineer exam.

Questions

1. Which of the following statements is inaccurate about Software as a Service?

    A. It is delivered to users through the Internet using a browser-based interface.

    B. Software does not require an active Internet connection.

    C. The software vendor updates the applications on a rolling basis.

    D. The software vendors may charge a recurring fee for SaaS software.

2. Which Google Cloud Platform database offering is best suited for low-latency content management and e-commerce?

    A. Cloud Spanner *distributed SQL DB management*

    B. Cloud Memorystore

    C. Cloud SQL —

    D. Cloud Datastore

3. Which Google Cloud Platform storage offering provides high-performance, transient, local block storage?

    A. Filestore

    B. Regional persistent disk and regional SSD persistent disk

    C. Local SSD —

    D. Zonal standard persistent disk and zonal SSD persistent disk

4. Acme, Inc., is developing a new website. The company has decided to use GCP to host the website using a WordPress virtual machine within the Google Compute Engine. What feature would you recommend Acme, Inc., implement to ensure optimal content distribution to its global audience?

    A. Cloud Armor

    B. Cloud CDN -

    C. Cloud SQL

    D. Cloud Interconnect

5. Jim is having a discussion with Jane on identity and access management best practices. They are trying to decide how to organize the employees who work in the New York and Boston offices. What security term describes how IT administrators organize the employees by office?

   A. Group

   B. Roles

   C. Users

   D. Domain

6. What specialized service offering helps administrators evaluate performance metrics by creating useful analytic reports from metrics, logs, and event data across Google Cloud Engine and Google App Engine?

   A. BigQuery

   B. Bigtable

   C. Datastore

   D. Operations Suite — metrics, logs, & Metadata

7. What system component is shared in a managed Kubernetes cluster although it is a dedicated component in a virtual machine?

   A. Hypervisor

   B. Operating system

   C. Library/bin

   D. Applications

8. A company has decided it wants to host its website using Google Cloud Platform. Which platform would be best suited to host the website?

   A. Google App Engine

   B. Google Cloud Engine

   C. Google Kubernetes Engine

   D. Google Cloud Functions

Answers

1. **B.** All of the conditions are correct except for answer B. While some applications have an offline mode, the delivery of all cloud applications is through the Internet, which requires an active Internet connection.

2. **C.** Cloud SQL and Cloud Spanner are the only two relational database systems. However, Cloud Spanner is for high-volume activity, whereas Cloud SQL is for low-latency activities such as CMS and e-commerce systems. Cloud Memorystore is an in-memory database option, and Cloud Datastore in a non-relational option.

3. C. Local SSD is the GCP storage offering that provides high performance, transient, local block storage. Zonal emphasizes efficient storage, not high performance. Regional is also incorrect because of the description of zones. Finally, Filestore is a different kind of storage type in GCP.

4. B. Cloud CDN is a content delivery network, making answer B the best choice. Cloud Armor is a network security protocol with GCP. Cloud SQL is likely the type of database that the WordPress instance utilizes; however, this is not the correct answer. Cloud Interconnect enables connections with GCP infrastructure and an internal organization.

5. A. A group is the highest level in the organization that Jim and Jane assign each employee to a bucket category, making this the correct answer. Each employee is considered a user who is then assigned fine-grained roles. Therefore, answers B and C are not appropriate. A group gets access to a domain, a lower-level part of an organization.

6. D. Google Cloud Operations Suite is an analytics tool that helps administrators and end users monitor metrics, logs, and event data activity across GCE and GAE. Because Operations Suite is the only option having to do with logging and metrics management, it is the most logical answer. BigQuery is the data warehouse solution available within GCP. Bigtable is a highly scalable storage system for machine learning/artificial intelligence–based data. Such data stored in Bigtable is associated with large datasets. Datastore is a NoSQL database intended for significant data document management handling.

7. B. Managed Kubernetes clusters do not include hypervisors. All virtual environments contain library/bins and applications to run. Libraries cannot be shared across applications either. The only component that can utilize all containers, applications, and library instances is an operating system. Therefore, answer B is correct.

8. A. Applications that have extended use and require low-touch maintenance given they are self-contained are suited for the Google App Engine (GAE), which is the GCP PaaS offering. Google Cloud Functions are specific cluster-based applications associated with events, triggers, and activities. Google Compute Engine is the IaaS offering, which is where all virtual machines are created and managed. Google Kubernetes Engine (GKE) is another IaaS offering that allows for server clustering and containerization.

hypervisor - virtual machine monitor (VMM) - software running VM

compute Engine (IaaS) - VM are created + managed

Setup, Projects, and Billing

In this chapter you will learn to
- Describe the different architecture options for a GCP project
- Describe the different account types available for a GCP project
- Explain how to assign credentials to a GCP project and account –
- Understand how to configure billing management in GCP
- Learn the importance of APIs and Monitoring (formerly Stackdriver) to projects

Before we address any of the technology capabilities within the Google Cloud Platform (GCP), it is critical to discuss how to prepare your GCP environment for its first project. You are always required to connect your credentials to the GCP payment system, a prerequisite for conducting any form of activity on the platform. Table 2-1 introduces several terms you need to familiarize yourself with when using GCP.

Term	Definition
Organization	Root of the resource hierarchy.
Folders	Group resources that share standard identity and access management (IAM) policies.
Resource	A compute object such as an application programming interface (API) or virtual machine (VM) associated with a project.
Project	The approach GCP uses to organize all resources. A project contains users, APIs, billing, authentication, compute capacity, and monitoring among its resources.
Application programming interface	A programmatic approach that explains how software components should interact. An API combines sets of routines, protocols, and tools.
Service account	A designated GCP account that belongs to your application or virtual machine instance instead of an end user. An application assumes the account role to call one or more APIs so that a user does not need to be directly involved.
Super administrator	Administrative user who has complete control over an entire organization and all of its projects.

Table 2-1 GCP Fundamental Terminology *(continued)*

Term	Definition
Identity and access management	A method to provide fine-grained access control and accessibility for centrally managing cloud resources.
Role	A set of clearly defined permissions that establish user relationships.
Identities	The digital records of the user or account within GCP.
Billing account	The central hub to associate payment details for all projects. GCP charges users for the utilization of resources and services unless provided free of charge.

Table 2-1   GCP Fundamental Terminology

The chapter introduces you to the GCP *organization hierarchy,* which consists of organizations, folders, and projects. The organization hierarchy must also have an assigned service account, as this is the only way to manage role assignments for Google Compute Engine (GCE) and Google App Engine (GAE) resources. The last section of this chapter discusses billing management. Every project is associated with a billing account; therefore, one of the first steps in setting up a GCP account is to configure your billing information.

Projects and Accounts

To complete any activity in GCP, the user must first set up an initial cloud project and the appropriate user accounts, which includes billing management responsibilities. Figure 2-1 explains the basic structure of a GCP resource hierarchy with a typical organization utilizing one or more resources. At the top, you see that there is only one organization (a single node). An *organization* is the root of the resource hierarchy. Under every organization you have resources such as folders and projects that map to the organization. *Folders* group resources that share standard IAM policies and might contain multiple subfolders or resources. Note that a given folder can only maintain a single parent relationship.

It is essential to understand the definition of project in GCP. A *project* is the foundation for every facet of business operation in GCP, including creating, enabling, and using all Google Cloud services. It is technically impossible to utilize any service without setting up a project, as there is no way to track activity unless a project can associate APIs, enable billing, or manage credentials for Google Cloud resources against a project ID. A project always consists of a project name, project ID, and project number.

 NOTE   Across the GCP, the project ID and project number are unique. Be sure to create a project name that is meaningful and doesn't contain any sensitive data. The project name is editable at any time in the life cycle of the cloud deployment.

Resources are part of an organization, including projects. You associate GCP resources by attaching them to or enabling them within a GCP project. Examples include enabling

Figure 2-1
GCP
organizational
hierarchy

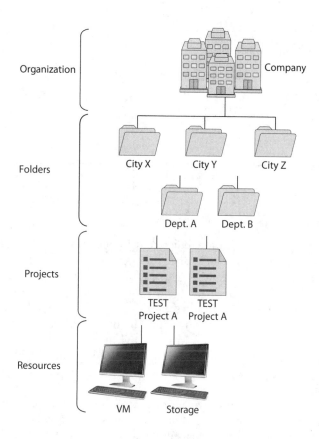

an API in a GCP project and creating a virtual machine within a GCP project. The only way Google can track and bill a customer for services rendered as well as correctly assign permissions is to associate such resources to a project. Here are some points to remember in creating a project:

- All projects are part of an organizational hierarchy.
- All items reside under an organizational node, as there can only be one organization associated to a project.
- Folders organize an organization structure in a more granular fashion (that is, by department) to support permissions.
- It is helpful to decide upfront who should do what within the organization to assign roles.
- Permissions are inheritable, which means each resource or folder sitting below another gets access to its parent's permissions.
- Children permissions may have resources that a parent might not have access to, resulting in fine-grained system control of resources within GCP.

Select from	DYNALEARNING.COM ▼	NEW PROJECT	⋮

dynalearning.com

🔍 Search projec

No organization

RECENT

Name	ID

Figure 2-2 Assigning an organization in the GCP console

Organization

You can build an organizational hierarchy in one of two ways: creating the organizational structure in G Suite (Google's office productivity platform) or creating the security mapping in Google Cloud Identity, which is Google's Identity as a Service (IDaaS) platform and part of the IAM offering.

Presumably, you have already set up a Google Cloud Platform account at this point.

As shown in Figure 2-2, you switch the organization for the project from No Organization to dynalearning.com. In your environment, you would switch from No Organization to the organization name you created during GCP setup. Making such an adjustment is required to associate your organization to a GCP project, a necessity when managing roles.

Once you select your organization, go to the left-hand column and select Identity & Organization. You are now ready to set permissions for your organization. Cloud identity accounts, as well as management of G Suite user actions, can be completed by accessing the Identity & Organization page found in the GCP console, as illustrated in Figure 2-3.

Organization Configuration

A project can only have one organization; therefore, only a single cloud identity can exist. Cloud identities are initially managed by the *super administrator,* who can assign roles to anyone in an organization. The super administrator can even create other organizational administrator users with the intention of managing aspects of a project under a given folder. A super administrator yields significant control over a GCP instance. Their capabilities exceed the typical permissions of a daily administrative user. During the initial setup, best practices suggest using the super administrator as a way to set up the initial projects and accounts. Then, you need a means of implementing policies that secure the super administrator accounts so that access to highly sensitive configurations being available for day-to-day operations is restricted.

By default, GCP provides all users currently assigned to a project the role of Project Creator and Billing Account Creator within the domain. What does this mean? If you create a new resource within a project or decide to create another project inside the GCP

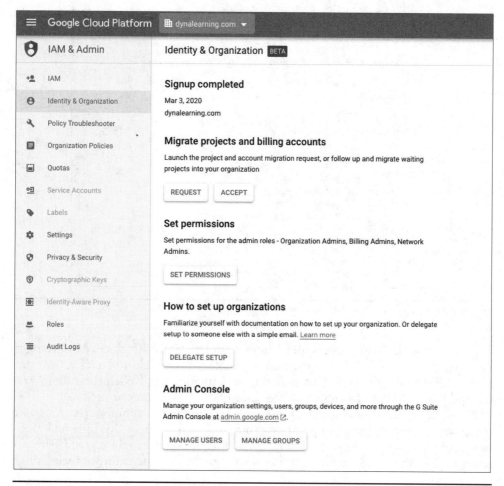

Figure 2-3 The Identity & Organization page

domain owned by the organization, you pay for the services incurred. The super administrator is in charge of the following tasks:

- Defining the initial structure of the resource hierarchy
- Creating the identity access management policies necessary for the resource hierarchy
- Delegating management roles to users within the project

When the super administrator is assigned to the organization, a couple things must occur first: the organization must already be in existence and a new GCP project should already be created. In the example in Figure 2-4, a new project called eDynaLearn has been created and the user jack@dynalearning.com has been added and assigned the Folder Admin role.

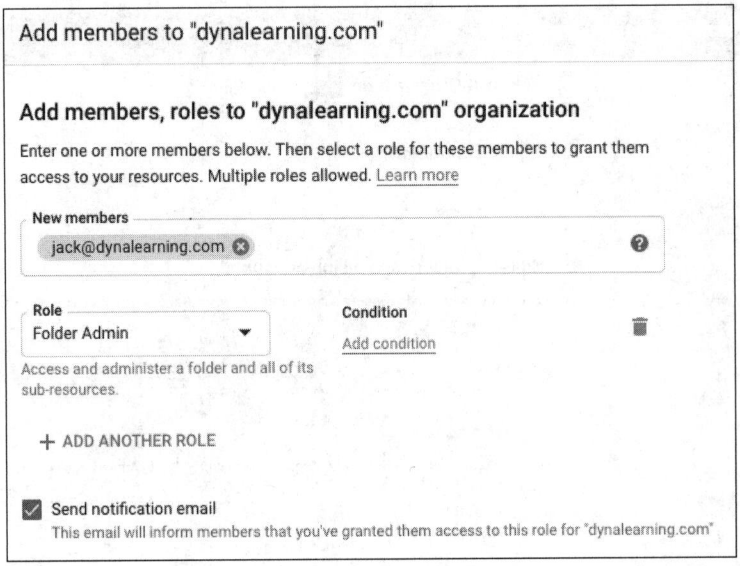

Figure 2-4   Assigning Folder Admin role

At a minimum, the user role Folder Admin, found under the Resource Manager, must be added to create folders at the top-level organization. You should add roles at this time, such as Billing Administrator, Compute Engine Administrator, Kubernetes Administrator, and Project Editor, depending on the scope of your organization's needs.

Once the organizational hierarchy is established, the super administrator can create the folder structure to better support fine-grained role management. To create folders, go to the console and select Resource Manager. An interface similar to the one in Figure 2-5 appears. The super administrator can then configure the folder structure to their liking.

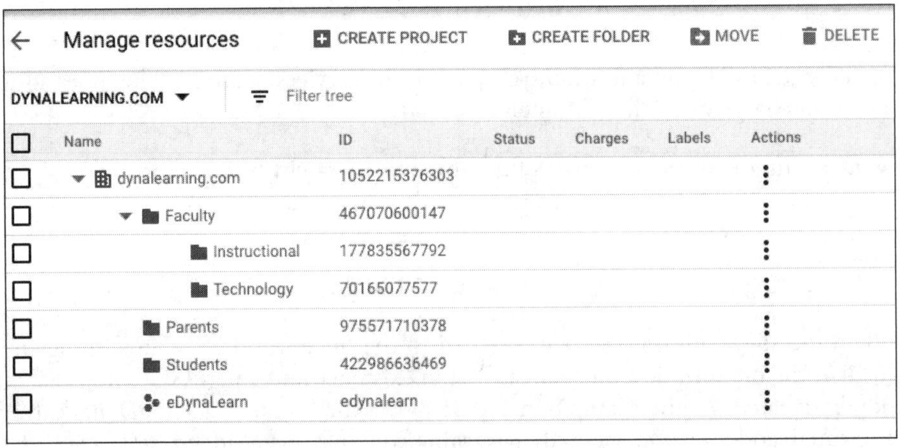

Figure 2-5   Example of how to create folders in GCP

In the scenario presented, dynalearning.com has three folders: Faculty, Parents, and Students. Under Faculty, you find two subfolders: Instructional and Technology. The hierarchy contains one project: eDynaLearn.

Project Configuration

Whereas the organizational hierarchy is the foundation for managing permissions, roles, and resources, the orchestrator is the project. A project handles the resource creation and utilization process, supports billing operations, manages permissions, and controls all facets of GCP service usage. When your organization creates a GCP account, a project called My First Project is created. You likely want to delete that project title and start fresh. As long as the administrator has provisioned you with `resource manager.projects.create` IAM permission, you are capable of creating a new project in GCP. By default, all super administrator users are provisioned at the organizational level to create projects.

NOTE   When you sign up for a Google Cloud Platform account, your organization is allocated a certain number of projects. Think of it as a credit placeholder. GCP generally starts users out with 12 projects. As an organization increases its usage of the platform, it can request more projects if it feels there is a need for additional capacity.

Organizational Policies

You should be familiar with organizational policy controls in GCP to assign resources to services throughout the entire platform. Every resource requires specific role-based policy assignments. The policy service is part of the IAM section within the GCP console. The nature of policy management in GCP is to create constraints on resources, not users. Examples of constraints might include allowing or denying a set of values when associating them to a resource using Boolean logic.

Organizing Security Policy

As part of the organizational hierarchy design process, you must identify who in the organization can use what resources. Often, putting constraints on independent resources can be time-consuming and likely prone to error. A better approach is to create a policy that attaches to an ordinary identifier within the resource hierarchy. That way, the execution is consistent when many resources are utilizing the same policy process.

Another essential thing to consider is that all folders and projects inherit a policy from an organization. A policy created cannot be disabled or removed by an object lower in the organizational hierarchy once created. All policies leverage the Organization Policies page shown in Figure 2-6, which is accessible from the IAM section within the GCP console.

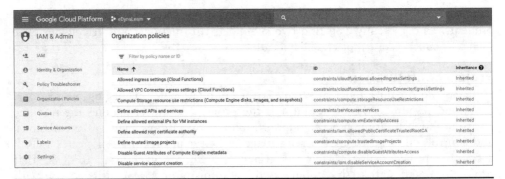

Figure 2-6   Example of the Organization Policies page

Projects

As mentioned earlier in the chapter, a project is a master organizer for all Google Cloud resources associated with a focal purpose. Projects contain resources, including APIs, billing information, authentication credentials, and monitoring settings, among other details. Projects are basic organizational building blocks used to support a virtual cloud environment. Under a project, the use of an organization and folder is a way to organize resources and apply governance within the cloud environment. Measuring day-to-day activities, however, is based on how one consumes project resources.

Once your organizational hierarchy and folder structure are aligned, you should navigate to the Google Cloud Platform console. The home page initially appears where you open the console. Select the option IAM & Admin. Then select Manage Resources so that you can create new projects (see Figure 2-7).

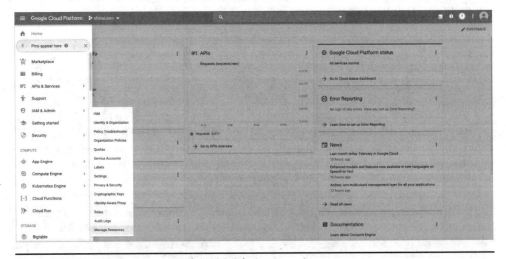

Figure 2-7   Console home page with IAM & Admin menu view

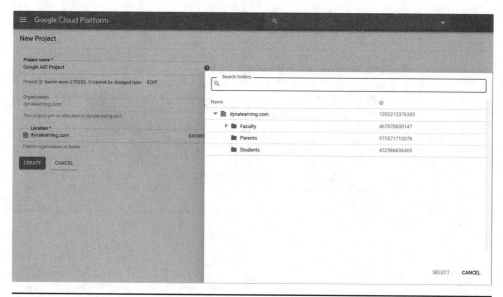

Figure 2-8 Selecting the location for a new project in GCP

Once the screen appears, click the Create Project button. A new window appears where you can fill in the project name and select a project location. The project must have a unique name. The location must point to an existing organization or folder within the hierarchy. Select Browse to pick the location (see Figure 2-8). Once you have completed both tasks, click Create. You have now created a new project.

Roles and Permissions

As a Google Cloud Certified Associate Cloud Engineer, your responsibility does not end with merely managing resources. You must also control who gains access to those resources. The terms GCP formally uses to describe this responsibility is *roles* and *identities*. A role is a set of clearly defined permissions that establish user relationships. Identities are the digital records of the user or account within GCP. As part of the exam, you need to understand the three GCP roles. Table 2-2 defines each type.

 EXAM TIP Make sure to know the difference between the three roles described in Table 2-2—specifically, the predefined and custom roles—as IAM is an integral part of the Associate Cloud Engineer exam. In particular, know the difference between predefined user-, viewer-, and admin-based roles.

User roles are assigned using the IAM section of the GCP console. A project can have one or more permissions assigned. As the administrator, you assign a user and role to a project.

Type	Description of Role and Approach
Primitive role	Basic level of access: owner, editor, and viewer. Can be applied to most GCP resources. Grants more control to resources than users often require. Although this role is still available, GCP does not recommend its use because it is a legacy capability. The primitive role was available long before general availability of Cloud Identity Access Manager. The functionality provided by primitive roles does not align with best practices.
Predefined role	Best approach to securing resources as it follows the principle of least privilege. Only allows users to gain access to resources they require. Permissions are updated by Google and tied to Google-built resources found in the console.
Custom role	User-defined and self-maintained permissions. Roles are bundled using existing predefined roles. Can only be applied at the organization and project levels.

Table 2-2 Roles Available in GCP

To assign user permission at the organization or project level, you would go to the IAM section of the GCP console. The top-level page, IAM, has the option *Permissions for your organization* displayed. To add a new user, click Add. Next, fill in the e-mail address and select the appropriate user roles (see Figure 2-9). You can add as many roles as necessary. The user must have a valid Cloud Identity account to be added to the project. Once those tasks are complete, click Save. The new account is now available on the IAM Permissions lists.

Figure 2-9
Assigning roles
to new users

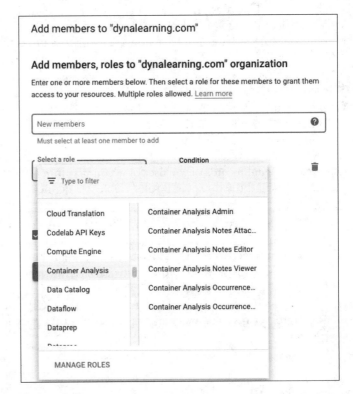

Service Accounts

In some instances, an application is needed to initiate a specific action. A user does not have to complete this interaction; it may be done via an API call instead. One example where this is the case is the execution of a virtual machine (VM). A *service account* is assigned permissions to access only those resources it needs. The service account permissions also limit the resources that services control. Service accounts have a unique e-mail address; however, they do not constitute user accounts. Unique attributes of a service include the following:

- Service accounts do not have passwords.
- A service account does not allow for a browser- or cookie-based login.
- Service accounts are associated with private/public RSA key pairs for Google authentication only.
- Service accounts are not part of a G Suite domain.

Of all these attributes, *key pairs* are critical to the authentication process within a GCP service account setting.

Service Account Keys

Each service account has two sets of private/public RSA key pairs. The first key pair type is a *Google-managed key pair*. The second type is *user-managed key pairs*.

 EXAM TIP Service accounts have two types of key pairs: user-managed and Google-managed. Understanding the difference between the two is critical for the exam.

Google-managed service accounts run internal Google processes on behalf of the user. Such service accounts are publicly viewable, although they are also viewable in IAM. All Google-managed accounts are granted Project Editor role by default. You cannot delete a service account unless a project is deleted as well.

User-managed service accounts can be created any time after a project is created, whereas a default service account is created at the same time as a project. For example, assuming a project contains Compute Engine or App Engine, the default service accounts for both Compute and App Engine are made available as well. A user can view the credential by locating the project-generated e-mail address. A hypothetical e-mail address would be Project_Number-compute@eDynaLearn.iam.gservieceaccount.com for the sample project created earlier in the chapter. You can create up to 100 service accounts per project, including any of the default accounts, such as the Compute Engine and Apps Engine, using the IAM API, the `gcloud` command-line tool, or the Service Accounts page on the IAM & Admin section of the GCP console.

EXAM TIP You are limited to creating 10 service account keys to ensure a proper service account key rotation. At times, it may still be challenging to manage your service account keys. Using the Cloud Key Management Service (KMS) is a great way to store and manage keys in a single location securely. Additionally, it is a best practice to protect your service account keys. Also, be careful not to hardcode your service account keys into public repositories such as GitHub, as this presents your organization with a security vulnerability.

Billing Management

One of the first tasks a user must complete when signing up for GCP is setting up their billing information. Google immediately tracks the activity of all chargeable services enabled in a project. An example of a chargeable resource is a VM created in Compute Engine. Associated with the creation of the VM might also be storage, bandwidth, and database utilization. Resources and services tied to a given project are how GCP monitors cost utilization for customer billing. This section reviews the use of the GCP Billing API functionality during the setup of an account.

Billing Accounts

A *billing account* is the central hub to associate payment information with one or more projects. GCP charges users for the utilization of resources and services (unless free), which are often noted as "alpha" or "beta." Alpha and beta services mean that these are currently in trial mode. Often, these are either free to try or the price of such services is significantly reduced. Users should be careful, though, as there is little indication when a feature becomes generally available. Billing options include the creation of a single invoice, where all charges appear against a single account. Smaller organizations with cloud footprints requiring one or two projects and containing minimal folder hierarchies often follow this billing model.

Enterprise organizations that require a separation of billing details based on an organizational entity such as department or team may consider creating multiple billing accounts. Each billing account can be associated with a specific entity. Only resources and services for that specific entity pay for GCP utilization.

There are two ways organizations can pay for their GCP resources and services: self-service and invoiced. A *self-service billing account* is ideal when an organization sets up a form of payment with Google. At the end of each month, the organization automatically pays Google with the form of payment setup. Using an *invoiced billing account* is the second approach. When an organization is large, consumes enormous GCP resources, or has multiple billing statements under one organizational hierarchy, invoiced billing is a good option. Google sets up payment terms with the organization to pay its invoices. The payment is not automatic.

To set up an account, go to the GCP console. Locate the menu option Billing. Under the option Overview, you can follow all of the prompts to create or modify a billing

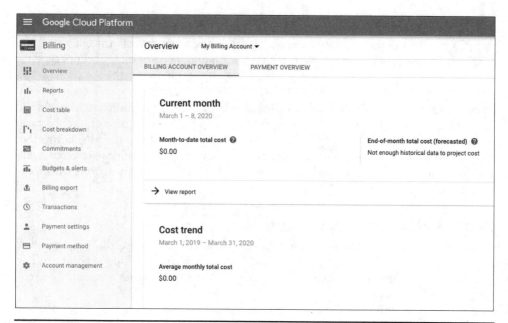

Figure 2-10   Billing menu and partial view of Overview screen

account (see Figure 2-10). An organization that requires multiple billing accounts can complete the creation of multiple accounts under the single organizational hierarchy under "My Billing Account." Select Manage Billing Accounts. On the resulting page, the entire billing account hierarchy is available. You can add as many accounts against a single project as necessary.

Billing Roles

Members of an organization who are responsible for billing fall into one of four categories in GCP: creator, administrator, user, and viewer. Like other roles mentioned throughout this chapter, billing management roles are also critical to remember for the Associate Cloud Engineer exam. Table 2-3 defines each role.

Role	Responsibility
Billing Account Creator	Creates new self-service accounts.
Billing Account Administrator	Manages self-service accounts. Does not have the ability to create new accounts.
Billing Account User	Enables user to link projects to a billing account.
Billing Account Viewer	Allows user to view transactional and billing data associated to GCP account.

Table 2-3   Billing Account User Types

EXAM TIP Make sure you study the various billing roles as defined in Table 2-3. It is not uncommon to see questions on the exam that discuss billing management and how to obtain pricing under one or more account type.

In any organization, you may find only one or two people who have creator privileges. Administrators usually hold a technical role in the organization, such as a cloud administrator managing account resources. Users who can create a project have account user credentials. The only way to make a project operational is to tie the project together with a billing account for payment recognition. Viewer responsibilities are often available for auditors, accounting, and those who handle specific fiduciary actions within the organization.

Budget Alerts and Data Exports

GCP allows organizations to create budget alerts for accounts. Budget alerts are not project specific, because they are associated with a single billing account. When configuring a budget alert, make sure to recognize the overall spend across all projects, not just a single instance.

You have two options in creating a budget alert. The first option is to set a spending threshold. The other option is to set the budget for the amount from the previous month. Once you know how much you want to spend, the next decision is to determine the action thresholds. In Figure 2-11, you need to fill out the fields "Percent of budget" (at what percent of the budget you want to be notified), "Amount" (at what amount of the budget you should be notified), and "Triggered on" (either forecasted or actual dollars spent).

Finally, if you also decide to activate Pub/Sub, click the checkbox. Pub/Sub is a Google-managed real-time messaging service allowing users to send and receive messages between one or more self-contained applications. If you are satisfied with your selection, click the Finish button. A budget is now active for a specific project based on the parameters established.

Exporting Data

Data source and file type output are two areas of exporting billing data that may come up on the exam. GCP allows a user to store exported billing data either in BigQuery dataset or a Cloud Storage bucket. To export data, go to the Billing menu and select Billing Export.

TIP A Cloud Storage bucket or BigQuery dataset must exist prior to a billing export. If this is your first time completing an export, you can follow the prompts inside the Billing Export window to create the storage option.

In order to export information, you must associate the export against a specific project. To create the association, select the Edit menu under either export option. Each export option walks you through the storage-specific requirements. Once this is complete, click Save.

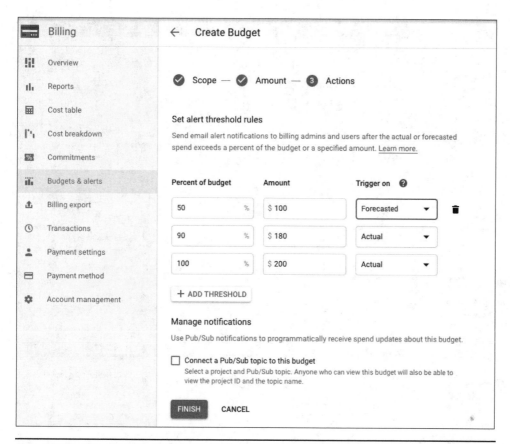

Figure 2-11 Creating a budget alert in GCP

API Functions

Every GCP service offering is programmatically enabled by application programming interface (API) functions. Whether you are looking to create a new virtual machine, build a new database, or manage security, API functions are involved in the execution of each service or resource activity in your project. All GCP services have API requirements. It is up to the user to enable each API on a project basis. All APIs are associated with cloud utilization; therefore, enablement leads to tracking for billing purposes.

During project creation, GCP enables core storage, database, and monitoring API functions. Examples include BigQuery API, Cloud Datastore API, Cloud Logging API, and Service Usage API. You are responsible for enabling the remainder of the API services in GCP. Figure 2-12 presents the API Library, which contains over 200 API options in GCP broken out into categories.

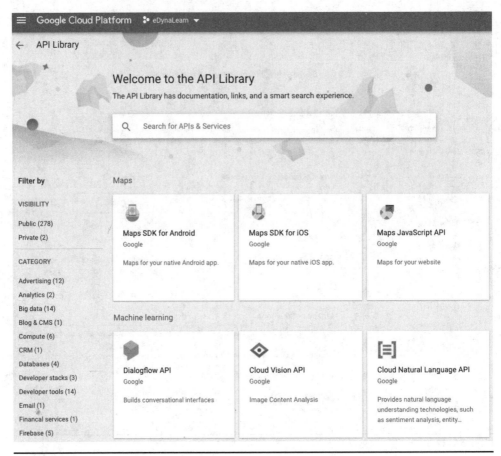

Figure 2-12 GCP API Library catalog

To enable an API, follow these steps:

1. Go to the GCP console.

2. Select APIs & Services.

3. A page with all API and service activity appears.

4. Click Enable APIs and Services at the top of the page.

5. To enable an API, select the appropriate API box.

6. Read the information on the next page on the usage rights.

7. If you agree, click Enable.

Once the API is enabled, you can track the activity on the APIs & Services page.

At any time, an API or service can be disabled. To disable a service, go to the page. Click the link for the API or service that you want to disable. On top of the next page,

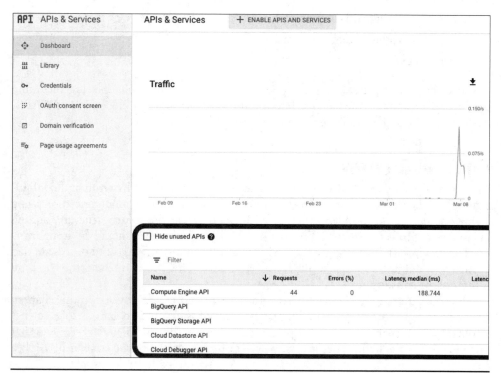

Figure 2-13   APIs & Services page showing the enabled APIs

click Disable. It is important to note that if a service requires an API, a prompt appears asking you to enable the API or service. Similarly, if you choose to disable an API or service but there is a prerequisite, you see a notification stating the need to run the resource. Finally, if you are looking to understand all the activity associated with a specific API, click one of the names under the Name column at the bottom of the APIs & Services page, as shown in Figure 2-13.

Provisioning Monitoring

Throughout the chapter, we have covered the setup and configuration of the projects, roles, and billing. While Cloud Monitoring (formerly Stackdriver) is not covered in detail until later in the book, it is essential to discuss the setup process now. Monitoring is a service that helps monitor, log, trace, and debug applications or resources. When a user starts a project, it is ideal to begin monitoring and logging with a Monitoring workspace. To create the workspace for data collection, follow these steps:

1. Go to APIs & Services in the GCP console.

2. Click the Library option.

3. Search for and select the option Monitoring API.

4. The Monitoring API loads.

5. GCP asks you to create a workspace.

6. Select Yes.

Once this is complete, you see a page that collects performance metrics, including traffic rate, error rate, and latency rate against variables such as credentials and APIs. Activity monitoring is available for both service and user accounts.

Chapter Review

The chapter begins with a discussion of the organizational hierarchy setup and configuration. You should be able to define the resource hierarchy within an organization using a single-folder or multifolder structure. Once you create the folder structure, adding one or more projects to it based on the organizational structure should be straightforward. Organizations must figure out what a project contains, as project resources are tied explicitly to billing accounts. While some resources are free, costs often accrue based on utilization or consumption.

The configuration of roles and permissions is the second area covered in this chapter. At the start of a project, a super administrator must assign users to various roles so that resources are accessible to the appropriate individuals within the hierarchy. Policies that include constraints define user access to system functionality. In the context of GCP, a constraint may include blocking access to specific functionality in a virtual machine or not being able to access a network port within a project. The three role types associated with policy management in GCP are primitive, predefined, and custom. Most users follow predefined policies as established by GCP, given access is limited to what the user needs and nothing more. Primitive controls often provide more than a user might need, and custom roles can be either too flexible or too rigid.

Another type of account is the service account, which is not associated with a specific user but helps to manage resources such as Compute Engine and App Engine. Service accounts are useful for using resources to perform specific operations without user intervention. Service accounts have two types of key pairs: user-managed and Google-managed.

Before you can utilize any features within GCP, you must set up billing account information to associate a payment method to all services and resources that are not free within the GCP. All billing charges are associated with a project and the resources and services consumed. A project can have more than one billing account, which is typical for an enterprise client. GCP offers two types of billing statements: self-service and invoiced. Most clients utilize self-service, which means at the end of each month, they automatically get charged for services consumed by the payment method submitted. Invoiced billing is intended for large enterprise clients or clients with complex billing requirements. The Billing API handles all billing transactions.

The last section of this chapter introduced you to APIs and Monitoring (Google Cloud Operations Suite). APIs are available throughout GCP supporting specific application functionality. All APIs are located in a central library where you can enable them as necessary. Most APIs, applications, services, and resources, once consumed, cost money.

Monitoring, logging, tracing, and debugging applications and resources using Monitoring, a service available in GCP, ensures optimal performance. Setting up a Monitoring workspace early in the project life cycle is considered a best practice.

Questions

1. DynaLearning.com is looking to establish its billing accounts against its current organizational hierarchy. It presently has faculty, parents, and student folders under the organization dynalearning.com. Two subfolders exist under the faculty folder: instructional and technology. A project exists under the subfolder instructional. Assuming that DynaLearning.com does not have a business need for separate invoices, where would a billing account be established?

   A. Organization: Dynalearning.com

   B. Folders: Student, Faculty, Parents

   C. Subfolder: Instructional

   D. Project: eDynaLearn

2. Two conditions must be met in order for a billing export to occur. What are these conditions?

   A. A Cloud Storage bucket and BigQuery dataset must exist prior to a billing export.

   B. A Cloud Storage bucket and organizational hierarchy must exist prior to a billing export.

   C. An organizational hierarchy and project must exist prior to a billing export.

   D. A Monitoring workspace and project must exist prior to a billing export.

3. Which feature is a key component of GCP operations and must be enabled by a user?

   A. VM

   B. SDKs

   C. APIs

   D. Storage

4. Tim has been assigned to set up a new GCP account for his company, Tim Corp. As part of the account setup, he creates an organization. Since the purpose of this GCP account is for Tim to create virtual machines to support his business needs, he does not foresee a need for any folders. If Tim does not need to create folders, what should he do next?

   A. Create a project under the organization, Tim Corp.

   B. Create a billing account under the organization, Tim Corp.

   C. Create a service account for the organization, Tim Corp.

   D. Create a Monitoring workspace for the organization, Tim Corp.

5. ACE, Inc., recently implemented GCP. It assigned a cloud administrator to apply the appropriate roles and permissions in the system. One of the tasks is to establish the billing roles and responsibilities. The cloud administrator is not sure which role to assign for the following description found in the requirements specification: "User shall not be allowed to create accounts. User should only be able to manage service accounts." Which role should the cloud administrator choose?

   A. Account Creator

   B. Account Administrator

   C. Account User

   D. Account Viewer

6. DynaLearning.com has a single monthly invoice for all services utilized on GCP. What type of billing arrangement should it utilize?

   A. Invoiced billing

   B. Credit card

   C. Self-service billing

   D. Electronic funds transfer

7. How many user-managed service accounts can be created for a given project?

   A. 12

   B. 100

   C. 200

   D. 10

8. Which of the following is not a method for creating a service account?

   A. IAM API

   B. The `gcloud` command-line tool

   C. Service Accounts page

   D. Compute Engine API

9. The principle of least privilege states that users should only gain access to those resources they require. Which role is this aligned with?

   A. Primitive

   B. Predefined

   C. Custom

   D. Service

10. Which role is a Google-managed service accoun␣␣␣␣␣␣␣␣␣ account creation?

    A. Administrator

    B. Viewer

    C. Editor

    D. Creator

Answers

1. **D.** Project: eDynaLearn is the correct answer be␣␣␣␣␣␣ billing accounts against a single project. An ent␣␣␣␣␣ many projects, folders, and subfolders. An orga␣␣␣␣␣ correlates with a project for billing purposes. Yc␣␣␣␣␣ under an organization. Billing always correlates␣␣␣␣␣

2. **A.** Billing exports require a means to query and␣␣␣␣␣␣ answer A the only logical answer. All other options do not make any sense. A Cloud Storage bucket is the storage option. BigQuery is a type of enterprise data warehouse that allows for fast SQL-based querying of datasets.

3. **C.** APIs are a key component of GCP operations and must be enabled by a user. There are over 200 APIs available in GCP, and each function inside of GCP somehow ties to an API. While GCP does offer a combination of free and paid SDKs to develop applications, this is not a predominant feature of the platform. You always pay for storage. A VM is a resource and service created as a result of the compute engine. However, this is just one use of the correct answer—APIs.

4. **A.** You cannot create a billing account unless a project exists, making answer A correct. A billing account is dependent on the creation of a project, not just an organization. A service account always maps to a project. Erasing a service account is dependent on a project's deletion. A monitoring workspace monitors, logs, and traces the activities specific to an individual project.

5. **B.** Administrator is the only role that accurately matches the definition given in the question, making answer B correct. Creators have super administrative abilities. They can manage and create accounts, including service accounts. Viewers are only able to see transactional and log data at most. Users are able and required to link a project to a billing account, but they cannot manage a service account.

6. **C.** GCP provides two options for billing: invoice or self-service. Unless an organization is an enterprise customer, self-service billing is generally how it pays for services, making answer C correct. Credit card and electronic fund transfers are two options available for self-service billing but are not specific billing options available in GCP.

7. B. The threshold is 100 user-managed service accounts per project, making answer B correct. By default, GCP starts an account with 12 projects, and you must request a bigger allotment of projects if you hit the threshold. There are over 200 APIs available in the GCP, and you can only create 10 key pairs per project.

8. D. Compute Engine is an API for a GCP resource. It is not responsible for creating any accounts, making answer D correct. IAM API, the `gcloud` command-line tool, and the Service Accounts page are all methods for creating a service account.

9. B. The service role is aligned with the principle of least privilege. Primitive accounts provide too much access per the definition. Custom roles may provide too much control or restrict access to the end user beyond what's necessary. Google manages predefined roles, which offer "just enough access."

10. C. The only account created by default is Project Editor, and you are unable to delete the role unless you delete the project. All the other roles must be assigned by the organizational administrator at the project inception manually using the IAM & Admin console.

Compute Engine | 995

In this chapter you will learn to
- Determine when to use Compute Engine for the Google Cloud Platform (GCP)
- Plan and configure compute resources in the GPC
- Understand what type of virtual machine to implement
- Describe management practices for virtual machines in GCP

A common concept associated with cloud computing is virtualization. The Google Cloud Platform Compute Engine service offers virtual machine provisioning. There are several ways one can virtualize an environment in Compute Engine. A complete list of features accessible through the GCP console is presented in Figure 3-1.

Figure 3-1
Compute Engine
navigation in
GCP console

Reason for Using Compute Engine	Use Cases for Using Compute Engine
Complete control Need to make OS-level modifications Need to move from desktop or data center to cloud without code rewrite Desire to use customized virtual environment	Requires specific OS type and configuration On-premises software that can potentially run in the cloud

Table 3-1 Reasons and Use Cases for Compute Engine Usage

In GCP, virtual machines are called *instances*. Most organizations create one or more instances in GCP. Table 3-1 states the reasons when it is best to use Compute Engine and typical use cases.

Fundamental Concepts in Compute Engine

You associate a virtual machine instance within a project. Since a virtual machine instance is a project resource, it is essential to align the instance properly within the organizational hierarchy and match resources with policies. By default, the GCP console either opens up at the organization level or to a specific project.

To be associated with a project, instances should tie to a zone or region. Think of a zone and region as the geographic parameters. Why? These are the data centers the virtual machine will be most aligned to during a deployment. *Zones* are data center–specific resource targets that share specific configuration attributes. A zone is located within a region. *Regions* are geographical areas that house the cloud infrastructure for a compute engine. Examples might include asia-east1 and us-east1. Zone speed and network connectivity vary within a region. An important activity that must occur as part of any configuration is selecting the geography parameters where the instance will reside. It is suggested that you locate your instance in the geography closest to where a majority of the traffic resides. As you learn in the next sections, you have several considerations during the deployment of a virtual machine instance. These include cost based on geography, data locality, availability, latency, and infrastructure requirements.

Security Privileges

To create a virtual machine within Compute Engine, a user must be a team member on the project or a specific resource at a minimum. Assuming the user receives the appropriate permission within a project, they can assign roles to other users or apply the proper permissions to the resources required to initiate virtual machine creation. There are several predefined roles for Compute Engine that a user may want at the onset that will help with the rapid deployment and configuration of the features discussed in this chapter:

- **Compute Engine Admin**   Full control of Compute Engine resources
- **Compute Engine Network Admin**   Full control of all Compute Engine networking resources
- **Compute Engine Security Admin**   Full control of all Compute Engine security resources

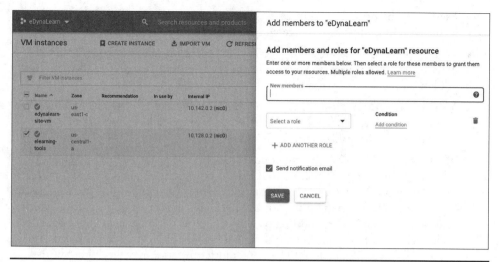

Figure 3-2   Permission modification on a VM instance

- **Compute Engine Viewer**   Read-only access to get and list information about all Compute Engine resources, including instances, disks, and firewalls. Allows getting and listing information about disks, images, and snapshots, but does not allow reading the data stored on them.

- **Compute Service Agent**   Gives Compute Engine Service Account access to assert service account authority. Includes access to service accounts.

Should there be a desire for granular access, an administrator can directly apply permissions to resources versus granting project-level access. This way, a user can only manage a specific resource within a project instead of all assets. For example, there may be two virtual machine instances within a project. The administrator may not want all users to have access to both instances. Applying permissions through identity and access management (IAM) allows for the tailoring of resources. Figure 3-2 shows an example of two different virtual machines in two different zones. Each VM instance allows for independent permission modification.

Virtual Machines Instances

As previously mentioned, GCP refers to a virtual machine as an instance. Virtual machines run within the Google infrastructure. Compute Engine is in line with the Infrastructure as a Service architecture. A user or organization can create a virtual environment that is micro in size or enterprise in scale supporting high availability. When creating a virtual machine instance, you must determine the following parameters (see Figure 3-3):

- **Name**   What is the name of your virtual machine environment?

- **Labels**   How would you want to organize your virtual machine if there is more than one? Using a label is a useful naming convention method.

- **Region**   The primary region where your virtual machine will run. Locate the virtual machine closest to the geography where it operates optimally.

- **Zone**   A specific location within a region. A region may have one or more data centers. A user can pick which of the data centers they prefer. You can find guidance on the GCP website describing each zone.

- **Machine Configuration**   The overarching configuration of the virtual machine that determines the monthly spend based on storage capacity, operating system selection, memory utilization, and services in use.

- **Machine Family**   This parameter has three options: general-purpose, memory-optimized, and compute-optimized. General-purpose is a standard configuration where all options aim for cost and system efficiency. Memory-optimized emphasizes higher-level utilization of CPU and RAM. The result is faster performance, which leads to a much higher monthly expense—intended for large memory workloads exclusively. Compute-optimized is designed for high-performance workloads, not necessarily large workloads. CPU and memory utilization remains high, but the requirement is not as excessive. Storage capacity is also more significant than in the general-purpose configuration.

- **Series**   This is the generation of the type of system processor utilized in the system configuration. A second-generation instance will be more expensive.

- **Machine Type**   Describes the different packaged configurations offered by GCP combining CPU and memory. Machine Type ties back to the Machine Family options, memory-optimized or compute-optimized.

- **Container**   You have the option to create a container image for the VM instance. Only select this option if that is your preference.

- **Boot Disk**   You have more than ten operating system choices to select from in GCP, including various Windows OS–, Linux OS–, and Unix OS–based options. You pick the OS and baseline storage capacity you prefer in this section.

- **Identity and API Access**   Options under this group all relate to IAM and API-based access.

- **Service Account**   You can select if you want to create a system user service account, a compute engine service account, or no service account at all. A best practice is to select a system service account at the minimum.

- **Firewall**   Select whether the allowable traffic to the VM should only be secure (HTTPS) or if unsecured traffic is permissible (HTTP).

- **Management, Security, Disks, Networking, and Sole Tenancy**   Additional configuration and policies to support VM management.

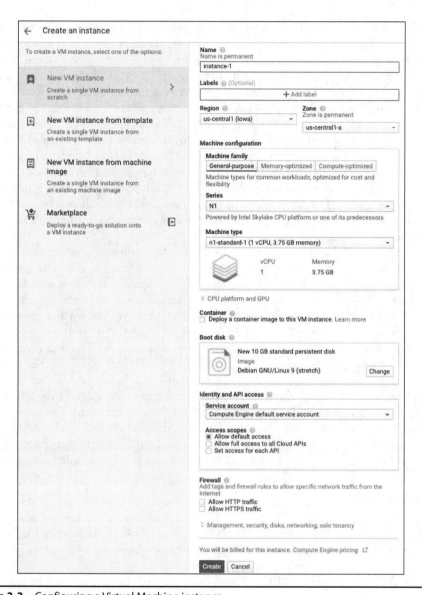

Figure 3-3 Configuring a Virtual Machine instance

 EXAM TIP Make sure you know the difference between the four instance types: a new instance, an instance template, a virtual machine image, and a virtual machine deployed from the Marketplace. You must become familiar with each configuration setting in creating a machine instance. Each of the configuration settings is available in some capacity under one or more of these sections.

Most users create a new image whereby they only install a base operating system and standard configuration on a virtual machine to meet their organizational needs combining a mix of the configurations listed. Custom images are appropriate when there is a need for a specific operating system and application that must run in a dedicated environment and configured in a particular way. If the system configuration can be customized and reproducable, it should be possible to create a custom image from the boot disk of the instance. Without having to start another instance, the configured environment with specific operating system and application settings can be made available to users.

An instance template is a global resource in GCP that is useful if the end goal is to standardize configuration settings such as the machine type, boot disk image or container image, labels, and other instance properties. The virtual machine instance is not bound to the operating system or application configurations. The environment deployed under the Compute Engine requires a few settings, such as where the image will be hosted (region and zonal location).

There are several factors to consider in the configuration of your virtual machine instance. Cost is a significant decision point that varies across regions. The location of data regulation also influences price. For example, it costs more to host data in Europe because of GDPR (General Data Protection Regulation) than it does in North America or South America. High availability is a third consideration should the organization require system redundancy. Focusing on having instances in more than one zone or potentially more than one region can almost guarantee zero chance of an outage, even though one environment might be inaccessible. System latency is yet another consideration. If your organization does not implement content delivery network services, then geography matters. Keeping the data as close to the users who intend to use it most is critical to the success of a cloud implementation. Should the cloud instances be distributed across many locations, the instances should be where user demand is highest, not necessarily where consumption is cheapest. Finally, different regions have different hardware configurations. It is vital to pick the best setup for the intended system need.

Instance Groups

An instance group is a collection of virtual machine instances that are available within a single unit. The instance group either acts as a form of system redundancy or coexists with one or more virtual machines to support a complete enterprise system. There are two types of instance groups: managed and unmanaged.

A *managed instance group* (MIG) enables one or more virtual machines to operate at a given time. Workloads support scalability, high availability, and autonomous services within GCP, including regional deployments, autoscaling, autohealing, and updating. An unmanaged instance group is a collection of virtual machines that are self-maintained as well as contain heterogeneous instances you can arbitrarily add and remove from the group. *Unmanaged instance groups* do not offer any automated features like MIGs do. Using unmanaged instance groups is not an ideal fit for deploying highly available and scalable workloads. The only time you should consider using unmanaged instance groups is when there is a need to apply load balancing to groups of heterogeneous instances, or if a cloud administrator must manage the instances themselves.

TIP The only time unmanaged instance groups are optimal is for load-balancing groups of varying instance types. If you are also balancing cloud instances yourself, you should use unmanaged instances. Otherwise, use managed instance groups because they provide the high availability and autonomous features not offered in unmanaged instances.

Autohealing

Highly available applications are always available and running on a virtual machine instance. If a managed instance group stops running, the MIG upon system restart automatically re-creates the virtual machine instance that experiences errors. The problem often encountered is that the application's health is not dependable. The instance may run, but it usually does not detect system errors post-startup, such as freezes and crashes. To ensure that an application runs properly and remains available, a cloud engineer should configure an autohealing policy for a managed instance group.

Autohealing ensures the system is always operational by relying on health check signals sent to an application. When the signals are sent to make sure the application does not freeze, crash, or load with errors, a health check determines if a virtual machine instance is unhealthy. Should the VM fail or appear unhealthy, the group automatically initiates the creation of the virtual machine instance. Oftentimes, the reasons why an environment is unhealthy is due to improper workload fit, issues with network configuration, or rules management issues. With zonal managed instance groups, where there is a single instance, or regional managed instance groups, where only one instance per zone exists, autohealing only re-creates instances when deemed unhealthy. Preemptible instances allow autohealing from the restart of a VM instance, assuming resources are available.

Autoscaling

Autoscaling is appropriate when there is a need to add or remove instances from a MIG. Load capacity determines the use of autoscaling. A policy can be applied to specify how to group one or more instances if autoscaling. It is appropriate to use autoscaling policies for actions such as load balancing, utilization monitoring, metrics monitoring, or to support workloads associated with zonal MIGs.

Automatic Updating

MIGs allow for the automatic updating of instances. Based on self-determined configurations, it is possible to deploy a new version of software to one or more instances in a MIG. The speed and scope of deployment are parameters that change based on preference to minimize application interruption. A cloud engineer can deploy partial rollouts, which encourage canary testing.

Stateful Workloads

Stateful workloads allow for saving data to a persistent disk for its use with a service. With GCP, it is possible to build and deploy highly available stateful workloads on virtual machine instances by applying stateful managed instance groups. Stateful workloads can be optimized using autohealing and autoupdating to increase application uptime and resiliency.

Preemptible Instances

Compute Engine has a unique feature called a preemptible virtual machine (PVM). A PVM allows for the creation of virtual machines that will terminate after 24 hours. These VMs are available for purchase at a significant discount to the customer with the condition that excess capacity requirements from other workloads can lead to an immediate shutdown of these temporary instances. The purpose of these instances is for application testing, quick batch jobs, and to support fault-tolerant applications. A PVM can save a customer as much as 80 percent in the deployment of a Google Compute Engine resource. Autohealing and autoscaling are available for preemptible VM instances as well.

Instance Templates -

You can create a repeatable virtual machine or managed instance group (MIG) resource called an *instance template*. An instance template requires an administrator to identify the machine type, boot disk image or container image, labels, and relevant VM properties just one time. If an organization frequently uses a standard configuration, then using instance templates is a way to save the configuration without having to re-create a VM instance or group of VMs several times.

Instance templates are global resources. When an administrator creates a template, they are not bound to any geography. Each time an instance template is deployed, however, one of the specifications required is to determine the zonal or regional parameters to which the resource will be bound. A template is unable to correlate with another zone if tied to a given geography. For example, a disk in us-central1-a can only have a template used in that same region or zone.

Sole-Tenant Nodes —

At times you may require a dedicated physical server for a VM instance in which a specific project resides. Compute Engine offers an option called *sole-tenant nodes* so that an instance does not share any physical hardware with other VM projects. A cloud engineer isolates this instance from the rest of the projects within a node group. The sole node can be a distinct size from the rest of the nodes or of similar capacity with other isolated projects. A node group can support multiple instances; the key to isolation is to ensure that a sole tenant is isolated and run separate from all shared node groups.

Disks -Block, Object storage

Compute Engine deploys with a single persistent bootable disk. Often, this is not enough for most enterprise-scale projects. The deployed disks contain the operating system at the time you configure the virtual machine instances. Should there be a need for more storage, there are several supplemental options available with Google Compute Engine. Two types of storage are associated with Compute Engine: block storage and object storage. Table 3-2 illustrates the choices a cloud engineer can pick from when implementing a VM instance requiring additional disk capacity. Throughout this section, you will learn how Compute Engine utilizes each disk type for an instance.

	Zonal Standard Persistent Disk	Regional Standard Persistent Disk	Zonal SSD Persistent Disk	Regional SSD Persistent Disk	Local SSD	Cloud Storage Bucket
Type	Efficient and reliable block storage	Efficient and reliable block storage with synchronous replication across two zones in a region	Fast and reliable block storage	Efficient and reliable block storage with synchronous replication across two zones in a region	High-performance local block storage	Affordable object storage
Minimum Disk Capacity	10GB	200GB	10GB	10GB	375GB	As needed
Maximum Disk Capacity	64TB	64TB	64TB	64TB	375GB	As needed
Incremental Capacity	1GB	1GB	1GB	1GB	375GB	As needed
Maximum Capacity per instance	257TB	257TB	257TB	257TB	3TB	As needed
Scope of Access	Zone	Zone	Zone	Zone	Instance	Global
Data Redundancy	Zonal	Multizonal	Zonal	Multizonal	None	Regional, dual-regional, or multiregional
Encryption at Rest	Yes	Yes	Yes	Yes	Yes	Yes
Custom Encryption Keys	Yes	Yes	Yes	Yes	No	Yes
Machine Type Support	All	All	Most	Most	Most	All

Table 3-2 Disk Storage Comparison

Zonal Standard Persistent Disk and Zonal SSD Persistent Disk

A *standard persistent disk* is similar to a physical disk one might find internally in a desktop, laptop, or server. The difference, though, is data distribution across several disks. A standard disk is the equivalent of a *standard hard disk drive* (HDD), which is composed of magnetic media, whereas *solid-state drive* (SSD) persistent disks are flash based. Persistent disks are not dependent on the virtual machine instance. Persistent disks can be detached or moved to retain data post-instance deletion. Persistent disks scale based on available disk size. An instance can expand or contract with more persistent disks to meet performance and storage requirements.

Regional Standard Persistent and Regional SSD Persistent Disk

Similar to zonal persistent disks, regional persistent disks are available as both standard and solid-state options. Storage qualities are also consistent with zonal attributes. The difference between zonal and regional persistence disks is the ability to provide storage and replication of data between two zones versus one. The objective is to build an enterprise system on Compute Engine with high availability that can support resources in many zones. An example of when regional persistent disks are appropriate is to support workloads needing failover capabilities in multiple zones. When more than one disk is needed to support more than once instance, which is the case with regional managed instance groups, regional persistent disk options are optimal. Using regional persistent disks is also suitable when databases and enterprise applications need high availability.

Local SSD

If a virtual machine instance requires high performance, local block storage intended for short-term use is the best option. The first option is that the instance-hosting server physically connects to the local SSD. When this configuration is in place, a local SSD offers higher throughput and lower latency than either standard or SSD persistent disks. Alternately, the data stored in a local SSD remains active until the instance is either terminated or deleted. Storage capacity in GCP is 375GB per drive. An instance leveraging local SSD disks has a capacity limit of eight local SSDs, or 3TB at present.

Cloud Storage Bucket

GCP offers an affordable solution referred to as Cloud Storage buckets for enterprise solutions that require flexible, scalable, and durable storage without the requirements of persistent disk latency. Unlike the other storage options discussed, Cloud Storage buckets utilize an object storage model to manage data. Additionally, Cloud Storage buckets are mountable to virtual machine instances for read/write usage activities. A typical use case is for a log to be written once to a Cloud Storage bucket but then read many times thereafter.

Every piece of data constitutes an individual object in a storage container. Object creation is limitless with Cloud Storage buckets. *Objects* consist of two parts: object data and object metadata. Data is the actual file in the cloud storage. Metadata consists of attributes that describe the various data objects in the storage. Buckets do not allow for nesting, although they do allow for data organization and access control capabilities.

Furthermore, there are creation and deletion limits with Cloud Storage buckets because of nesting parameters. It is essential to design storage applications that encourage object-level operations rather than bucket options.

Snapshots

Taking a snapshot of the Compute Engine persistent disk has several purposes. The first purpose is to quickly back up a disk to mitigate any potential lost data. Another aim is to transfer data from an original disk to a new disk instance. Finally, if there is a need to make a disk available across several nodes, a snapshot is an easy way to replicate data consistently and affordably.

Organizations will want to create a snapshot from time to time of their persistent disk instances. While cloud computing ensures almost constant system uptime, it does not guarantee unexpected data loss if many people are interacting with an environment in unexpected ways. A best practice is to set up a snapshot schedule. Scheduling is a method in which a backup of a virtual machine is made on an interval basis. To create a snapshot, the cloud engineer will need to use a command-line tool to execute the process thoroughly.

Should an organization ever require the need to restore data from a snapshot, it can procure the persistent disk from a given point in time from a restore point. Similarly, if the data in the system has little value, a cloud administrator can delete all files to free up storage capacity.

During an initial snapshot capture, the system creates a full virtual machine copy. Subsequent snapshots will only capture changes in the environment to reduce the expense of maintaining the environment backup. The housed location of the snapshot determines the cost incurred for the backup. Another factor is the network requirements to restore the environment. The snapshot location is either multiregional or regional. For example, snapshots may associate with a cloud storage multiregional location such as europe or regional location such as europe-north1. Multiregional locations often provide for higher availability and reduced costs when supporting snapshot re-creation and restoration.

There are exceptions, however, when multiregional location defaults may pose a challenge. When there is no default location available in your designated region, the closest region is what GCP associates with your snapshot. Using an alternate region incurs a network charge given the location is multiregional. An example of such a case is that southamerica-east1 will incur a network charge given the location is multiregion us.

On the other hand, a regional storage location gives an engineer more control because the location is specific. A default location assignment is assigned to a snapshot, which is the multiregion that is closest to your currently assigned persistent disk. Using the previous example, if an engineer has a persistent disk stored in the europe-north1 region, the snapshot is stored in the eu multiregion by default. There is an exception, however. If there is no default location near your persistent disk (for example, southamerica-east1), the closest region will incur a network charge given the location is multiregion us.

Images

GCP offers two types of images: public and custom images. Public images are supported and maintained by Google and the open source community. Third-party vendors also make these images available in the GCP Marketplace. Anyone can access these predefined images to create a new instance. All projects can consume these images using the preconfigured settings or modify the configuration at the time of instance deployment. Examples of some prebuilt image instances are seen in Figure 3-4.

Custom images are images created by a cloud administrator and only available to the organization's projects. It is possible to create a custom image from one or more other images. Public images do not incur any additional cost unless there is some use of premium services. Custom images imported or created in Compute Engine do not actually incur a development fee. The only fee associated with a custom image is the hosting fee incurred with the project.

All configurations are preconfigured with a specific boot disk. Should running on a bigger persistent disk be required, the administrator can resize the disk at any time. All public images are frequently updated, including the size requirements. Such features are available in the list of public images on the images page accessible via Google Cloud console.

Compute Engine supports *Shielded VM images* (64-bit images) in some instances. These images are notated in the images list table with the notation `gce-uefi-images` as part of a project. All 64-bit projects must maintain UEFI-compatible firmware. If a cloud engineer would like to use these images, they can filter for images using the `gce-uefi-images` parameter within the project name. Support for all

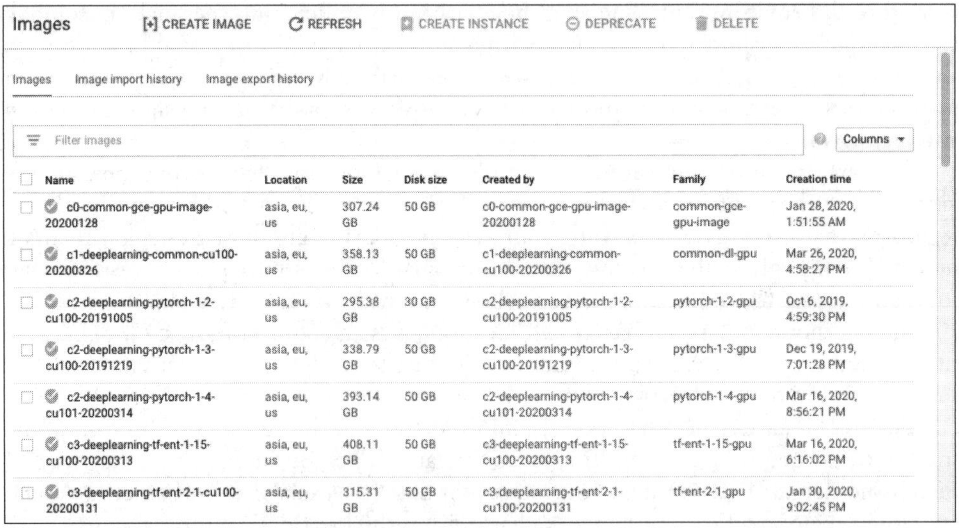
Images [+] CREATE IMAGE REFRESH CREATE INSTANCE DEPRECATE DELETE

Images Image import history Image export history

Filter images Columns

Name	Location	Size	Disk size	Created by	Family	Creation time
c0-common-gce-gpu-image-20200128	asia, eu, us	307.24 GB	50 GB	c0-common-gce-gpu-image-20200128	common-gce-gpu-image	Jan 28, 2020, 1:51:55 AM
c1-deeplearning-common-cu100-20200326	asia, eu, us	358.13 GB	50 GB	c1-deeplearning-common-cu100-20200326	common-dl-gpu	Mar 26, 2020, 4:58:27 PM
c2-deeplearning-pytorch-1-2-cu100-20191005	asia, eu, us	295.38 GB	30 GB	c2-deeplearning-pytorch-1-2-cu100-20191005	pytorch-1-2-gpu	Oct 6, 2019, 4:59:30 PM
c2-deeplearning-pytorch-1-3-cu100-20191219	asia, eu, us	338.79 GB	50 GB	c2-deeplearning-pytorch-1-3-cu100-20191219	pytorch-1-3-gpu	Dec 19, 2019, 7:01:28 PM
c2-deeplearning-pytorch-1-4-cu101-20200314	asia, eu, us	393.14 GB	50 GB	c2-deeplearning-pytorch-1-4-cu101-20200314	pytorch-1-4-gpu	Mar 16, 2020, 8:56:21 PM
c3-deeplearning-tf-ent-1-15-cu100-20200313	asia, eu, us	408.11 GB	50 GB	c3-deeplearning-tf-ent-1-15-cu100-20200313	tf-ent-1-15-gpu	Mar 16, 2020, 6:16:02 PM
c3-deeplearning-tf-ent-2-1-cu100-20200131	asia, eu, us	315.31 GB	50 GB	c3-deeplearning-tf-ent-2-1-cu100-20200131	tf-ent-2-1-gpu	Jan 30, 2020, 9:02:45 PM

Figure 3-4 Public images under Compute Engine in GCP

images, including UEFI-compatible products, is pending the support of the operating system vendor.

Virtual Machine Maintenance

Regardless of image type, an engineer must routinely maintain the health of their running virtual machine instances by implementing a strong patching strategy. While GCP does offer capabilities, including autohealing, autoscaling, and health checks, it is essential to make sure that an instance remains secure and stable. Engineers are still responsible for maintaining instance security posture; this is not an activity handled through instance automation.

Health Checks

There are times when a virtual machine instance may not respond to traffic appropriately. It may be challenging for the cloud administrator to determine the cause of the unusual behavior. GCE offers a feature called *health checks* to evaluate how a virtual machine is responding to traffic. Most times, engineers look at health checks in conjunction with load balancers and firewall rules.

There are two health check categories: health check and legacy health check. Depending on the category, the protocol and load balancing port used is different during the health check. Under most circumstances, load balancing correlates with non-legacy health checks. The exception is network load balancing, where legacy health checks are appropriate.

Health checks must match the load balancer configuration and backend (that is, instance groups and zonal endpoint groups). Three considerations are category, protocol, and port specification. Except for network load balancers, all health checks fall under non-legacy. Supported protocols include HTTP, HTTPS, HTTP/2 with TLS, SSL, and TCP. Legacy health checks only support HTTP and HTTPS. Health checks support three port modes, whereas legacy health checks only support one. Port specifications for standard health checks include the following:

- **--port**   For TCP port number
- **--port-name**   For any named port set or instance group
- **--use-serving-port**   For instance groups, backend services, zonal network endpoint groups, and a port defined at each endpoint

Once the three parameters are determined to complete the backend configuration, an engineer can create a health check. Health checks are deployable in one of three ways: Cloud Console, the `gcloud` command-line tool, and the REST APIs. Legacy health checks can only use the `gcloud` command-line tool or the REST APIs. Health check scope is either global or regional.

Figure 3-5
Compute Engine
global settings

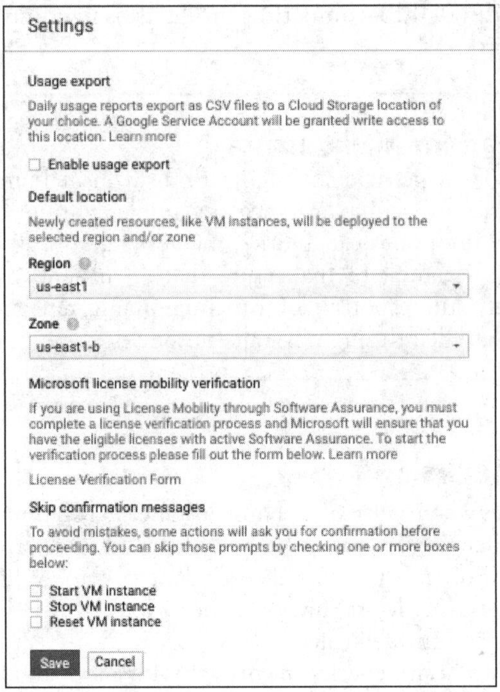

Settings

Settings allow a cloud engineer to create a GCP default for the region and zone in which they would prefer their instances be located during creation. Instead of the administrator having to configure an instance or instance group each time, settings under Compute Engine allow for a global default. Furthermore, if a cloud engineer intends to utilize a Microsoft license through Software Assurance, the key can be entered here instead of having to enter the information several times. Finally, Google Compute Engine often provides a user prompt upon start, stop, and reset of a virtual machine. Instead of having to confirm the prompt each time, an administrator can select the appropriate checkboxes in the settings interface to avoid the initiation process. As shown in Figure 3-5, global settings for Google Compute Engine include the region selected (us-east1) and zone selected (us-east1-b).

Planning, Managing, and Monitoring Virtual Machines

Throughout the chapter, you read about the different types of virtual machine instances available in GCP. Once an instance is in place, ensuring it runs optimally is par for the course. All cloud engineers must consider operational cost, usage metrics, and performance metrics.

Planning Considerations

When focusing on a single instance or a small compute footprint, you can use virtual machine instances to help streamline many infrastructure needs for the modern technology organization. In upcoming chapters, you will learn more about other enterprise-class hosting options within GCP. Regardless of the solution class, there are common considerations across all platforms.

Capacity Planning

If scalability and high availability are mandatory requirements for a Compute Engine project using one or more virtual machine instances, consider solutions with managed instance groups. The only way to support autoscaling, load balancing, health checks, and autohealing is with the use of managed instance groups. Additionally, memory-intensive compute solutions should integrate the use of processing based on graphics processing unit (GPU). *GPU-based computing* accelerates high-performance compute capacity in environments that require intense computational and analytics interfacing.

Operating System vs. Virtual Machine Tasks

There are three options for maintaining a virtual machine instance using GCP: Cloud Console, Cloud SDK, and Cloud Shell:

- **Cloud Console**   An interactive web-based interface that allows users to deploy, scale, and diagnose production issues using a browser. *gui*
- **Cloud SDK**   A collection of command-line tools that support development across the Google Cloud Platform. *Tools*
- **Cloud Shell**   A web-based interactive shell environment specific to the Google Cloud Platform. Users can manage projects and resources without having to install an SDK on their computers.   *command prompt*

All three of these options are useful for virtual machine tasks exclusively, whereas activities requiring interaction at the operating system level should use the Secure Shell (SSH) or Remote Desktop Protocol (RDP) tools provided by a virtual machine instance, depending on the preloaded operating system. Linux OS–based virtual environments include SSH via a browser. Windows OS–based virtual environments offer RDP-based clients.

Instance Monitoring

Whether you are looking to view the state of a single instance, managed instance group, unmanaged instance, or snapshot, monitoring tools are available across each of the respective sections within the Cloud Console. Each reporting component allows for an administrator to evaluate CPU utilization, disk activity, and network load. To access monitoring activity, click the Monitoring link available under one of the instance types. An example of a monitoring output is available in Figure 3-6.

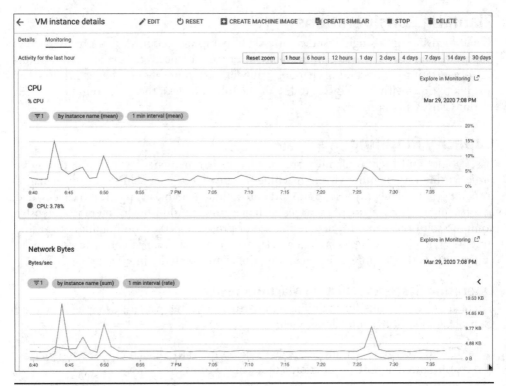

Figure 3-6 Example of VM instance monitoring within Compute Engine

Cost Management

In previous chapters, you were introduced to the concept of billing management against projects and resources. A virtual machine is a resource. It is suggested that you track the cost of a virtual machine instance to ensure that your budget is in line with your expectations. The reason being is that when an instance is available for deployment, there is a set amount of CPU utilization and memory assigned to a virtual machine instance. Similarly, there is a specific amount of disk allocation per instance initially. Should the instance exceed capacity or the utilization spike, you do not want to be surprised when receiving a monthly billing statement.

Google bills virtual machine instances in one-second increments; however, there is a minimum charge of one minutes' worth of usage. The cost of an instance increases exponentially with higher CPU utilization, memory utilization, and storage usage. The type of disk and the location of the data center also influence the price of the virtual machine instance. With that said, if your instance continually runs, Google does provide usage discounts. Finally, as mentioned earlier in the chapter, the implementation of preemptive virtual machine instances is a way to reduce expenses. Should an organization need a virtual machine for a short duration with the intent of disposal relatively quickly, using a preemptive virtual machine can reduce expenses by as much as 80 percent, depending on the infrastructure and location requirements needed to host the instance.

Exercise 3-1: Creating and Managing Instances

In this section, you will complete an exercise. The intent of the exercise is for you to become familiar with the GCP Cloud Shell command-line tool, `gcloud`, by creating a virtual machine instance. You will also become familiar with basic virtual machine maintenance operations and how to access network resources using SSH in GCP using the console.

Follow these steps to complete the exercise:

1. Go to the top right corner of the GCP console and select Activate Cloud Shell (see Figure 3-7).

2. Go to the bottom of the page, where you will be prompted to open the Cloud Shell interface.

3. Click the Continue button.

4. Enter the following command:

```
gcloud compute instances
```
(Error: command/name argument expected)

5. A list of all the commands available will appear in the Cloud Shell (see Table 3-3). You will need to use a combination of these commands to create and manage the virtual machine instances for this exercise.

6. We need to find out two parameters before creating our new virtual instance: machine type and disk type. To locate these parameters, enter the following in Cloud Shell:

```
gcloud compute machine-types list
gcloud compute disk-types list
```

The output you will find appears in Figures 3-8 and 3-9 for your machine type and disk type. Our machine type for this example will be f1-micro, and our disk type will be pd-standard.

7. You want to determine the best region for your virtual machine instance as well. For this exercise, we will also need to select the zone. Once you have identified the machine type, disk type, and specific location, you are able to create a virtual machine instance using Cloud Shell.

8. Type the following:

```
gcloud compute instances create examtools-instance-1 testtools-
instance-2 --zone us-central1-a --machine-type=f1-micro
```

Figure 3-7
Activate
Cloud Shell

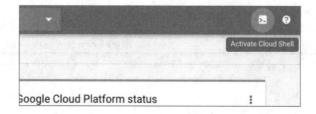

Command Function	Command-Line Description
add-access-config	Create a Google Compute Engine virtual machine access configuration
add-iam-policy-binding	Add IAM policy binding to a Google Compute Engine instance
add-labels	Add labels to Google Compute Engine virtual machine instances
add-metadata	Add or update instance metadata
add-tags	Add tags to Google Compute Engine virtual machine instances
attach-disk	Attach a disk to an instance
create	Create Google Compute Engine virtual machine instances
create-with-container	Create Google Compute engine virtual machine instances running container images
delete	Delete Google Compute Engine virtual machine instances
delete-access-config	Delete an access configuration from a virtual machine network interface
describe	Describe a virtual machine instance
detach-disk	Detach disks from Google Compute Engine virtual machine instances
export	Export a Google Compute Engine virtual machine instance's configuration to a file
get-guest-attributes	Get the guest attributes for a compute instance
get-iam-policy	Get the IAM policy for a Google Compute Engine instance
get-serial-port-output	Read output from a virtual machine instance's serial port
get-shielded-identity	Get the Shielded identity for a Google Compute Engine instance
import	Create Google Compute Engine virtual machine instances from a virtual appliance in OVA/OVF format
list	List Google Compute Engine instances
move	Move an instance and its attached persistent disks between zones
network-interfaces	Read and manipulate Google Compute Engine instance network interfaces
os-inventory	Read Google Compute Engine OS inventory data and related resources
remove-iam-policy-binding	Remove IAM policy binding from a Google Compute Engine instance
remove-labels	Remove labels from Google Compute Engine virtual machine instances
remove-metadata	Remove instance metadata
remove-tags	Remove tags from Google Compute Engine virtual machine instances
reset	Reset a virtual machine instance
set-disk-auto-delete	Set autodelete behavior for disks
set-iam-policy	Set IAM policy for a Google Compute Engine instance
set-machine-type	Set machine type for Google Compute Engine virtual machines

Table 3-3 Available Commands and Groups for `gcloud` Compute Instance

Command Function	Command-Line Description
set-scheduling	Set scheduling options for Google Compute Engine virtual machines
set-service-account	Set service account and scopes for a Google Compute Engine instance
simulate-maintenance-event	Simulate maintenance of virtual machine instances
start	Start a stopped virtual machine instance
stop	Stop a virtual machine instance
tail-serial-port-output	Periodically fetch new output from a virtual machine instance's serial port and display it as it becomes available
update	Update a Google Compute Engine virtual machine
update-access-config	Update a Google Compute Engine virtual machine access configuration
update-container	Update Google Compute Engine virtual machine instances running container images
update-from-file	Update a Google Compute Engine virtual machine instance using a configuration file

Table 3-3 Available Commands and Groups for `gcloud` Compute Instance

The output is shown in Figure 3-10. You can see that two virtual machine instances are created: examtools-instance-1 and testtools-instance-2. Each machine has 0.6GB in boot disk capacity. The machine type is f1-micro, and it has one CPU in the micro configuration. The location is the us-central1-a region. By default, pd-standard is the disk type utilized.

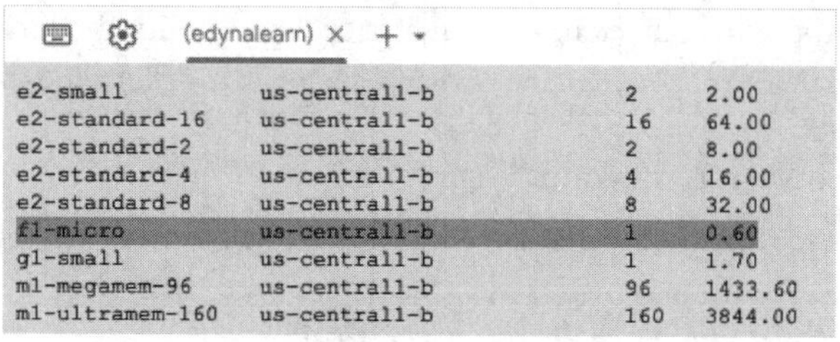

Figure 3-8
Output for machine types list

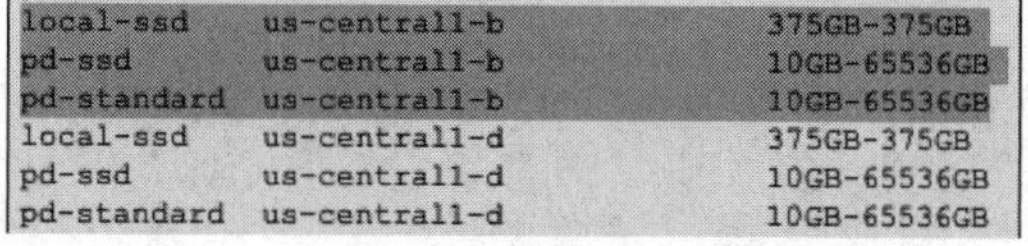

```
                                (edynalearn)  ×   +  ▾

        e2-small              us-central1-b              2      2.00
        e2-standard-16        us-central1-b             16     64.00
        e2-standard-2         us-central1-b              2      8.00
        e2-standard-4         us-central1-b              4     16.00
        e2-standard-8         us-central1-b              8     32.00
        f1-micro              us-central1-b              1      0.60
        g1-small              us-central1-b              1      1.70
        m1-megamem-96         us-central1-b             96   1433.60
        m1-ultramem-160       us-central1-b            160   3844.00
```

Figure 3-9
Output for disk types list

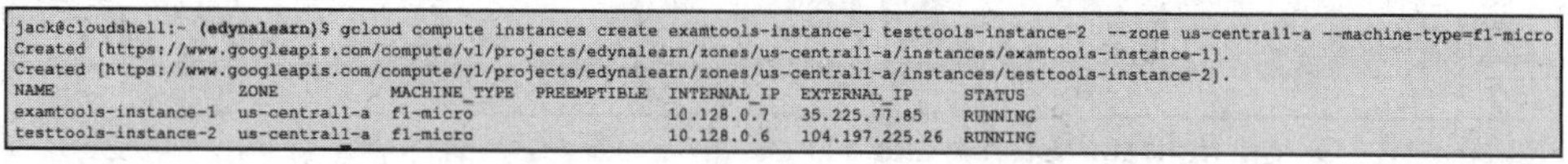

```
        pd-standard  us-central1-c              10GB-65536GB
        local-ssd    us-central1-b              375GB-375GB
        pd-ssd       us-central1-b              10GB-65536GB
        pd-standard  us-central1-b              10GB-65536GB
        local-ssd    us-central1-d              375GB-375GB
        pd-ssd       us-central1-d              10GB-65536GB
        pd-standard  us-central1-d              10GB-65536GB
```

```
jack@cloudshell:~ (edynalearn)$ gcloud compute instances create examtools-instance-1 testtools-instance-2  --zone us-central1-a --machine-type=f1-micro
Created [https://www.googleapis.com/compute/v1/projects/edynalearn/zones/us-central1-a/instances/examtools-instance-1].
Created [https://www.googleapis.com/compute/v1/projects/edynalearn/zones/us-central1-a/instances/testtools-instance-2].
NAME                   ZONE           MACHINE_TYPE  PREEMPTIBLE  INTERNAL_IP  EXTERNAL_IP     STATUS
examtools-instance-1   us-central1-a  f1-micro                   10.128.0.7   35.225.77.85    RUNNING
testtools-instance-2   us-central1-a  f1-micro                   10.128.0.6   104.197.225.26  RUNNING
```

Figure 3-10 VM creation output

```
Welcome to Cloud Shell! Type "help" to get started.
Your Cloud Platform project in this session is set to edynalearn.
Use "gcloud config set project [PROJECT_ID]" to change to a different project.
jack@cloudshell:~ (edynalearn)$ gcloud compute instances list
NAME                  ZONE            MACHINE_TYPE  PREEMPTIBLE  INTERNAL_IP  EXTERNAL_IP     STATUS
examtools-instance-1  us-central1-a   f1-micro                   10.128.0.7   35.192.141.234  RUNNING
testtools-instance-2  us-central1-a   f1-micro                   10.128.0.6   104.197.225.26  RUNNING
edynalearn-site-vm    us-east1-c      g1-small                   10.142.0.2   34.74.25.85     RUNNING
jack@cloudshell:~ (edynalearn)$
```

Figure 3-11   Virtual machine inventory

9. Maintaining and inventorying your virtual machine instances is just as important as the creation process. To conduct a virtual machine instance inventory, enter the following command in Cloud Shell:

```
gcloud compute instances list
```

The output is shown in Figure 3-11. For our system, you can see there are three virtual machines. Two virtual machines are found in the us-central1-a zone, and one virtual machine is located in us-east1-c.

The next activity you will want to become familiar with is how to operate the instances as an engineer. Starting, stopping, and resetting a virtual machine in Cloud Shell is a fairly simple process—it requires a single command. The only thing you must know is the name of your virtual machine instance and the zone in which the instance currently runs.

In this part of the exercise, you will utilize the two recently created VM instances: examtools-instance-1 and testtools-instance-2. You will start and stop examtools-instance-1 in us-central1-a as well as reset testtools-instance-2 in us-central1-a.

10. To stop and start examtools-instance-1 in Cloud Shell, enter the following:

```
gcloud compute instances stop examtools-instance-1 --zone us-central1-a
gcloud compute instances start examtools-instance-1 --zone us-central1-a
```

The output is shown in Figure 3-12.

11. To reset testtools-instance-2 in Cloud Shell, enter the following:

```
gcloud compute instances reset testtools-instance-2 --zone us-central1-a
```

The output is shown in Figure 3-13.

```
Your Cloud Platform project in this session is set to edynalearn.
Use "gcloud config set project [PROJECT_ID]" to change to a different project.
jack@cloudshell:~ (edynalearn)$ gcloud compute instances stop examtools-instance-1 --zone us-central1-a
Stopping instance(s) examtools-instance-1...done.
Updated [https://compute.googleapis.com/compute/v1/projects/edynalearn/zones/us-central1-a/instances/examtools-instance-1].
jack@cloudshell:~ (edynalearn)$ gcloud compute instances start examtools-instance-1 --zone us-central1-a
Starting instance(s) examtools-instance-1...done.
Updated [https://compute.googleapis.com/compute/v1/projects/edynalearn/zones/us-central1-a/instances/examtools-instance-1].
Instance internal IP is 10.128.0.7
Instance external IP is 34.68.28.166
jack@cloudshell:~ (edynalearn)$
```

Figure 3-12   Output from start/stop in Cloud Shell

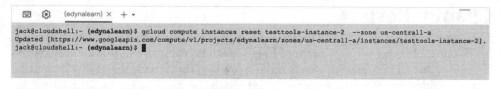

Figure 3-13 Output from reset in Cloud Shell

One final activity that you need to be familiar with is gaining access to the network of your virtual machine instance in order to complete operating system administrative activities. The quickest way to access the network is using SSH when your instance supports Linux OS or through the Remote Desktop Protocol (RDP) for a Windows-based system. Initiating a new SSH session can be done directly from the console window.

12. To initiate an SSH session, find the virtual machine instance you would like to access within your project. In this exercise, we will initiate a session for elearning-tools, as seen in Figure 3-14.

13. A new terminal window will open.

You are now able to create a single instance virtual machine using the `gcloud` parameters within Cloud Shell. You are now familiar with how to manage your instances as well as connect to the VM using the SSH client using the console.

EXAM TIP While there are other graphical ways to create virtual machine instances within GCP, you are likely to be tested using command-line examples exclusively. It is essential to become familiar with the concepts earlier in the chapter on how to create a single virtual machine instance, instance groups, and snapshot under the Compute Engine menu. Each of the terms mentioned throughout the exercises is mentioned across the Compute Engine console options.

Name ^	Zone	Recommendation	In use by	Internal IP	External IP	Connect	
elearning-site-vm	us-central1-a			10.128.0.31 (nic0)	34.68.159.221	SSH ▾	⋮
elearning-tools	us-central1-a			10.128.0.32 (nic0)	104.197.52.27	SSH ▾	⋮

Open in browser window
Open in browser window on custom port
Open in browser window using provided private SSH key
View gcloud command
Use another SSH client

Related Actions

Figure 3-14 SSH menu in Google Cloud Compute Engine console

Chapter Review

Compute Engine is GCP's virtualization platform. Google refers to a virtual machine as an instance. Reasons to use Compute Engine include complete infrastructure control, the ability for an administrator to make OS-level modifications, the ability to quickly transfer workloads from a data center or desktop to the cloud without code rewrite, and the desire to customize a virtual environment once provisioned.

A virtual machine is a resource within a GCP project. A project requires alignment with an organizational hierarchy. Every resource must have specific permissions assigned to operate. A virtual machine can assume the permissions of a project, or an administrator may assign user-specific permissions to an instance.

Throughout the chapter, you became familiar with several virtual machine types, including a single instance virtual machine, instance templates, managed instance group, unmanaged instance, snapshots, sole-tenant node, and preemptive instance. When configuring each instance type, parameters to take into account include zone, region, machine type, boot disk type, and machine family. Each of these factors may influence the cost and geographic availability of a deployable instance. Instances that require lower memory and CPU utilization are less expensive. When considering what type of virtual machine to use, implement a solution that meets current needs and allow for growth to avoid unnecessary spending. Locating an instance closest in geography to where most users will access it also ensures optimal performance and often less expensive network costs.

Managed instance groups vary from unmanaged instance groups primarily due to their ability to handle autonomous support features such as autohealing, autoscaling, automatic updating, and load balancing. Unmanaged instance groups require administrative control. Other unique instance types include preemptive instances and sole-tenant nodes. Preemptive instances are specifically for short-term use with the intent of being disposed of. A preemptive virtual machine can integrate enhanced features, including GPU. Sole-tenant nodes are stand-alone, isolated virtual machine instances operating on their dedicated hosting environment. Administrators separate these instances from a project group with a node group.

GCP makes available prebuilt images containing a variety of general-purpose, memory-optimized, and compute-optimized instances. These instances are deployable through the image catalog in Compute Engine. There is a specific subset of images called Shielded VMs. These images include the `gce-uefi-images` parameter in their name. A Shielded VM is a particular type of 64-bit VM that supports advanced security controls, including integrity monitoring, to ensure boot images are not compromised.

Regardless of the type of instance one deploys, a prerequisite is storage selection. The chapter introduces you to two types of storage: object storage and block storage. Both storage types are available among different types of disks. Except for Cloud Storage buckets, which is a type of object storage offering almost unlimited capacity to an instance, a virtual machine instance does have a storage attach limit depending on the type of disk utilized. Disk types include zonal standard persistent, regional standard persistent, zonal SSD persistent, regional SSD persistent, and local SSD.

At the end of the chapter, an extended exercise demonstrated how to create and manage a single instance virtual machine using Google Cloud Shell. There are three ways a cloud administrator can interact with GCP virtual machines: Cloud Console, Cloud Shell, and Cloud SDK. Should an administrator want to make operating system changes to a virtual machine, built-in SSH or RDP clients are available for use.

Cloud Shell has a command-line language. All command-line entries begin with `gcloud` compute instances when referencing a virtual instance. Create, delete, start, stop, reset, list, and describe are examples of functions to complete repeatable tasks using Cloud Shell. When a user is trying to complete an ad hoc action, it is recommended they use Cloud Console rather than Cloud Shell.

Questions

1. Which Google Cloud Platform feature should you use to create a virtual machine?

   A. Cloud Functions

   B. Compute Engine ‑

   C. Cloud SDK

   D. App Engine

2. Your organization takes weekly snapshots of its environment. The initial snapshot size is 200GB. Two later snapshots include an additional 27GB and 3GB of data. How much storage will be necessary for the three snapshots?

   A. 230GB. 230GB for the third snapshot, as the previous snapshots are purged upon the creation of the final snapshot.

   B. 657GB. 200GB for the initial snapshot, 227GB for the second snapshot, and 230GB for the third snapshot.

   C. 230GB. 200GB for the initial snapshot plus 30GB for the subsequent snapshots.

   D. 3GB. 3GB because the only thing that will need to be captured is the final snapshot.

3. You want to delete a virtual machine instance in the us-east1-b zone named systools-instance-1. What command line would you enter into Cloud Shell?

   A. `gcloud compute instances delete systools-instance-1 zone us-east1-b`

   B. `gcloud compute instances delete systools-instance-1`

   C. `gcloud compute instances delete-access-config systools-instance-1 zone us-east1-b`

   D. `gcloud compute instances delete systools-instance-1 zone us-east1`

4. Which of the following parameters can you use if you want to see an inventory of all project instances?

   A. list

   B. describe

   C. os-inventory

   D. network-interfaces

5. Which of the following command lines starts a server with the name webtools-instance-1?

   A. gcloud compute instances reset webtools-instance-1

   B. gcloud compute instances start webtools-instance-1

   C. gcloud compute instances move webtools-instance-1

   D. gcloud compute instances update webtools-instance-1

6. The CIO of DynaLearning asked his IT staff why GCP Compute Engine is a great alternative from maintaining in-house servers. The organization is looking to virtualize most of its infrastructure. Which of the following answers would *not* be a valid reason for DynaLearning to use Compute Engine?

   A. Compute Engine offers engineers complete control of their infrastructure.

   B. Compute Engine allows engineers to make OS-level modifications.

   C. Most organizations have a desire to move their desktops and data centers to the cloud without code rewrite.

   D. Virtualized instances are not customizable once configured.

7. Joe is trying to optimize his public-facing website. He anticipates that the website will receive 50,000 users a month. Most users will come from the southeastern part of the United States. What zonal/regional configuration would best suit optimal content delivery?

   A. southamerica-east1/southamerica-east1-b

   B. us-east1 (South Carolina)/us-east1-b

   C. us-east4 (Northern Virginia)/us-east4-b

   D. northamerica-northeast1/northamerica-northeast1

8. Within the project eDynaLearn, there are three instances: examtools-instance-1, systool-instance-2, and dynatools-instance-3. Each of these instances is currently running except for dynatools-instance-3. All instances have specific management responsibilities. How would a cloud administrator be able to easily determine administrative and system status details through filtering?

   A. Status and members of the managed groups

   B. Labels only

    C. Metadata

    D. Status only

9. A cloud architect was recently asked to determine the best approach on moving an analytics-intensive, high-performance, IoT-based application from the company's data center in Boise, Idaho, to the public cloud. The application only has ten internal company users. The architect must decide what instance type is most appropriate to handle the workload. What would you recommend to the architect?

    A. General-purpose machine configuration

    B. Memory-optimized compute configuration

    C. Compute-optimized configuration

    D. General-purpose machine configuration with GPU attached

10. Autoscaling should be considered based on all the following conditions except which one?

    A. Additional load balancing

    B. Observed high CPU utilization

    C. High memory utilization

    D. Frequent system updates

11. Of all the disks types available for Compute Engine, which offers the most flexibility?

    A. Cloud Storage buckets

    B. Zonal standard persistent disk

    C. Zonal persistent SSD

    D. Local SSD

12. How would one go about finding a Shielded VM in the Compute Engine image library?

    A. All Linux VMs are shielded by default.

    B. Using the filter function, search for the phrase "64-bit."

    C. Search for "64-bit" in the description of a VM name.

    D. Using the filter function, search for `gce-uefi-images`.

13. In order for a health check to run properly, what condition must be met?

    A. The load balancer and backend configuration must match the health check configuration.

    B. The load balancer must match the health check configuration.

    C. The backend configuration must match the health check configuration.

    D. There are no prerequisites for a health check.

14. The team at DynaLearning is building a gradebook application. They are looking to complete some application testing in a self-contained virtual machine instance. The team will not use the instance once the application is in production. What type of virtual machine is optimal for the team to use from a cost and productivity perspective?

    A. Sole-tenant nodes

    B. Preemptible

    C. Unmanaged instance group

    D. Snapshot

15. A cloud architect has been tasked with designing a highly available solution that supports memory-intensive compute functionality. The architect must include autoscaling, load balancing, health checks, and autohealing into the solution to ensure a stable environment. What two attributes best describe the architecture to be used?

    A. Unmanaged instance groups, GPU-based processing

    B. Managed instance groups, GPU-based processing

    C. Snapshots, additional storage

    D. Preemptible instances, GPU-based processing

16. A cloud engineer must make custom updates to the Windows 2012 operating systems. Which tool would best suit the engineer's need using Compute Engine?

    A. SSH   *Linux*

    B. RDP   *Windows*

    C. Cloud Shell

    D. Cloud Console

17. You recently noticed that your virtual machines instance that runs analytics-oriented operations is not performing optimally. Many organizational users are complaining that during peak usage times, they experience performance degradation. Recently, the organization added additional zonal SSD storage and CPU capacity to the virtual machine instances. However, such changes are not improving performance. What additional changes can be made to correct performance degradation?

    A. Attach a GPU and install necessary libraries onto the instance.

    B. Migrate all data to Cloud Storage buckets.

    C. Add CPU capacity.

    D. Move virtual machine instances to another GCP data center.

18. The organizational cloud engineer of DynaLearning is delegating project-level authority to individuals at the resource level, not project level. What role should the cloud engineer assign to each user if the objective is to get information about an instance only without editable permissions?

    A. Compute Resource Manager

    B. Compute Project Admin

    C. Compute Viewer

    D. Compute Instance Admin

19. An organization that is looking to optimize Compute Engine cost savings should consider taking all of the following actions except which one during the planning stage?

    A. Select the smallest footprint necessary to operate your virtual machine instances.

    B. Utilize preemptive instances for temporary use of virtual machine instances.

    C. Set up billing alerts to ensure cost containment with resources.

    D. Select a data center based on the lowest cost of a deployable resource per month.

Answers

1. **B.** Compute Engine is the only feature listed that offers virtual machine instance support and deployment options. Cloud Functions is GCP's serverless compute platform. Cloud SDK is the command-line tool that enables a user to create a virtual machine instance within Compute Engine. App Engine is GCP's Platform as a Service offering to develop custom-hosted web applications.

2. **C.** Although answer A may appear to be the same storage capacity, answer C is correct because all snapshots are saved. A snapshot is never purged unless a cloud administrator manually completes such a task. Similarly, all snapshots are not deleted except for the last one. Therefore, answer D is incorrect. Finally, answer B is incorrect as each time a copy is made, a complete copy of an instance is not captured.

3. **A.** Unless all images are located in a specific region and zone, you must be explicit in the zone and region you want to delete an image from using Cloud Shell. The difference between us-east1 and us-east1-b is that -b denotes zone and us-east1 denotes region. You can automatically eliminate answer B as there is no zone or region identified. Answer C does not delete an image. Answer D only identifies the region, whereas answer A identifies the zone. Therefore, A is the correct answer.

4. **A.** `list` allows an administrator to review all virtual machine instances. `describe` allows an administrator to understand the features of one or more virtual machine instances. `os-inventory` is a read-only function allowing administrators to understand operating system data and resources better, and `networking-interfaces` enables administrators to understand all details regarding network interfaces across instances.

5. **B.** start is the actual command to start the server. reset restarts the virtual machine instance by clearing the memory of an active virtual machine. Neither move nor update starts or restarts a virtual machine.

6. **D.** The only inaccurate statement is answer D because a cloud engineer can modify a virtual instance at any time by adding storage capacity, memory capacity, and CPU utilization if necessary. OS-level changes can also be made using an SSH or RDP client, depending on the type of virtual machine deployed in GCP.

7. **B.** The closest data center to the southeast United States is currently South Carolina. The most cost-efficient way to deliver and ensure optimal performance is to select the GCP data center that is closest to the majority of your user traffic. While the northern Virginia data center may be an attractive option, it is further north than South Carolina. Both the southamerica-east1 and northamerica-northeast1 may reside in the Eastern time zone; however, the data centers are outside the United States, so there will be a premium cost for network traffic.

8. **A.** The question is asking for two attributes: system status and user access. You can filter on a given project based on status and members within a managed group. Labels may be provided as part of a virtual machine instance, but they are not specific to the requirement. Metadata may or may not be included within the instance description. Finally, status does not provide a managed instance group user data.

9. **C.** There are two distinguishable characteristics in the question—a small number of users and a high-performance requirement. By definition, compute-optimized is designed for high-performance workloads, but not necessarily large workloads. CPU and memory utilization remains high, but the need is not excessive. Storage capacity is also more significant than in the general-purpose configuration. Memory-optimized computing assumes high-performance, high-volume computing requirements. General-purpose computing will not be sufficient for a high-volume workload. Even if the architect added GPU capacity load, the high-volume throughput requirements are better suited for compute-optimized configurations.

10. **D.** Frequent system updates is not a reason to consider autoscaling. All other metrics listed have a strong correlation with the need to autoscale a managed instance group or virtualized instance.

11. **A.** Cloud Storage buckets can scale as necessary, whereas all other formats have storage limitations. Furthermore, all the other disk types are block based, whereas Cloud Storage buckets are object based. Cloud Storage buckets offer a global footprint in terms of scope of access. All other formats have limitations. Cloud Storage buckets support all machine types, whereas other storage types often have limits. Data redundancy for all examples provided is either zonal, multizonal, or none. Only Cloud Storage buckets offer regional, dual-regional, or multiregional data redundancy support. Where Cloud Storage buckets are not ideal is when there are high input/output use cases. Cloud Storage buckets do not allow for direct mounting in comparison to standard storage devices.

12. **D.** A Shielded VM is correctly titled within the image library with the `gce-uefi-images` parameter in the name. A Shielded VM is a particular type of 64-bit VM that supports advanced security controls, including integrity monitoring, to ensure boot images are not compromised. Therefore, answer A is incorrect because not all VMs include Shielded functionality. GCP does not include the phrase "64-bit" in the title or family name of an image.

13. **A.** Two preconditions exist: the load balancer and backend configuration must match the virtual machine instance. You cannot have one condition be met without the other for a health check to run in a standard or legacy mode. Given both conditions must be met, making answers B, C, and D incorrect.

14. **B.** When an organization intends to use a virtual machine instance for a short period of time, a preemptive instance can save the organization as much as 80 percent in cost. It also allows for the environment to be self-contained from production. A sole-tenant node is a dedicated virtual machine instance that does not share any physical hardware with other projects. It may not be intended for short-term use. There are, however, costs associated with utilizing a sole-tenant node, given the dedicated infrastructure requirements. A snapshot is a form of backup, which makes answer D incorrect. An unmanaged instance group should only be applicable when an organization requires load balancing to groups of heterogeneous instances, or an administrator must manage the instances themselves. An unmanaged instance group is seldom appropriate as a short-term cost-efficient solution.

15. **B.** Managed instance groups support autoscaling, load balancing, health checks, and autohealing. Also, it is a fairly routine process to add GPU capacity to a MIG. An unmanaged instance does not support autonomous features. Preemptive instances are not intended for high availability, and snapshots are a backup of an instance.

16. **B.** When a cloud administrator needs to make OS-based updates to a Windows system, they use an RDP client. SSH clients are used for Linux-based systems. Cloud Shell is a web-based interactive shell environment specific to the Google Cloud Platform. Users can manage projects and resources without having to install an SDK on their computers. Cloud Console is an interactive web-based interface that allows users to deploy, scale, and diagnose production issues using a browser.

17. **A.** Adding a GPU and the additional CUDA libraries is the appropriate response. Migrating data from one type of disk to another is unlikely to improve system performance. The organization already added CPU capacity without much success. Moving the instances to a new data center may improve performance only if the data center is closer to where most activities reside. However, one would assume that the data center selected during the configuration defaulted to the closest geography possible. Given that adding a GPU is intended to accelerate the speed of complex processing, this is the most logical response.

18. **C.** Compute Viewer is a read-only user. Compute Instance Admin is a type of administrator who has both read and write permissions over a compute instance. The other two roles, Compute Resource Manager and Compute Project Admin, are both fictitious.

19. **D.** Not all data centers have the same project resources. Prices also vary based on location. Just because an image may be slightly cheaper in another region does not mean the final price will be more affordable. Network traffic activity contributes to the final price. All other options are contributory factors to cost optimization.

Kubernetes Engine

In this chapter you will learn to
- Determine when to use Kubernetes Engine for the Google Cloud Platform
- Plan, deploy, and configure a Kubernetes Engine cluster
- Manage Kubernetes Engine resources
- Deploy a container application to Kubernetes Engine using Pods
- Implement monitoring and logging options for Kubernetes Engine applications

Kubernetes is a container orchestration system created by Google. A Kubernetes cluster consists of several machines accessible from Compute Engine that work together to form a cluster. A Google Kubernetes cluster leverages the Kubernetes cluster management system to interact with one or more clusters. An engineer uses specific Kubernetes commands and resources in order to support application actions such as completing tasks, setting policies, and enabling cluster health monitoring. Kubernetes applies many of the same principles discussed in Chapter 3, such as autoscaling, automatic updates, and monitoring.

Google founded Kubernetes technology back in 2014 as a means of supporting container orchestration for automating processes such as application deployments, scaling, and system management. Kubernetes became freely available to the technology community because Google felt it offered enormous potential for managing workloads across nodes in one or more clusters. Kubernetes is now maintained by the Cloud Native Computing Foundation.

Many individuals confuse the concepts of instance groups and Kubernetes clusters. There are many distinctions between the two. In this chapter, you learn about Kubernetes fundamentals and architecture principles. Additionally, you become acclimated with deployment and management practices for Kubernetes resources using Cloud Console, Cloud SDK, and Cloud Shell. At the end of the chapter, you will complete an exercise to become familiar with how to deploy and manage Kubernetes clusters using the Google Kubernetes Engine (GKE).

Fundamentals of Google Kubernetes Engine

GKE is Google Cloud Platform's (GCP's) managed Kubernetes service. With this service, GCP customers can create and maintain their Kubernetes clusters without having to manage the Kubernetes platform.

Kubernetes, at the most fundamental level, is characterized by various capabilities that are representative of the system state. States include the deployable application container and workloads, network, disk resources, and monitoring behaviors, all of which are objects available using the Kubernetes API. Object abstractions might include Pods, Services, Volumes, and Namespaces. Object controllers, which enable advanced functionality in GKE, include ReplicaSet, Deployment, StatefulSet, DaemonSet, and Jobs.

GKE is the right choice if you need a container orchestration platform that provides scalability and flexibility. If you require a platform that provides complete control over every facet of container orchestration, including networking, storage, maintenance, and support for traditional stateful applications, the GKE platform is an ideal fit. Should your application require less hands-on support, there are other offerings, such as Cloud Run, within GCP that may better suit your organizational needs.

Objects

Objects are persistent entities within Google Kubernetes Engine. Kubernetes uses objects as a means to manage the operational state of a cluster. A Kubernetes object has three main purposes:

- It helps identify what containerized applications are running.
- It provides resource availability among those applications.
- It supports policy assignment around those applications.

When you're working with Kubernetes, the use of an object acts as a record of intent. If you create an object in GKE, the system ensures the object remains in place. The object should describe the state of the workload. To complete any form of function with GKE, a cloud engineer must invoke the Kubernetes API using Cloud Console or Cloud Shell.

Workloads

Workloads are the packaging of containerized, hardware-independent, isolated applications. Each container, whether it contains an application or batch job, is known as a workload. Before executing a workload in the Kubernetes Engine cluster, an administrator must package all requirements for the workload inside the container.

At this time, GKE only supports Docker containers, containerd on container-optimized OSs (cos_containerd), and containerd on Ubuntu node images for workloads. In the future, GCP intends to increase its portfolio of additional container options. Solutions such as Cloud Build and Container Registry are also available to handle the container image life cycle for building, storing, and serving images.

Pods

Pods are single instances in a cluster where a process is actively operating. A Pod must contain at least one container. Pods typically operate in a single container, although they can run in many when resources are shared. Pods share container resources, including networking and storage capacity. Here are some considerations about shared resources among Pods:

- **Networks** Unique IP addresses are associated with a Pod. Shared objects might consist of network namespaces, IP addresses, and network ports. Containers inside a Pod communicate with one another using localhost.
- **Storage** Pod shared-storage volumes are available between one or more containers.

Pods run a single instance of an application on a Kubernetes cluster. However, creating individual Pods is not a standard or recommended practice. You will often find that Pods are established in sets, referred to as replicas. A controller manages the full set of replicated Pods. The management process includes the Pod deployment. Controllers support horizontal scaling based on the number of Pods needed to run the cluster successfully. Pods will automatically be terminated if they exhibit signs of being unhealthy. Collectively, the controller is responsible for health and scaling management.

Although Kubernetes Engine shares many similar attributes with Compute Engine managed instance groups, there are two key differences. First, Pods execute applications in containers and are placed on cluster nodes. Managed instance groups use the same code across each node. Second, controllers manage all Pod activity. Managed instance groups require a user to execute commands using Cloud Console, Cloud SDK, or Cloud Shell.

 TIP Unless you need to debug, troubleshoot, or inspect unusual behavior, the controller should always manage the Pods within a Kubernetes cluster. Furthermore, remember that a Pod remains active on a given node until one of four conditions occurs: process completion, Pod deletion, Pod eviction due to a reduction in resources, or a failed node. When a node fails, a Pod automatically is set for removal.

Services

Services in Kubernetes Engine enable many sets of Pod endpoints to become a single resource using configurable grouping options. The default design of a Service includes a stable cluster IP address that a client may use to contact other Pods using the same Service. Through a send request to the IP address, the request is directed to one or more Pods in the available Service. Selectors allow for the identification of member Pods within the grouping. Labeling must be part of the selectors for it to be part of a Service. Unlike labels in Compute Engine, which constitute a form of metadata, a label for Kubernetes Engine Pods is an arbitrary key–value pair that is attached to an object.

Pod deployments are temporary and their IP addresses is dynamic; therefore, using an IP address does not make sense often. By utilizing Services, there is a stable IP address available for however long the Service is active. Another advantage of using Services rather than Pods in a standalone manner is load balancing, because you can call a single, constant IP address that balances requests from Pod Services. IP addresses are used in a variety of ways depending on one of the five types of services available in Kubernetes Engine. When using Services, you have five options to choose from:

- **ClusterIP**   The default option for a Service. A stable internal IP address receives a send request from an internal client under these conditions.

- **NodePort**   NodePort values are defined by the Service. The client must send the IP address requests to a node or one or more NodePort values.

- **LoadBalancer**   A network load balancer's send request comes from a client to a given IP address.

- **ExternalName**   An internal client is likely to use the DNS name of a Service as an alias for an external DNS name.

- **Headless**   Using a headless Service is appropriate when you require a Pod grouping, but a stable IP address is not necessary.

ReplicaSet

The purpose of the *ReplicaSet* is to ensure a stable set of Pods run perpetually. ReplicaSets are associated with fields, including a selector to set parameters such as the number of Pods that can be acquired, the number of replicas that can be maintained, and a template for establishing the creation of new replicas should new Pods be required. ReplicaSets satisfy creation, deletion, and maintenance using stated requirements. ReplicaSets use a Pod template to meet the needs of creating new Pods.

ReplicaSet is a controller, as mentioned earlier in the chapter, that is capable of identifying when there are not enough Pods available for a running application or workload. If such a condition is recognized, a ReplicaSet will create one or more Pods. ReplicaSets can also update and delete Pods.

There are many advantages, including declarative updates to using ReplicaSets with Pods; however, Deployments have many advanced features that should be considered first. If the intent is to focus on custom orchestration and the Kubernetes Engine does not require updates, ReplicaSets are adequate. Otherwise, Deployments are a more appropriate approach to cluster orchestration as there is likely to be little reason to manipulate ReplicaSet objects.

Deployments

Deployments are sets of like-kind Pods managed by the Kubernetes Deployment controller that does not have any unique characteristics. When an instance becomes unhealthy, a Deployment can run one or more replicas of an application to replace failed or unresponsive instances. Deployments ensure that application instances are available to serve user requests as necessary.

Deployments makes use of the Pod template to describe a Pod specification. The Pod specification acts as a blueprint detailing what the Pod should act and look like throughout its entire life cycle. The specification makes clear how an application should operate, the prerequisites for volume mounting, and labeling conventions among specific details. New Pods are automatically created any time a template is modified.

StatefulSet

Pods that maintain unique, persistent identities as well as stable hostnames that Kubernetes Engine can support regardless of schedule are known as a *StatefulSet*. The use of StatefulSets is similar to Deployments; however, unique identifiers are available to each Pod. StatefulSets apply ordinal indexing to manage the identity and ordering of Pods. Pods are deployed sequentially but terminated in reverse. Similar to Deployments, StatefulSets also use a Pod template containing a Pod specification. What distinguishes StatefulSets is data maintenance behaviors. All state information is accessible from persistent disk storage.

DaemonSet

Making sure that all nodes run Pods is essential to container management. The use of a *DaemonSet* ensures that if Pods are added to a node, similar actions occur with a cluster. A deletion of a Pod from a cluster results in removal. Deleted Pods are accessible through garbage collection. A DaemonSet acts as a clean-up mechanism for those instances it creates. Should a cloud engineer decide to use a DaemonSet for GKE, it has many applications, including establishing shared storage, running logs per node in a cluster, and enabling node-based monitoring agents. DaemonSets use a Pod specification to maintain Pod requirements.

Jobs

Jobs are another type of controller object in GKE. Unlike other controller objects, a Job will operate until completion instead of ceasing when it reaches a given state. Jobs are most often associated with the handling with finite tasks, although they are quite useful for complex operational activities such as computational and batch-oriented tasks. While Jobs support parallel execution of Pods, there are only a few occasions where using Jobs will closely align with processes.

Two types of Jobs are available in GKE: Non-parallel Jobs and Parallel Jobs with completion count. A Non-parallel Job creates a single Pod. Once the Job is complete, the Pod terminates. If the Job terminates because of unsuccessful activity, the Pod is re-created. Parallel Jobs with creation count are appropriate when you look for several Pods to terminate after a given behavior occurs using completions field. Completion fields determine how many Pods should terminate successfully before the Job is complete. Like other controllers mentioned, Job controllers create a new Pod if the state of an existing Pod fails, gets deleted, or is unhealthy.

Kubernetes Architecture Principles

Google Kubernetes Engine consists of a combination of several objects and controllers. A cluster is the core object in the Google Kubernetes Engine that runs on top of the container application (see Figure 4-1). The cluster master is responsible for the Kubernetes control plane processes. A control plane process might include the API server, scheduler, and resource controllers. The cluster master life cycle occurs during the creation and deletion of a cluster.

The cluster master acts as the single endpoint for a cluster. Interactions across all clusters occur through API calls. The cluster master responds to the calls by handling all API server requests. Kubernetes API calls can be made directly via an API using HTTP/gRPC, using Cloud Console, or running command-line `kubectl`. The API server process acts as the communication hub for the cluster, given the API server acts as the source of truth. Additionally, the cluster master is also responsible for all operational activity across cluster nodes, which includes managing network and storage resource allocation across workloads.

A cluster contains one or more nodes. Each of the nodes acts as a machine that runs the containerized application. An individual machine consists of Compute Engine instances. Each time a cloud engineer creates a cluster, Kubernetes Engine creates these Compute Engine instances. The master is responsible for managing each node. When a node receives an update, it acts upon the update by responding accordingly. Control over nodes can either be manual or automatic, although Kubernetes Engine does allow for automatic repairs and upgrades to cluster nodes. Nodes are critical to the architecture of a Kubernetes Engine because they help run the services necessary to support the containers that make a cluster workload, including the runtime and node agent `kubelet`. A node communicates with a master that is responsible for container management against a schedule on a node.

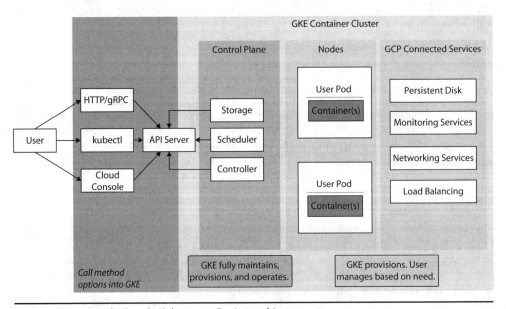

Figure 4-1   Example Google Kubernetes Engine architecture

By default, a standard node for a Compute Engine instance configuration is set to n1-standard-1 with one virtual CPU and 3.75GB of memory. A cloud engineer can modify this configuration for a cluster along with the selected operating system image needed to run the container. There are many advantages to choosing a specific CPU platform as well as memory configuration, especially if the cluster or node pool baseline requires a particular type of workload. Local ephemeral storage is also configured with Kubernetes Engine, similar to how CPU and memory resources are configurable.

Deployment Approaches

Google Kubernetes Engine provides two deployment options for Kubernetes clusters: using Cloud Console and via the command line if you use Cloud Shell or Cloud SDK. To begin deploying a cluster using Cloud Console, Cloud Shell, or Cloud SDK, there are prerequisite quotas that a cloud administrator should have in place. These include one Compute Engine CPU cluster in the region of choice and one in-use IP address. The Google Kubernetes Engine API is made available through the Cloud Console. You enable the API by going to the APIs & Services menu and selecting Library (see Figure 4-2). You need to search for the Kubernetes API.

Once you find the Kubernetes API (see Figure 4-3), you will enable it, which may take a few minutes. When the Kubernetes API is activated, the services will allow for the creation of Kubernetes clusters and deployable containers.

At this point, it may be necessary to add user credentials for the specific API (Kubernetes Engine API). You will select Create Credentials from the top of the

Figure 4-2
Choosing Library
from the APIs &
Services menu

Figure 4-3
Kubernetes
Engine API

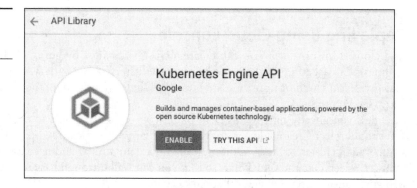

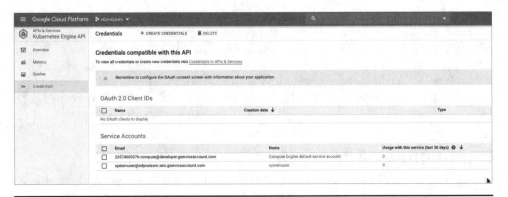

Figure 4-4   Create Credentials for Kubernetes Engine API

interface (see Figure 4-4). On the next page, you will have three choices: Service Accounts, Oauth, or Help Me Choose. Follow these steps to complete the credentialing process:

1. In the Credentials interface, you should pick API (Kubernetes Engine) if you intend to use the API with Compute Engine or App Engine.

2. The answer is Yes if you intend to create a minimum of one virtual machine instance for a cluster.

3. You need to select the What Credentials Do I Need Button? Follow the screen prompts. Once complete, click Save.

4. The API keys or systems accounts become active per system mandated needs.

You are now ready to create your first GKE cluster.

TIP   A project must always be associated with a GKE instance to ensure billing is appropriately set up. Assuming an API is configurable, necessary credentials are then related to the Kubernetes Engine API. Billing is also associated with the proper project so that an engineer can begin provisioning GKE clusters.

Deploying Using Cloud Console

As a cloud administrator, you can create a cluster instance by going to the Kubernetes Engine menu (see Figure 4-5) and selecting Clusters. A secondary screen will appear that gives you three options: Create Cluster, Deploy Container, and Take the Quick-Start (see Figure 4-6).

Unless you already have a cluster in place, you will not be able to deploy a container. You should select Create Cluster if you are familiar with the required parameters to create a Kubernetes cluster instance. Otherwise, if you are unfamiliar and need assistance creating a cluster, select Take the QuickStart so that you can walk through how to create a multitier web application using Google Kubernetes Engine.

Figure 4-5
Kubernetes
Engine menu in
Cloud Console

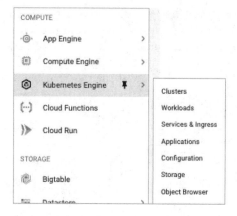

Figure 4-6
Create options
when selecting
Cluster in
Kubernetes
Engine

To begin creating a new Cluster Instance, click Create Cluster. A new interface will appear that presents you with the ability to configure the cluster (see Figure 4-7). As an administrator, you will need to go through each of the sections on the left to properly size your cluster instance.

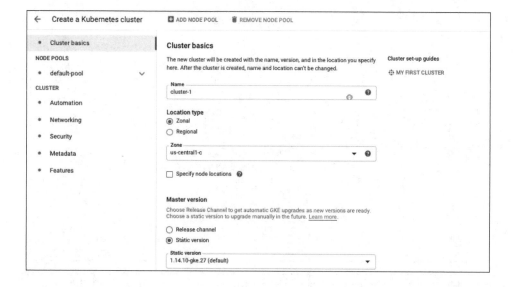

Figure 4-7 Cluster creation interface

You begin with the Cluster Basics tab, in which you name and select the region/zone where you want your cluster hosted. To properly size each node of your cluster, go to the Nodes tab found under default-pool (see Figure 4-8). It is on this tab where you decide the optimal machine configuration. By default, a cluster is configured as an n1-standard-1 (1 vCPU, 3.75GB memory) using a standard persistent disk with a 100GB boot disk.

Figure 4-8   Interface to configure cluster machine type

You can change this configuration to meet your organization's needs. There are numerous template configurations available under General-Purpose, Memory-Optimized, and Compute-Optimized. Based on other organizational needs, go to each of the other tabs to configure specific security and metadata parameters per node. To set node-specific requirements, tab through each of the items on the left. Pay particular attention to the Networking and Security tabs, given that an engineer will need to determine if the cluster will be public or private. Similarly, you should determine if the cluster will be shielded, providing extra security. Once this is complete, click Create at the bottom of the screen to create a cluster.

TIP If you are looking to optimize your cluster performance, you may consider tweaking the configuration of the template. To improve availability, you would modify the zone. Another option is to create node pools. If you are looking to automate specific cluster features such as maintenance, those options can be configured under the Maintenance tab. Logging and monitoring capabilities are also widely available. To configure such capabilities, select the appropriate options under Features in the Kubernetes navigation within the Cloud Console.

It will take several minutes for the newly configured cluster to become available. Once it is available, click Connect to enable the cluster. You will be prompted to select whether you would like to configure the `kubectl` command line or use Cloud Console to initiate and view the recently created workloads. In this case, choose Open Workloads Dashboard (see Figure 4-9).

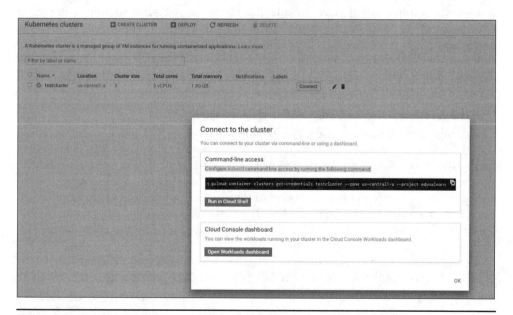

Figure 4-9 Newly created cluster example and interface to open the workload interface

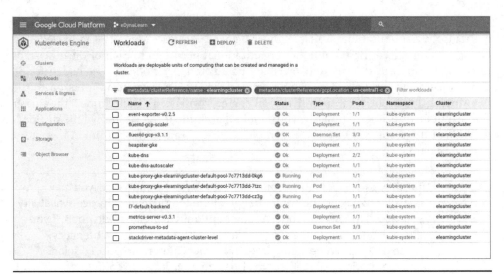

Figure 4-10 List of workloads currently available based on the newly created cluster

As you see in the background of Figure 4-9, the testcluster was successfully created. Once you select Open Workloads Dashboard, a new interface opens. The workloads, which are the deployable computing units, are created and managed in a cluster. These appear in the browser window (see Figure 4-10).

Depending on your configuration, you may need to make some configuration adjustments to ensure the environment is fully enabled. Reasons for needing to make configuration adjustments may include the template you selected might not have a sufficient amount of storage capacity for all Pods or the DaemonSets were never configured with specific nodes. These are activities that an engineer can complete post-deployment, and a Kubernetes cluster can be configured within Cloud Console using the graphical user interfaces.

Deploying Using Cloud Shell or Cloud SDK

Cloud engineers can create and manage Kubernetes activities using Cloud Shell or Cloud SDK via command-line operations. The command line for any Kubernetes Engine–based activity starts with `gcloud container`. If you were to type the `gcloud container` command into Cloud Shell or Cloud SDK, you would be provided with a listing of options to extend the command line. The available `gcloud container` groups are shown in Table 4-1.

If there is a need to see the current server configuration, use the command `get-server-config`.

The `gcloud container` command group supports the creation and management of GKE container and cluster instances. When creating a specific group, however, there is a need to apply cluster-specific configurations. Examples might include parameters

Group Command	Description
`binauthz`	Manage attestations for Binary Authorization on Google Cloud Platform
`clusters`	Deploy and tear down Google Kubernetes Engine clusters
`hub`	Centrally manage features and services on all your Kubernetes clusters with Hub
`images`	List and manipulate Google Container Registry images
`node-pools`	Create and delete operations for Google Kubernetes Engine node pools
`operations`	Get and list operations for Google Kubernetes Engine clusters
`subnets`	Manage subnets to be used by Google Kubernetes Engine clusters

Table 4-1   Kubernetes Group Commands

such as project, zone, disk size, machine type, and number of nodes. In the command line, you may find yourself entering a very long string. The command line will contain several parameters depending on how many customizations you intend to make to a standardized template. Figure 4-11 shows the output from creating a container using the following commands:

```
gcloud container --project "edynalearn" clusters create  "dynalearn-cluster"
--zone "us-central1-a" --username "admin"  --machine-type "n1-standard-1"
--image-type "COS" --disk-type "pd-standard" --disk-size "100"
--num-nodes "3" --enable-stackdriver-kubernetes --enable-autoupgrade
--enable-autorepair
```

When you submit the command line, specific parameters about your newly created cluster are made available. In this case, certain default conditions were not entered into the command line intentionally. The system provided relevant feedback on the default configurations as well as what features were enabled using the parameters specified.

It can be cumbersome to add parameters to the command line to create a more customized Kubernetes cluster group. Unless the intent is to deploy a reasonably vanilla cluster instance, you will likely find it much easier to complete a cluster configuration and deployment using Cloud Console. However, not everything can easily be completed in Cloud Console. For example, there will be instances where complex configurations require the use of certain automation tools only available using a command line such as Cloud Shell or Cloud SDK. Depending on the use case, select what tool best fits the need.

```
jack@cloudshell:~ (edynalearn)$ gcloud container --project "edynalearn" clusters create  "dynalearn-cluster" --zone "us-central1-a" --username "admin"  --machine-type "n1-standard-1"
   --image-type "COS" --disk-type "pd-standard" --disk-size "100" --num-nodes "3" --enable-stackdriver-kubernetes --enable-autoupgrade --enable-autorepair
WARNING: Currently VPC-native is not the default mode during cluster creation. In the future, this will become the default mode and can be disabled using `--no-enable-ip-alias` flag.
Use `--[no-]enable-ip-alias` flag to suppress this warning.
WARNING: Starting with version 1.18, clusters will have shielded GKE nodes by default.
WARNING: Your Pod address range (`--cluster-ipv4-cidr`) can accommodate at most 1008 node(s).
This will enable the autorepair feature for nodes. Please see https://cloud.google.com/kubernetes-engine/docs/node-auto-repair for more information on node autorepairs.
Creating cluster dynalearn-cluster in us-central1-a... Cluster is being health-checked (master is healthy)...done.
Created [https://container.googleapis.com/v1/projects/edynalearn/zones/us-central1-a/clusters/dynalearn-cluster].
To inspect the contents of your cluster, go to: https://console.cloud.google.com/kubernetes/workload_/gcloud/us-central1-a/dynalearn-cluster?project=edynalearn
kubeconfig entry generated for dynalearn-cluster.
NAME               LOCATION       MASTER_VERSION  MASTER_IP      MACHINE_TYPE   NODE_VERSION   NUM_NODES  STATUS
dynalearn-cluster  us-central1-a  1.14.10-gke.27  104.154.178.17 n1-standard-1  1.14.10-gke.27 3          RUNNING
jack@cloudshell:~ (edynalearn)$
```

Figure 4-11   Command-line output in Cloud Shell to create a new `gcloud` container

Application Pods and Kubernetes

It is not possible to create a container until at least one cluster is assigned to a GCP project. Once a cluster is available, the cloud engineer is then able to deploy a container. If the intent is to deploy a container using Cloud Shell or Cloud SDK, a prerequisite is to install the `kubectl` command-line tool. Otherwise, to deploy a cluster using Cloud Console, follows these steps:

1. Go to the Kubernetes Engine menu and select Cluster. A list of the existing cluster instances will appear.

2. Click the Deploy button at the top of the interface.

3. A new screen will appear that allows for the creation of a container (see Figure 4-12).

   You will need to configure parameters such as the container name, environmental variables (key, value), initial commands, application name, labels, and namespace.

Figure 4-12
Container
creation interface

4. The next step is to select the cluster in which the container is deployed upon creation. If an additional cluster is necessary, you can create a new cluster from the interface by clicking New Container Image. You would work through each prompt until all sections are complete.

5. Finally, it is suggested that the YAML file be evaluated before container creation. A YAML file includes all parameters associated with the configuration defined in the deployed container (see Figure 4-13).

Once all values are reviewed, and you are satisfied with the system entries, click Continue until all items are deployed.

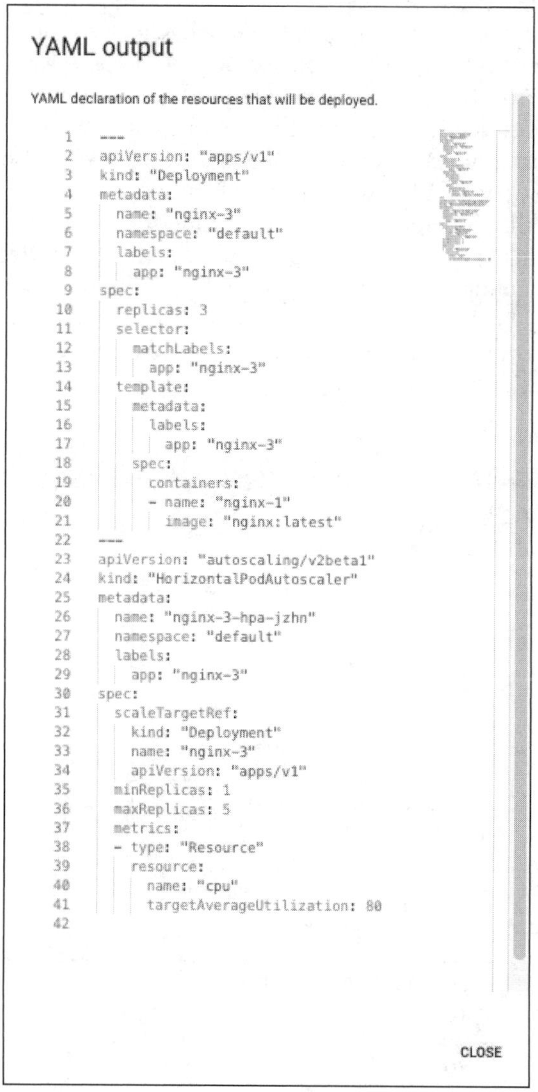

Figure 4-13
Example
YAML file

```
YAML output

YAML declaration of the resources that will be deployed.

1    ---
2    apiVersion: "apps/v1"
3    kind: "Deployment"
4    metadata:
5      name: "nginx-3"
6      namespace: "default"
7      labels:
8        app: "nginx-3"
9    spec:
10     replicas: 3
11     selector:
12       matchLabels:
13         app: "nginx-3"
14     template:
15       metadata:
16         labels:
17           app: "nginx-3"
18       spec:
19         containers:
20         - name: "nginx-1"
21           image: "nginx:latest"
22    ---
23    apiVersion: "autoscaling/v2beta1"
24    kind: "HorizontalPodAutoscaler"
25    metadata:
26      name: "nginx-3-hpa-jzhn"
27      namespace: "default"
28      labels:
29        app: "nginx-3"
30    spec:
31      scaleTargetRef:
32        kind: "Deployment"
33        name: "nginx-3"
34        apiVersion: "apps/v1"
35      minReplicas: 1
36      maxReplicas: 5
37      metrics:
38      - type: "Resource"
39        resource:
40          name: "cpu"
41          targetAverageUtilization: 80
42
```

CLOSE

EXAM TIP   It is essential that you know what is in a YAML file and its purpose. A YAML file is a script to create configuration and settings. The first time you create a container, it is a good idea to go through the steps of setting up the YAML file using Cloud Console. Once you have created a configurable YAML file, it can be modified and reused for subsequent container deployments using Cloud Shell or Cloud SDK. The script presents all the parameters available in the graphic UI of Cloud Console. The file can be stored and treated as a repeatable template.

Monitoring Principles and Kubernetes

Kubernetes Engine Monitoring uses Google Cloud's Operations Suite (formerly Stackdriver) to aggregate log, event, and metrics data across a Kubernetes environment to help a cloud engineer better understand the performance state in a production environment. It is possible to identify issues with application behavior quickly using the monitoring tools. Accessing information on Kubernetes Engine–specific resources can be found on the Overview page under Resource (see Figure 4-14).

Clicking the Kubernetes Engine link under the Resource will provide a detailed view of all GKE instances. A cloud engineer can evaluate workload and service performance metrics, including incidents, current CPU utilization, and memory utilization (see Figure 4-15).

Numerous monitoring tools can help an engineer ensure the system remains operational, including uptime checks and alerting policies. Uptime checks and alerting

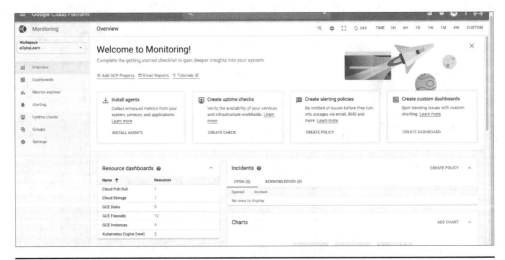

Figure 4-14   Resources on the Monitoring console

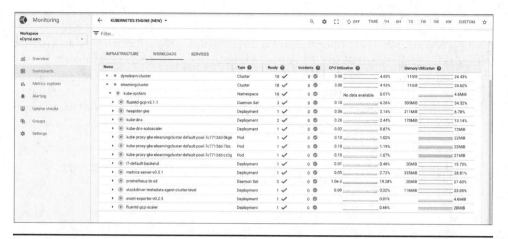

Figure 4-15 Kubernetes Engine Monitoring Workload status example

policies can be applied to a single instance within a cluster or to measure the performance of the entire cluster.

Uptime Checks

Resource health is an integral part of cloud administration. Operations Suite can validate if a service is available by ensuring it can be accessed from any GCP data center globally. A best practice is to configure an uptime check, which is an alerting policy to ensure the system properly utilizes the default configuration. An uptime check can be created directly from the navigation pane in Operations Suite or using the Alerting Policy interface. You will need to provide the following parameters to configure the uptime check:

- Name of the uptime check
- Check type (HTTP, HTTPS, TCP)
- Resource type (URL, App Engine, Elastic Load Balancer, Instance)
- URL path or configurable instance name
- Path (subdirectory)
- Check time (1–15 minutes)
- Log check failure

You can configure advanced settings such as authentication, networking, and geographic target settings by selecting the Advanced drop-down menu. Once each form field is filled out, you should complete a health check. Assuming the health check passes, click Save. Based on the time interval selected, the uptime check will evaluate the VM instance or cluster during the given time internal selected.

Alerting Policies

Alerting policies, similar to uptime checks, inform you if the performance of an instance within a cluster, an entire cluster, or a container breaches an expected performance threshold. Measures evaluated include metrics such as CPU utilization, memory utilization, disk capacity, and disk utilization. You can configure an alert based on a specific condition should performance deviate from expected performance levels. Configuration parameters include Conditions, Notifications, and Documentation (see Figure 4-16).

Figure 4-16
Alerting Policy
Configuration
interface

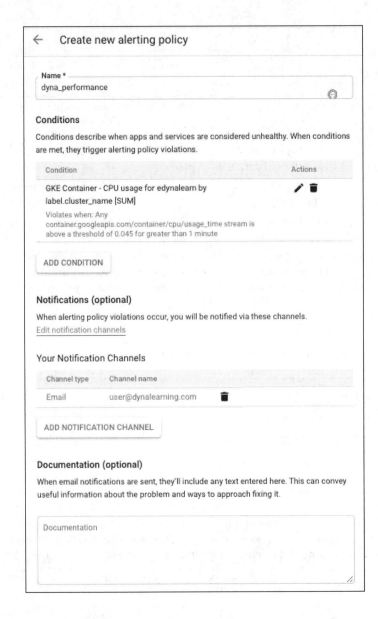

While it is essential to know what is occurring in the system by accessing the Cloud Console, you need to be alerted in real-time on the state of the system should performance degradation occur. Notifications can be configured for various communications platforms beyond e-mail, including Slack, SMS, Mobile, and PagerDuty, to name a few. Should an alerting policy breach an acceptable threshold, all users who are on a notification list will receive an immediate alert to the platform configured.

Once you save an alerting policy, a separate monitoring agent is also made available that provides a visual review of system conditions, incident logs, access to the notification channel, and relevant documentation for the specific alert.

Managing Kubernetes Clusters

At this point in the chapter, the process on how to create and configure a Kubernetes cluster should be clear. A detailed presentation on the use of Kubernetes Engine Monitoring using Operations Suite has shown you ways in which you would be able to configure alerts and notifications should a cluster or container experience performance challenges. From time to time, you will want to see the specific status of a cluster, not just rely on a monitoring agent. To view the status of a cluster using Cloud Console, you need to go to the Kubernetes Engine navigation area under Compute Engine and then click Clusters. The Clusters Overview page will appear. Once it is loaded, locate where the Kubernetes clusters are found in the interface. Under the Name column, you will find a link and an icon. Hover over the icon, and you will see the current state of the cluster. In the case of the clusters shown in Figure 4-17, both are running.

Clicking the link in the Overview screen will present a detailed view of the cluster on a subsequent page. As seen in Figure 4-18, the current state of the cluster, as well as its configuration, is made available. An administrator can identify all data on the state of the cluster in its hosted location, core infrastructure, storage, network settings, and security posture. Add-on features and permissions illustrate what services and APIs are active.

One additional area to review when managing a cluster using this interface is the node pools. Given a cluster is made up of several nodes, it only makes sense to evaluate the performance of each one. Scroll to the bottom of the cluster details page and then select the link under the node pool you would like to evaluate. Upon clicking the link, you will find details about the configuration of each node, the metadata parameters, security

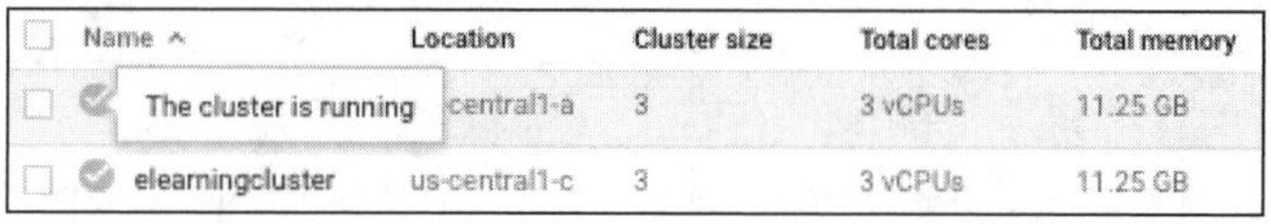

Figure 4-17
Checking
the current
cluster state

	Name ^	Location	Cluster size	Total cores	Total memory
	The cluster is running	central1-a	3	3 vCPUs	11.25 GB
	elearningcluster	us-central1-c	3	3 vCPUs	11.25 GB

Figure 4-18 Details for managing the cluster

configuration details, instance group details, and node-specific performance metrics (see Figure 4-19). It is possible to drill down further to see the performance of each node, including the state of CPU utilization, GPU utilization, ephemeral storage, memory utilization, Pod, and the current disk state.

You can also review the state of a Kubernetes cluster using the command `gcloud container clusters list`. The extent to which a user can review the details of the cluster using the `clusters list` command is limited to knowing if the cluster is

Figure 4-19   Node Pool Details interface

running or offline. To review the complete state of the cluster, enter the following on the command line:

```
gcloud container clusters describe <cluster name> --zone <zone name>
```

Not all the details are available in the single command line. You must use the `kubectl` command to access data on nodes and Pods.

Managing Kubernetes Nodes

Once you create a cluster in Kubernetes, adjust the number of nodes available using Cloud Console. You may also consider using a command-line tool such as Cloud Shell or Cloud SDK. This section will review how to add, modify, and remove nodes from a cluster using both methodologies.

Managing Kubernetes Nodes Using Cloud Console

Node details are available under the Kubernetes Engine | Cluster menu. Once you find this menu option in Cloud Console, select the cluster that requires modification. When the next window opens, you will see specific details about the infrastructure, storage, and

Figure 4-20
Managing
node pool
configuration in
Cloud Console

network configuration. First, click Edit at the top of the page. The page will refresh so that all fields are editable, including those under the node pool.

To modify the number of nodes in use per cluster, you need to scroll to the bottom of the page. You should click the relevant node pool that requires modification. On the Node Pool Details screen, look for the Edit button on the top and click it. Adjust the number of nodes as necessary (see Figure 4-20).

Bear in mind that a sufficient node pool quota must be available if the intent is to add nodes. Click Save. It will take a few minutes to update the node pool. Higher node consumption will increase GCP costs, while a reduction in node consumption will reduce GCP costs. During the save process, GCP is applying the appropriate configuration details to the cluster, including project and billing updates.

Managing Kubernetes Nodes Using Cloud Shell or Cloud SDK

Modifying a node pool using the command line requires you to identify four distinct parameters: cluster name, node pool name, cluster size, and zone or region. The command for adding or deleting nodes is different from updating nodes using Cloud Shell or Cloud SDK. When adding or deleting nodes, you would use the `gcloud container clusters resize` command. If updates are necessary (for example, if you want to attach add-on functionality such as autoscale), the command to use would be the following:

```
gcloud container clusters update
```

An example of resizing a node pool from three nodes to two nodes (a reduction in nodes) in the us-central1-a zone for cluster dynalearn-cluster would be as follows:

```
gcloud container clusters resize dynalearn-cluster --node-pool default-pool
--num-nodes=2 --zone us-central1-a
```

An example of updating the clusters by adding autoscaling and maximum of six nodes to zone us-cental1-a for cluster dynalearn-cluster would be this:

```
gcloud container clusters update dynalearn-cluster
--enable-autoscaling --min-nodes 1 --max-nodes 6 --zone us-central1-a
--node-pool default-pool
```

In summary, both methods accomplish the same task. If add, delete, or update requirements are cumbersome, it makes more sense to use Cloud Console rather than Cloud Shell or Cloud SDK to manage nodes.

Managing Kubernetes Pods

Pods can be managed directly in Cloud Console or using the command-line tool provided by Cloud Shell or Cloud SDK. Best practices encourage that a cloud engineer not directly modify Pods because Kubernetes maintains the entire deployment configuration. Instead, the approach to take is changing the deployment configuration. The next section addresses how to manage Pods using Cloud Console as well through the command-line tools using Cloud Shell or Cloud SDK.

Managing Pods Using Cloud Console

If you recall, a Pod is the smallest object that is deployable within a cluster. Pods are similar to a single instance process within the Kubernetes Engine. Making modifications to a Pod requires proper configuration across all objects, not just a single instance process. Otherwise, a configuration will likely error and cause a system outage. Pods are related to workloads in Kubernetes Engine. To manage a Pod, you need to navigate your way to the Kubernetes Engine | Workloads menu. Upon clicking the Workloads menu, you should see a screen with all active workloads. Next, select the link of an active workload that requires review so you can make configuration modifications (see Figure 4-21).

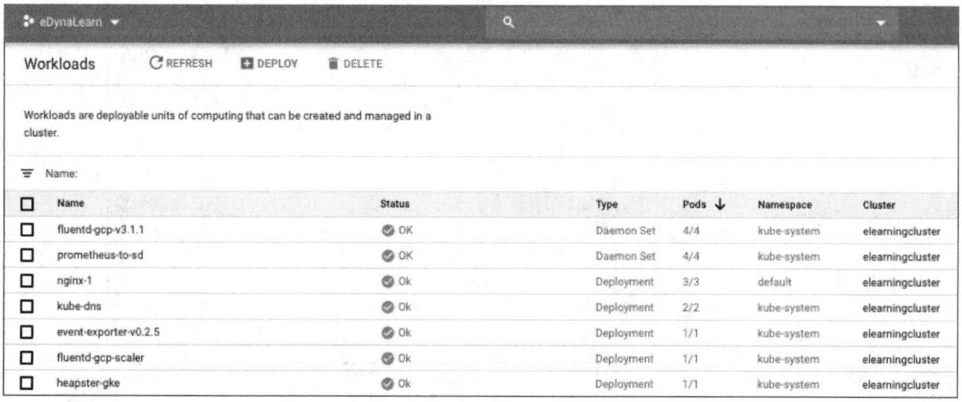

Figure 4-21   Workloads overview interface

Figure 4-22
Scale interface
under the
Action menu

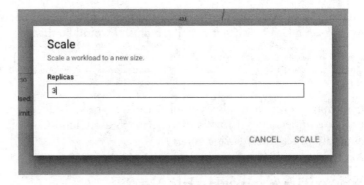

Pods are deployable managed objects. Each Pod has a configuration parameter called a Replica, which is a measure of how many applications can run concurrently in a Deployment. To modify the number of applications that can run in a Deployment, go to the Actions menu in the top-right corner of the screen. Upon selecting the drop-down menu, you have two options to resize the number of Replicas. You can choose to either scale or autoscale. When scale is selected, the only parameter that is modified is the number of Replicas. It can either increase or decrease (see Figure 4-22).

On the other hand, when autoscaling is selected, several parameters are configurable. Not only are Replicas adjustable, but parameters including CPU and memory utilization are adjustable as well (see Figure 4-23). Other actions include exposing a Service on a port and deploying code updates through the use of the rolling updates feature. A rolling update measures the wait time before a Pod can update, the maximum number of Pods allowable, and a minimum number of unavailable Pods permissible.

Figure 4-23
Autoscale
interface under
the Actions
menu

Autoscale
Automatically increase or decrease the number of replicated pods to maintain
performance and minimize cost. Horizontal Pod Autoscaling

Minimum number of replicas ⓘ   Maximum number of replicas ⓘ

1| 5

Autoscaling metrics
Use metrics to determine when to autoscale the deployment

CPU (80%)   ✎

＋ Add metric

CANCEL   DELETE   UPDATE

Figure 4-24
Output of Pod
deployments
using Cloud Shell

```
jack@cloudshell:~ (edynalearn)$ kubectl get deployments
NAME       READY   UP-TO-DATE   AVAILABLE   AGE
nginx-1    1/1     1            1           90m
```

Managing Pods Using Cloud Shell or Cloud SDK

Similar to managing nodes, the use of the `kubectl` command to work with Deployments. There is specific command-line terminology associated with Deployments as well. To identify what deployments are available currently, use the following command line:

```
kubectl get deployments
```

When you press ENTER, the output from the command line will appear in Cloud Shell or Cloud SDK (see Figure 4-24).

Defining the scaling and autoscaling parameters is similar for Cloud Console and command-line applications. For scaling, you must determine the name of the Deployment and the number of replicas. Autoscaling requires a more extensive set of parameters, including the minimum and maximum number of replicas available. Other parameters include CPU utilization within the command-line statement. Here are two examples of outputs—the first for scaling and the second for autoscaling:

- A Deployment named nginx-2 with four replicas:
  ```
  kubectl scale deployment nginx-2 --replicas 4
  ```
- A Deployment named nginx-2, with CPU utilization of 30 percent, a minimum of one replica, and a maximum of six replicas:
  ```
  kubectl autoscale deployment nginx-2 --max 6 --min 1 --CPU-percent 30
  ```

Regardless of which method is used to manage a Pod, there are numerous configuration options you can choose from when conducting maintenance. If Pod maintenance occurs at an individual level, it is possible system performance will be impacted by a misconfiguration given the numerous options available.

Managing Kubernetes Services

Services bring a set of Pods together and treat them as a single resource. Deployments and Services are available as a single package. An example Service that comes with a Kubernetes Deployment is a load balancer. Whether the purpose is to add, modify, or delete a Service, other parameters will also be updated.

Managing Services Using Cloud Console

Services are made available in Deployments. In Cloud Console, you need to select the Workloads menu option under the Kubernetes Engine to display a list of Deployments. For you to create a Service, a container must exist or be created with an image stored in a Google Container Registry. Other alternatives include GitHub and BitBucket.

Figure 4-25
Deployment
interface
illustrating
the required
repository/
URL path

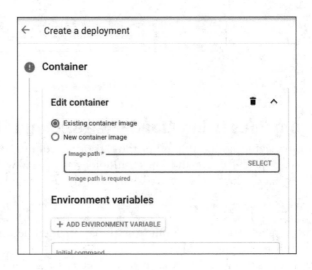

Alternately, if there is a direct URL path to an image, enter that in the image path instead of using the Deployment (see Figure 4-25).

Should there be a need for unique labels, to provide initial commands to run the Deployment, or a specific name for the application, this is the opportunity to make such changes. It will take a few moments to create the new instance, including the required Services.

Clicking the new Deployment provides a list of all Services as part of the Deployment details.

There are two ways to manage and review the Service details. The first option is to click the link under Exposing Services found on the Deployments page, accessible via the Workloads menu. The second option is to go to the Services & Ingress tab.

Should there be a need to delete a Service, go to the specific Service detail page and click the Delete button in the top navigation bar (see Figure 4-26). The Service container-application-service is deleted in this figure.

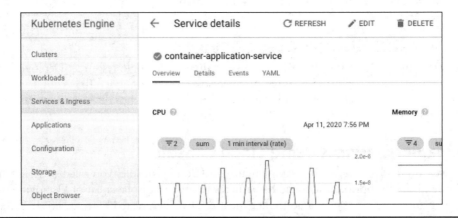

Figure 4-26   Service detail page example and navigation options

Command	Purpose	Command Line
list	Provides a description of all available Services	kubectl get services
add	Adds a new Service	kubectl run <service name> --image=<location> --port <port number>
expose	Exposes Services to resources outside a cluster	kubectl expose deployment <service name> --type=<service type>
delete	Deletes a Service	kubectl delete service <service name>

Table 4-2 Commands for Services and Example Command Lines

Managing Services Using Cloud Shell or Cloud SDK

The kubectl command is helpful when you're trying to manage all Service activity. There, of course, is specific terminology related to Services. Furthermore, the pertinent parameters to apply to the command line vary slightly. Table 4-2 provides the command lines for listing, adding, exposing, and deleting Services. Across all examples, the parameters require the Service name, path to the deployment, the network port, and the type of Service.

Image Repository Management

In the preceding three sections, several references were made to the Google Container Registry to support the deployment of Containers, Pods, and Services. Google Container Registry is a GCP API-based service that must be enabled before it is used to store container images across any containerized deployments. Once the Google Container Registry is enabled, make sure that the project using the Container Registry is provisioned with the billing and security credentials.

Image Repository and Image Details with Cloud Console

To view the Container Registry from the navigation area in Cloud Console, look under the Tools menu (see Figure 4-27). You will be able to review all images placed in the repository as well as corresponding configurations. Two specific settings are available: Vulnerability Scanning and Setting Images Available For Public Access. Under the Images

Figure 4-27
Container Registry navigation in Cloud Console

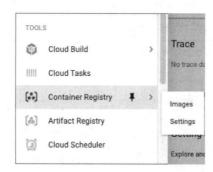

tab, a user can review details regarding the images available in the repository, such as name, hostname, and version.

Image Repository and Image Details Using Cloud Shell or Cloud SDK

Assuming that there are images in a given Cloud Container Registry, it is possible to query the image repository. The command line that allows a user to query the registry is `gcloud container images list`. Should there be a need to access a specific repository, the use of the `--repository` extension is appropriate. Bear in mind that it is necessary to add the location extension to the repository entry. For example, should you want access to the Google Container Registry, the command-line entry is `gcloud container images list --repository gcr.io/google-containers` (see Figure 4-28).

Two other commands that are relevant using Cloud Shell or Cloud SDK are `delete` and `describe`. The `delete` command removes an existing image from the repository, whereas `describe` provides a detailed overview of a given image.

Here's a sample statement illustrating the deletion of an image from the Container Registry:

```
gcloud container images delete gcr.io/edynalearn/library-vm
```

And here's a sample statement that describes an image in the Container Registry:

```
gcloud container images describe gcr.io/edynalearn/library-vm
```

Cloud Console, Cloud Shell, and Cloud SDK can all be used to query the Container Registry as a way to manage containerized images for Kubernetes Engine. There are several prerequisites, including security credentialing with IAM, billing setup, and the initial configuration of Docker to push and pull images to the Container Registry. Once all of these prerequisites are complete, you can easily support image management using this centralized cloud Container Registry.

```
jack@cloudshell:~ (edynalearn)$ gcloud container images list --repository gcr.io/google-containers
NAME
gcr.io/google-containers/addon-builder
gcr.io/google-containers/addon-resizer
gcr.io/google-containers/addon-resizer-amd64
gcr.io/google-containers/addon-resizer-arm
gcr.io/google-containers/addon-resizer-arm64
gcr.io/google-containers/addon-resizer-ppc641e
gcr.io/google-containers/addon-resizer-s390x
```

Figure 4-28   Example of Container Registry images using Cloud Shell

Exercise 4-1: Creating and Managing Kubernetes Engine Clusters

Throughout the chapter, you were introduced to many Google Kubernetes Engine concepts. This exercise brings together many of these concepts. At the completion of this exercise, you should be able to perform the following tasks:

- Create a Kubernetes Engine cluster
- Establish authentication credentials for the cluster
- Modify the Deployment
- Deploy an application to the cluster
- Expose a Service
- Describe a Service and Deployment
- Delete the cluster

The first part of the exercise is to identify where the Kubernetes Engine project is stored:

1. Open Google Cloud Shell and enter the following command line:

   ```
   gcloud config list project
   ```

2. The command line will validate what project you are in. For this exercise, the project is edynalearn.

The next part of the exercise involves creating the Kubernetes cluster:

3. Use the following parameters to create the cluster:

   ```
   gcloud container --project "edynalearn" clusters create  "exercise-cluster"
   --zone "us-central1-c" --username "admin"  --machine-type "n1-standard-1"
   --image-type "COS" --disk-type "pd-standard" --disk-size "100" --num-nodes "3"
   --enable-stackdriver-kubernetes --enable-autoupgrade --enable-autorepair
   ```

   It may take a few minutes to load. A few warnings may appear; you can ignore them as these are informational in nature. The output from creating the gcloud container, which includes the created clusters, appears in Figure 4-29.

```
NAME              LOCATION        MASTER_VERSION   MASTER_IP       MACHINE_TYPE   NODE_VERSION    NUM_NODES   STATUS
exercise-cluster  us-central1-c   1.14.10-gke.27   104.197.35.180  n1-standard-1  1.14.10-gke.27  3           RUNNING
```

Figure 4-29 Output of created exercise-cluster container

NOTE The command line specifies the project name, zone, username, machine type, image type, disk type, disk size, number of nodes required for the cluster, enablement of Google Operations for monitoring, enablement of autoupgrade, and enablement of autorepair. If you were to complete this activity using Cloud Console, all of these options would be entered on a single interface screen.

4. Once you execute the `gcloud` command to create your cluster, credentials must be added. Enter the following on the command line. Always include the zone unless otherwise noted (see Figure 4-30).

```
gcloud container clusters get-credentials exercise-cluster --zone us-central1-c
```

So far you have created the necessary container, which contains a series of clusters and credentials. The next step is to deploy a containerized application.

The exercise utilizes the Google Apps sample library. You will run the paymentservice app in your cluster. If you recall, a Kubernetes object creates and manages cluster resources. Kubernetes is a framework that creates a single deployable object to support an application such as the paymentservice app. Objects such as Services provide configuration rules and parameters to access the application across your platform of choice.

5. Run the following `kubectl run` command in Cloud Shell to create a new Deployment exercise-server from the paymentservice container image:

```
kubectl run exercise-server --image=gcr.io/google-samples/paymentservice
```

6. Although the command line creates a Deployment object that represents the paymentservice app, the port is not exposed. The next query exposes the port:

```
kubectl expose deployment exercise-server --port 80
```

You've created a standard container. However, there is a need to modify the Deployment.

7. The following command line will allow you to autoscale the number of Pods from three to five. It also configures the clusters so that it can perform with a CPU utilization up to 70 percent.

```
kubectl autoscale deployment exercise-server --max 5 --min 1 --cpu-percent 70
```

8. The system will return a response indicating the following:

```
horizontalpodautoscaler.autoscaling/exercise-server autoscaled
```

9. To validate all changes have been accurately made to your containers Services and Deployment, enter these two statements and review the output:

```
kubectl describe service
kubectl describe deployment
```

```
jack@cloudshell:~ (edynalearn)$ gcloud container clusters get-credentials exercise-cluster --zone us-central1-c
Fetching cluster endpoint and auth data.
kubeconfig entry generated for exercise-cluster.
```

Figure 4-30 Output of bound credentials for exercise-cluster container

```
jack@cloudshell:~ (edynalearn)$ gcloud container clusters delete exercise-cluster --zone us-central1-c
The following clusters will be deleted.
 - [exercise-cluster] in [us-central1-c]

Do you want to continue (Y/n)?  y

Deleting cluster exercise-cluster...done.
Deleted [https://container.googleapis.com/v1/projects/edynalearn/zones/us-central1-c/clusters/exercise-cluster].
```

Figure 4-31   Output confirmation of cluster deletion

The last part of the exercise is to delete the Kubernetes instance:

10. In the Cloud Shell command line, enter the following:

```
gcloud container clusters delete exercise-cluster --zone us-central1-c
```

11. You will be asked to delete the cluster. Enter **Y**. All clusters will be deleted in a few minutes (see Figure 4-31). It should take several minutes to make these changes.

Once this is complete, all cluster instances for exercise-cluster will be deleted from project edynalearn on --zone us-central1-c.

Chapter Review

Google created Kubernetes as an open source project. Google made Kubernetes a freely available platform as it saw enormous potential because Kubernetes allows for containerized orchestration of deployable applications in a cluster. A cluster consists of several machines accessible from Compute Engine that work together in support of one or more applications. Often, it is common to find a single container in a Pod, although multiple container Pods are not uncommon. Kubernetes is defined by its system state, which might include the application container and workloads, network and disk resources, and monitoring behavior. Each of these attributes are known as objects, which are available through the Kubernetes API. Objects may include Pods, Services, Volume, and Namespace.

Container operations define specific processes that must communicate and coordinate activities with the Kubernetes API. Object controllers, including ReplicaSet, Deployment, StatefulSet, DaemonSet, and Jobs, support these actions. Kubernetes cluster actions such as create, update, and delete are all executed using Cloud Console. gcloud supports Kubernetes Engine command-line activity using Cloud Shell or Cloud SDK.

The second half of Chapter 4 covers the approaches to creating and maintaining Kubernetes Engine instances using Cloud Console, Cloud Shell, and Cloud SDK. Tasks that you became familiar with include cluster, node, Pod, service, and image repository management. You also evaluated various gcloud commands throughout the chapter. Finally, you became familiar with the benefits of managing Nodes and Pods, with an emphasis on automation and monitoring management.

Questions

1. A cloud engineer is trying to explain the benefits of GKE to a colleague. The colleague does not understand why his team should implement a cluster-based architecture using GKE to support their application versus a managed instance group. What is the primary reason GKE is more appropriate?

   A. Managed instance groups use the same code across each node, whereas in GKE, Pods execute applications in containers, which are placed in cluster nodes.

   B. Managed instance groups require a user to execute commands using Cloud Console, Cloud SDK, or Cloud Shell, whereas a controller manages all Pod activity in GKE.

   C. Managed instance groups do not offer monitoring, unlike GKE.

   D. A and B are correct.

2. Any time a new node for a Compute Engine instance is created within a cluster, what is the default configuration that the administrator should expect to see when reviewing the cluster details page?

   A. f1-micro-1, 1 CPU, 1.7GB

   B. n1-standard-1, 1 CPU, 3.75GB

   C. n2-standard-1, 1 CPU, 3.75GB

   D. n1-standard-1, 2 CPU, 3.75GB

3. Which of the following does not utilize a Pod specification in GKE to function?

   A. DaemonSet

   B. StatefulSet

   C. Workload

   D. Deployment

4. Which of the following statements is accurate about Pods?

   A. ReplicaSets use a template to meet the needs of creating new Pod.

   B. Pods are always established as the smallest single objects.

   C. Objects manage replicated Pods.

   D. Pods are only active on a node when it receives an API call.

5. An organization recently implemented GKE, which includes a service running an application within several clusters. The organization indicated that a stable IP address is not a necessarily requirement. Which service type did the organization decide would best suit its business requirements?

   A. ClusterIP

   B. LoadBalancer

   C. ExternalName

   D. Headless

6. A recent surge of calls has come into the IT helpdesk about an application that resides on a GKE cluster. The cloud engineer would like to know basic infrastructure data on each node because she suspects, as in the past, the system may need additional processing capacity. Which command line can the admin use to find out the state of the utilization?

    A. `gcloud container clusters project system-a -zone us-east1-a`

    B. `gcloud container clusters list`

    C. `gcloud container clusters describe system-a -zone us-east1-a`

    D. `gcloud container clusters get-credentials system-a -zone us-east1-a`

7. A mission-critical system running on GKE often requires system maintenance. Recently, the system administrator added GPU capacity and configured the system to autoscale storage capacity with the hope that there will be fewer required maintenance calls. What type of policy would best suit the IT operations team to ensure the system remains stable?

    A. Alerting policy

    B. Uptime check

    C. Notification

    D. System audit

8. A new set of Kubernetes clusters was configured for a school district by a Google Cloud Platform services provider. The school district did not pay for support services because they are under a budget crunch. Their IT administrator would like to monitor system performance of their GKE instances. What monitoring tool would best assist the IT administrator?

    A. Cloud Shell

    B. Cloud Console

    C. Operations Suite

    D. Notifications

9. What `kubectl` command would an administrator use to update a resource on a server?

    A. `apply`

    B. `edit`

    C. `annotate`

    D. `patch`

10. What type of file is created during containerization that can be reused to establish a template for reuse in creating additional containers, configurations, and settings?

    A. XML

    B. JSON

    C. EXE

    D. YAML

11. A cloud engineer would like to deploy a container using Cloud SDK. However, when he uses the command-line tool, he gets errors. Why is that the case?

    A. He must install the `kubectl` command-line tool.

    B. He needs to use the parameter `gcloud container clusters`.

    C. He can only use Cloud Console.

    D. He can only use Cloud Shell; Cloud SDK is not allowed for container deployments.

12. A cloud engineer is configuring a container to store images using Cloud Container Registry. So far, the administrator has enabled the Cloud Container Registry API and configured the IAM setting against the project that will handle the Container Registry. The administrator has assumed that, other than pushing images to the repository, all the prerequisites have been met. Something isn't working properly. What step did the administrator forget?

    A. The container is properly set up. Nothing is wrong.

    B. Billing information must be configured.

    C. Cloud Container Registry vulnerability scanning should be enabled.

    D. Docker configuration for pushing the images to the Cloud Container Registry may not be complete.

13. There has been a recent surge in activity on a Kubernetes Engine cluster running the corporate intranet. The IT administrators are looking to increase CPU utilization to 70 percent and the number of Pods from three to six. What command-line state would the administrators apply in Cloud SDK or Cloud Shell?

    A. `kubectl autoscale deployment intranet-site --max 6 --min 1 --cpu-percent 70`

    B. `kubectl autoscale deployment intranet-site --max 6 --min 3 --cpu-percent 90`

    C. `kubectl deployment intranet-site autoscale --max 6 --cpu-percent 70`

    D. `kubectl scale intranet-site --replicas 6`

14. You need to increase the number of Pods from three to six without autoscaling using Google Cloud Console. How would you go about doing that?

   A. Modify the Pod directly.

   B. Modify the Service.

   C. Modify the node.

   D. Modify the Deployment.

15. Which of the following is not an action that can be completed under Services?

   A. Autoscale

   B. Automatic Updates

   C. Rolling Update

   D. Expose

Answers

1. **D.** Answers A and B are correct as both conditions are accurate; therefore, answer D is the appropriate response. C is incorrect because Operations Suite can be utilized with managed instance groups.

2. **B.** The correct answer is one virtual CPU and 3.75GB. By process of elimination, the size of the virtual CPU instance is 1. That means answer D is incorrect because the configuration is wrong as the example reflects two CPUs. Next, answer C is incorrect because an n2-standard-1 is a higher-performance machine type. Unless the organization is looking to support compute-optimized or memory-optimized instances, this machine type is seldom used by default. Likewise, f1-micro-1 is a bare-minimum instance. Unless the organization specifically sets the configuration to this as the default, it is not a standard configuration.

3. **C.** A workload is the only one listed that is not a type of controller. The definition of workload is the packaging of containerized, hardware-independent, isolated applications. The package might contain a Pod specification, but it is simply a component of the package. A Deployment, DaemonSet, and StatefulSet, all of which are controllers, utilize Pod specifications.

4. **A.** Pods are created in sets, referred to as replicas (ReplicaSets). A Pod may be the smallest object deployable in a cluster; however, it is often not produced as a single object. Answer C is a false, ambiguous statement. Answer D is incorrect because a Pod always remains active on a node until one of the four conditions are met: process completion, Pod deletion, Pod eviction due to a reduction in resources, or node failure.

5. **D.** By definition, only headless meets the qualifier when a Pod requires a grouping but a stable IP address is not necessary. All the other answers do not fit all the requirements. Services allow for endpoints to discover how Pods run a particular application. There are five service types. Four of them were listed in this question.

ClusterIP is the default type of Service. However, the conditions do not necessarily meet the requisite because a stable IP address is not necessary. LoadBalancer requires a stable IP address in its ability to send a request from a client to a given IP address. ExternalName utilizes the DNS name of a Service as an alias for an external DNS name.

6. **C.** Although answer B provides the administrator information on the readiness of the system, answer C provides full details on the basic infrastructure of each cluster node. Answer D does not provide configuration information. Instead it generates a `kubeconfig` entry. Answer A is a fictious statement.

7. **A.** Alerting policy is the correct answer because an administrator can configure an alert to measure CPU utilization and disk capacity. Should either breach exceed limits, the administrator will be alerted by one or more forms of notification of the incident. Answer B is incorrect because the purpose of a health check is to determine whether an instance responds properly to traffic. Answer C is incorrect because the administrator will receive a notification based on the type of alerting policy. An example of an alert might be an e-mail, SMS, or Slack notification. Answer D is not applicable to this question.

8. **C.** Operations Suite allows an administrator to fully monitor the performance of the Google Kubernetes Engine instances configured by the Google Cloud Platform service provider. Cloud Shell is a Google's web-based command-line utility. Cloud Console is how the administrator would be able to access Operations Suite, via a graphical user interface. Notifications are a potential output from alerting policies and uptime checks configured within Operations Suite.

9. **B.** Although all of the commands allow for some form of updating, only answer B (`edit`) allows for the modifications of a definition of one or more resources on the server by using the default editor. Answer A (`apply`) allows for a configuration change to a resource from a file or stdin. Answer C (`annotate`) supports the modification of an annotation for one or more resources. Answer D (`patch`) is applicable for only updating one or more fields associated with a resource by using a specific merge process.

10. **D.** YAML files are created during containerization. A repeatable template is created that includes configuration and setting details should an administrator want to develop more containers later on. XML, JSON, and EXE are not applicable in this case.

11. **A.** Installing the `kubectl` command-line tool is a prerequisite for using Cloud SDK. Answer B is a command-line statement that is used, but it does not initiate any form of container deployment. Answers C and D are incorrect because you can use Cloud SDK.

12. **B** and **D.** Billing must be configured against a project, as any object or resource stored is considered billable. A Docker repository must be configured as well. This is the only way GCP will allow for the pushing and pulling of images. Answer A is incorrect because the statement is false. Answer C is also incorrect because vulnerability scanning is not a prerequisite.

13. A. Only answer A addresses autoscaling up to six containers and a 70 percent CPU utilization accurately. Answer B states 90 percent CPU utilization and does not properly autoscale. Answer C places autoscale and deployment in the command-line statement in the wrong place. Additionally, there is no --min parameter. Answer D only addresses scale without autoscaling. It also does not address CPU utilization.

14. D. You would modify a Deployment, as it is best practice to modify the entire Deployment, not just an individual Pod. Answer A goes against best practice. Answer B is a fictious response, and answer C is a subset of answer D. You update the node field; however, you are ultimately updating all nodes, not a single node.

15. B. Automatic Updates is not a Service action. Automatic Deployments, on the other hand, is a Service that is available under certain conditions. All other options are available under the Actions menu within Services.

App Engine

In this chapter you will learn to

- Determine when to use App Engine for the Google Cloud Platform (GCP)
- Identify key App Engine components and architecture types
- Understand how to deploy and scale an App Engine application using Cloud Shell, Cloud SDK, and Cloud Console
- Learn techniques and best practices to manage App Engine traffic

App Engine is Google Cloud Platform's Platform as a Service (PaaS) offering. App Engine is a serverless platform that allows developers and cloud engineers to create and deploy applications using web-based languages such as Node.js, PHP, Python, Java, and .NET. Unlike other GCP services, App Engine does not require the use of a virtual machine instance or Kubernetes Engine to operate successfully as it handles the underlying infrastructure requirements. If you are looking to deploy a custom web or mobile-backend application, App Engine is likely the appropriate GCP solution. This chapter addresses the delivery model, architecture, and deployment best practices for App Engine.

Delivery Environment

App Engine supports two delivery environments: standard and flexible. It is possible to run an application in an environment independently or concurrently. App Engine is ideal for applications built using a *microservices architecture,* which is a type of software development technique that allows for an application to be treated as a collection of lightweight, loosely coupled services. The *standard environment* is appropriate when you are looking to establish a sandbox environment supported by a standalone programming language–based application without a needed operating system or third-party software to run the application successfully. *Flexible environments* require supportable resources including Docker containers, code libraries, operating systems, and third-party applications. Applications utilizing the flexible environment will often support backend and background processes. Table 5-1 illustrates the principal differences among the two delivery environment types.

	Standard Environment	Flexible Environment
Typical setup	Runs in sandbox. Uses runtime environment for specific programming language only. Startup takes seconds.	Runs within a Docker container on a Compute Engine virtual machine. Startup takes minutes.
SSH debugging	No	Yes
Background activity	Threading allowed with restrictions. Processes not allowed.	Threading allowed. Processes allowed.
Scaling	Rapid scaling. Can scale to zero.	Receives consistent traffic. Experiences traffic fluctuation. Performance varies based on demand. Deployments and scaling are slower. Requires a minimum of one instance.
Source code requirements	Source code–specific requirements for Python, Java, Node.js, PHP, Ruby, and Go.	Source code is written in any supportable version of Python, Java, Node.js, Go, Ruby, PHP, or .NET.
Cost factors	Runs for free or the cost is minimal for the most part. Scalable as needed. Sudden and extreme spikes of traffic will cause immediate scaling dependencies. Based on instance hours.	Runs in Docker containers and depends on other frameworks. Requires the use of billable GCP resources using Compute Engine. Based on usage of vCPU, memory, and persistent disks.
Access to App Engine API and services	Limited language support	No
Supports installing third-party binaries	Limited language support	Yes

Table 5-1   Comparing Standard vs. Flexible Environments for App Engine

Choosing Between Compute Engine, Kubernetes Engine, and App Engine

A concern among developers and cloud engineers when creating and deploying applications is the need to support and control an application, including its baseline infrastructure. You have four options to consider when using Google Cloud Platform:

- Compute Engine
- Kubernetes Engine (container)
- App Engine (standard environment)
- App Engine (flexible environment)

The App Engine standard environment is considered the basic environment offering among the four. It offers almost all of the automatic features available in Compute Engine and Kubernetes Engine without sacrificing volume and growth, while also integrating services. The standard environment comes with a local software development kit (SDK) to help users begin coding their applications as well as includes a sandbox environment that allows for a smooth transition to the native Google Cloud Platform production environment. While the standard environment is robust, it does have limitations in terms of service and library availability and programmatic language support. An environment that does not require a significant workload and large deployment with minimal configuration effort is best suited for the standard environment.

You may choose Compute Engine or Kubernetes Engine over the App Engine flexible environment if there is a need for more control, scale, and orchestration. Compute Engine and App Engine flexible environment have many commonalities, even more so than App Engine standard environment. Most of the similarities have to do with maintenance and cost. With flexible environment, GCP manages basic virtual machine maintenance. The maintenance regiment includes security and operating system updates. In contrast, in Compute Engine, the responsibility is entirely on the system administrator, similar to that of an on-premises data center environment.

Traffic activity dictates what engine is best suited for an organization. If your app will have frequent, predictable activity, GCP offers committed-use discounts for users as part of the Compute Engine. The cost savings can be significant over time. That said, sustained use of a system, particularly the same type machine, will save an organization even more money. For those organizations that see a repeated use pattern and also believe they will have traffic spikes now and again will likely prefer Compute Engine–based support, which is offered using the flexible environment under certain conditions. When there is no traffic, and the organization can scale down, and the standard environment is adequate.

A final consideration between Compute Engine and the App Engine flexible environment is usage duration. If you intend to use the app for a short-lived period or if fault tolerance is critical for batch processing, a preemptible Compute Engine VM is probably a better-suited option than an App Engine flexible environment.

Modular structuring, where the concern is well beyond cost and maintenance, is when you should weigh the option between Kubernetes Engine and App Engine versus a flexible environment. Containerization and microservice architectures are a perfect option for complex large apps with many facets, such as the use of rendering multiple services. GKE supports a modular structure architecture. In GKE, an operating system is fully abstracted, which allows for a lightweight, single-service Pod for continuous app deployment. When each service needs to be managed independently, including the maintenance and feature set, Kubernetes Engine is more appropriate because you avoid breaking everything when you touch a single instance. GKE also offers a mix of both Compute Engine and App Engine attributes. Compute Engine allows for significant customization and is fully managed. On the other hand, with Kubernetes Engine, GCP still manages a node, and updates are automatically made in order to be current. With App Engine, you can leverage one or more of these environments; it really comes down to ongoing system performance requirements.

App Engine Components

When a developer builds on App Engine, they will implement a solution that contains four components:

- Application
- Service
- Version
- Instance

An *application* is a top-level container that houses the services, versions, and instances of an application (see Figure 5-1). An application is associated with resources tied to a billable region and its data center. Resources include an app's code, settings, credentials, and metadata.

An application must include one service. Each time a *service* is updated, it becomes a new *version,* usually containing the codebase of the application. The reason why version management within App Engine is useful is twofold. First, it offers the ability to support rollbacks when a developer identifies a bug during development or a control-based issue. Second, versions allow applications to more easily migrate features as well as support the splitting of application traffic. Each time a version is issued, it will include a slightly different variation of the application, often including new features, bug fixes, and product enhancements, and it will address earlier issues. As a version executes, it creates an *instance* of an application. Depending on how many locations you run the application, there may be one or more instances of an application. Applications scale up or down based on how many instances are created. App Engine instances are either resident or dynamic. A *resident instance* is one that runs continuously, whereas a *dynamic instance* is available based on load requirements.

 EXAM TIP For the exam, you are not expected to know how to develop an App Engine application, but only how to deploy, scale, and manage traffic for an App Engine application.

Figure 5-1
Example
App Engine
component
architecture

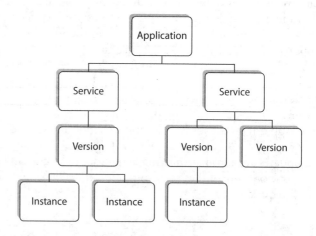

Deploying App Engine Applications

The current scope of Google's Associate Cloud Engineer certification only requires you to know how to deploy an App Engine application. The expectation is that you are able to demonstrate your ability to deploy an App Engine application using Cloud Shell or Cloud SDK. The next section demonstrates how to deploy a sample available App Engine app within the Cloud Shell environment.

Deploying an App Engine Application Using Cloud Shell or Cloud SDK

The first thing you must do when deploying an App Engine application is to install the App Engine components that support the application deployment activity. To determine what is already installed and what requires installation, execute the Cloud Shell and then following these steps:

1. Upon start up, enter the following command:

   ```
   gcloud components list
   ```

2. You should see a list of several App Engine extensions already installed (see Figure 5-2). The one you need to install is the Python extension. If it is not already installed, type the following into Cloud Shell:

   ```
   gcloud components install app-engine-python
   ```

```
For detailed information on this command and its flags, run:
  gcloud components --help
jack@cloudshell:~ (edynalearn)$ gcloud components list

Your current Cloud SDK version is: 289.0.0
The latest available version is: 290.0.0
```

	Components		
Status	Name	ID	Size
Update Available	Cloud SDK Core Libraries	core	14.3 MiB
Not Installed	Appctl	appctl	20.1 MiB
Not Installed	Cloud Bigtable Emulator	bigtable	6.6 MiB
Not Installed	Cloud Firestore Emulator	cloud-firestore-emulator	40.4 MiB
Not Installed	Cloud Spanner Emulator	cloud-spanner-emulator	21.3 MiB
Not Installed	Emulator Reverse Proxy	emulator-reverse-proxy	14.5 MiB
Not Installed	Minikube	minikube	22.1 MiB
Not Installed	anthos-auth	anthos-auth	8.7 MiB
Not Installed	kpt	kpt	19.6 MiB
Installed	App Engine Go Extensions	app-engine-go	4.9 MiB
Installed	BigQuery Command Line Tool	bq	< 1 MiB
Installed	Cloud Bigtable Command Line Tool	cbt	7.7 MiB
Installed	Cloud Datalab Command Line Tool	datalab	< 1 MiB
Installed	Cloud Datastore Emulator	cloud-datastore-emulator	18.4 MiB
Installed	Cloud Pub/Sub Emulator	pubsub-emulator	34.9 MiB
Installed	Cloud SQL Proxy	cloud_sql_proxy	3.8 MiB
Installed	Cloud Storage Command Line Tool	gsutil	3.6 MiB
Installed	Google Cloud Build Local Builder	cloud-build-local	6.0 MiB
Installed	Google Container Registry's Docker credential helper	docker-credential-gcr	1.8 MiB
Installed	Kind	kind	4.5 MiB
Installed	Skaffold	skaffold	12.0 MiB
Installed	gcloud Alpha Commands	alpha	< 1 MiB
Installed	gcloud Beta Commands	beta	< 1 MiB
Installed	gcloud app Java Extensions	app-engine-java	62.3 MiB
Installed	gcloud app PHP Extensions	app-engine-php	
Installed	gcloud app Python Extensions	app-engine-python	6.1 MiB
Installed	gcloud app Python Extensions (Extra Libraries)	app-engine-python-extras	27.1 MiB
Installed	kubectl	kubectl	< 1 MiB

Figure 5-2   List of installed extensions

3. If the application is already installed, it is still a good idea to make sure you have the latest extension library by reentering the command-line statement.

4. The next action you need to take is downloading an App Engine sample. Google provides numerous downloadable samples on GitHub, including the Hello World application. You can find the application at https://github.com/GoogleCloudPlatform/python-docs-samples.

5. Scroll to the end of the GitHub sample page. Click the button that allows you to open the Python App Engine sample that loads into Google Cloud Shell. A new screen will appear where the App Engine executable exports into Cloud Shell (see Figure 5-3).

6. Once this is complete, enter the following command into Cloud Shell at the command prompt:

```
cd cloudshell_open/python-docs-samples/appengine/standard/hello_world
```

7. You will then see the following files in the directory:

- app.yaml
- main.py
- main_test.py

Of the three files, the file you need to concern yourself with is the app.yaml file, which is the most important one. To view what is inside the app.yaml file, enter the following command:

```
cat app.yaml
```

Figure 5-4 is indicative of the Cloud Shell output.

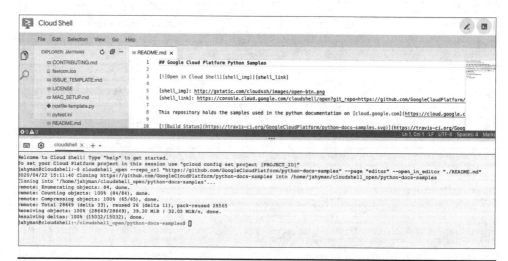

Figure 5-3   The GitHub deployment screen into Cloud Shell for the Hello World application

Figure 5-4
app.yaml Cloud
Shell output

```
runtime: python27
api_version: 1
threadsafe: true

handlers:
- url: /.*
  script: main.app
```

The app.yaml file contains the parameters for the deployment, including the version of Python, the API version, and the Python `threadsafe` parameter, which is set to true in the example. The run protocol is determined by the last three lines of the file.

8. You need to initially set the directory in which the application is found. To do so, enter the following:

   ```
   gcloud config set project <Project ID>
   ```

9. In this case, we are setting our project to edynalearn. Once you set the parameter, you can then deploy your application using the following command:

   ```
   gcloud app deploy app.yaml --project <project ID>
   ```

10. You can add optional parameters such as `--version` to better manage app version control and `--no-promote` to ensure that app traffic is not directed to the instances when executed. Sample output appears in Figure 5-5.

GCP-deployed App Engine projects have a deployable naming convention when accessed on the web. The convention is http://*<project name>*.appspot.com. As seen in Figure 5-5, our URL is https://edynalearn.uc.r.appspot.com. Under most circumstances, the app will be placed in a region. Using the provided example, UC reflects that the app

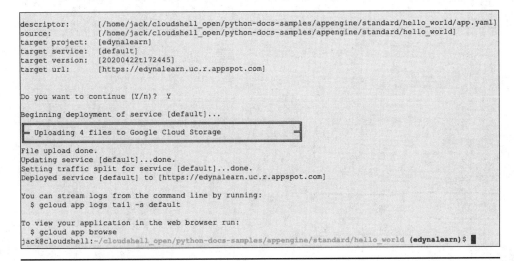

Figure 5-5 Complete App Engine deployment

is located in the US Central Data Center. Other countries' naming conventions exist with each data center being represented by a two-letter code. The URL also reflects that the user would find the deployable Hello World application using the App Engine standard environment.

Monitoring Deployed App Engine Applications Using Cloud Console

After you deploy an app, you can view the health of the application under several conditions, including service condition, version, and instance. To be able to review each of these metrics, go to the App Engine menu under the Google Cloud Platform Cloud Console and select Dashboard. Figure 5-6 presents a holistic view of the current state of all App Engine instances running across our current project.

You can then drill down on a per-app basis to better understand performance under the conditions described in Table 5-2.

Applications can be stopped and started under each of these areas under the Tools menu. Alternatively, you can use the Cloud Shell command line to stop an application version by entering the following:

```
gcloud app versions stop <version identifier>
```

To identify the specific app version, enter the following command:

```
gcloud app versions list
```

Disabling an application can only be accomplished by going to the Cloud Console and choosing App Engine | Settings. Click the Disable button on the resulting screen to stop all application activity completely.

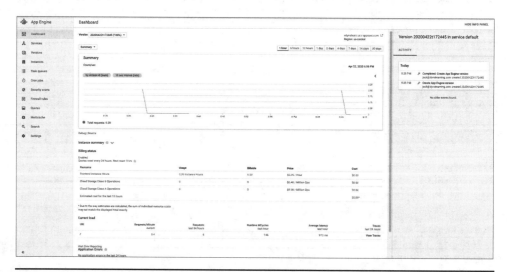

Figure 5-6 Dashboard to monitor the health of App Engine applications

App Engine	Performance Metric
Services	Current Version, Date/Time Deployed, and Tools to Manage Deployment
Version	Current Version, Status (Up/Down), Traffic Allocation, Number of Instances, Type of Instance, Environment, Programming Language Supported, App Size, Last Deployed Date
Instance	Performance by Uptime/Downtime Activity

Table 5-2 App Engine Performance Metrics Available in Google Cloud Console

Scaling and App Engine Applications

App Engine has three modes of scaling: automatic, basic, and manual. Each mode is identified within the app.yaml file:

- *Automatic scaling* creates an instance under several conditions: request rate, response latencies, and specific application metrics. Thresholds can be specific to ensure each metric is achievable. There is a minimum number of instances that must be available for automatic scaling to be available at all times.

- *Basic scaling* creates instances only when requests are received. Each instance shuts down when the application idles. Basic scaling is for intermittent or user-based activities.

- *Manual scaling* supports operational continuity based on how many instances run regardless of load level. Tasks that require systems to run based on complex capacity needs will best utilize manual scaling as the choice.

Table 5-3 presents the differences among the three scaling options.

Feature	Automatic	Basic	Manual
Request timeout	10 minutes for HTTP and task queue. 1 minute in select Java, PHP, and Python runtimes. Apps not returning a request within the timeline; App Engine interrupts the request handler and presents an error code.	24 hours for HTTP requests and task queue requests. App Engine interrupts request handler if no response is received. A basic scaled instance can handle a /_ah/start request and execute a program without returning a HTTP response code.	Same as basic scaling.

Table 5-3 Attributes of App Engine Scaling *(continued)*

Feature	Automatic	Basic	Manual
Background threads	N/A	Allowable	Allowable
Residence	Shutdown based on usage.	Shutdown based on idle-timeout parameter. If shutdown past idle-timeout window, instance will be shut down.	Stored in memory and state is preserved across requests. Upon restart, a `/_ah/stop` request appears in logs. If a registered shutdown hook exists, it has 30 seconds to execute before a complete shutdown.
Startup/shutdown	Created on demand to handle request. Automatically turned off when idle.	Created on demand for request and terminated when idle. Based on `idle_timeout` configuration parameter. Instance that has 30 seconds to stop before it is actively terminated.	Sent a start request automatically by App Engine using an empty GET request to `/_ah/start`. Follows same termination process as a basic scaling startup/shutdown.
Instance addressability	Anonymous	Instances are addressed at the URL based on https://<project_id>.*REGION_ID*.r.appspot.com. Configuration of wildcard of custom domains is also possible. Setup of an address or any instance via a URL is allowable.	Same as basic scaling.
Scalability	Scales automatically in response to processing volume. Scaling factors in `automatic_scaling` settings. Based on configuration output.	Service with basic scaling. Configured by setting maximum threshold in instances using `max_instances` parameter of `basic_scaling`. Instances scale with processing volume.	Configure number of instances for each version in service configuration file. Number corresponds to size of dataset held in memory or managed by offline work.

Table 5-3   Attributes of App Engine Scaling

Dynamic Scaling Principles

App Engine has the ability to scale by either basic or automatic scaling using any number of dynamic instances. Scaling often depends on incoming volume requests. Often, an increase in application requests will correlate to increases in dynamic instances.

With *basic scaling,* App Engine costs are often kept low. While the cost may be kept low, App Engine may actually end up experiencing high levels of latency and an increase of incoming volume requests at a given point in time. If an instance is not available to serve a request, App Engine will initiate a new instance. There are times, however, that instances may still be queued until the startup process is complete. Basic scaling is not appropriate when trying to achieve the lowest latency possible. Instead, consider *automatic scaling* because it supports preemptible instance creation.

Automatic scaling requires you to decide among a set of trade-offs. Performance and cost are often significant considerations. Unlike with basic scaling, load is handled automatically via the creation of new instances when the load queue of app requests increases.

As a cloud engineer, you have the ability to decide if you want the instance to be dynamic or not. If the instance is configured for automatic scaling or basic scaling, it is configured as dynamic. Otherwise, a manually scaled instance is deemed resident. To configure the app.yaml file for scaling, add the `automatic_scaling` parameter along with one of the key pairs in Table 5-4.

You can call one or more of the parameters listed in Table 5-4 for `automatic_scaling` and place them within the app.yaml file under the `automatic_scaling` configuration section. Should you decide to use `basic_scaling` instead, the only allowable parameters are `max_instances` and `idle_timeout`.

Parameter	Definition
max_instances	Maximum number of instances for App Engine to create for a given module version.
min_instances	Minimum number of instances for App Engine to create for a given module version.
max_idle_instances	Maximum number of idle instances to be kept running and capable of serving traffic.
min_idle_instances	Minimum number of idle instances to be kept running and capable of serving traffic.
target_cpu_utilization	Specifies the CPU threshold to start new instances in order to handle traffic. Balances performance and cost measures.
target_throughput_utilization	Used in conjunction with `max_concurrent_requests` to specify when a new instance starts a new request. When the number of concurrent requests reaches a value equal to `max_concurrent_requests` times `target_throughput_utilization`, the schedule initiates a new instance.
max_concurrent_requests	The number of concurrent requests an automatic scaling instance can accept before calling for a new instance.
max_pending_latency	Maximum time App Engine should allow a request to wait in the queue before starting new instances to handle requests, so pending latency issues are mitigated.
min_pending_latency	Minimum time that App Engine should allow a request to wait in the queue before starting a new instance.
idle_timeout	Shutdown time after receiving last request.

Table 5-4   Scaling Parameters

Traffic Handling and App Engine

When there is more than one version of an App Engine application, you may find it useful to split the traffic distribution. Reasons include conducting A/B testing, traffic management for even distribution of resource rollout, and performance opportunities for enhancing services. There are three options you can choose from to split traffic: IP address, HTTP cookie management, and random handling.

It is often easier to split traffic among IP addresses as it provides continuity and reliability, but HTTP cookie-based splitting is more precise because it offers better opportunities for version control management. Random offers a balance between the two. To split traffic among an App Engine app, follow these steps using Google Cloud Console:

1. Go to the Google Cloud Console and select App Engine | Versions.

2. On the Versions page, go to the top-right menu and click Split Traffic.

3. Select which option you want to split the traffic by—IP address, Cookie, or Random.

4. Once you've selected your option and completed the necessary configuration, click Save.

Alternatively, you can use Google Cloud Shell or Cloud SDK to enter the following command:

```
gcloud app services set-traffic
```

You can choose to split your traffic a few different ways using the command line. Your options are `ip`, `cookie`, and `random`. Enter the following command in Cloud Shell or Cloud SDK:

```
gcloud app services set-traffic --split-by <option>
```

To split traffic up proportionally, the command is

```
gcloud app services set-traffic --splits v1= <value>, v2 = <value>
```

For example, you might use the values `.7` and `.3`.

Should you need to migrate your traffic from one version of an App Engine application to a newer version, use `--migrate`. If you're trying to ensure traffic does not reach a service, the command-line parameter applied is `--no-promote`.

IP Address Splitting

An application that sends its traffic to an IP address is assigned a value between 0 and 999. An IP address hashes the number and then uses that assigned number to route the request. Assuming the IP remains static, the application should have no problem maintaining its performance. IP addresses can be considered static, but seldom are they permanent. If these conditions are met, IP address traffic splitting is an adequate approach.

There are some downsides to using IP traffic splitting. End-user activity across a session may cause a shift in the ability to stick to a single IP address. Also, holding onto a single IP address may not be viable. Furthermore, IP addresses are assigned at the version level of an application, which means that traffic splits will differ from what you often initially specify. Finally, managing internal requests between apps with IP addresses does not yield optimal behavior. It is better to use cookie management instead in these instances. When a request is sent between one or more App Engine instances running on GCP operating a small subset of IP addresses under the same version, you will often find the request behaves the same way. Requests are often sent to the same version of an App Engine app. The internal requests are often ignored, resulting in a complete avoidance of the percentage assigned for your assigned IP address traffic splits.

HTTP Cookie Splitting

With cookie splitting, an application will look in the HTTP request header for the cookie named GOOGAPPUID. It seeks to find a value between 0 and 999. If the cookie exists, the value is assigned to a cookie, and the request is routed. Otherwise, the request is randomly assigned and then routed. When the response cannot find GOOGAPPUID, the application will first append the instance by adding the cookie. Then it will assign a random value of 0–999 before sending the request. Cookie splitting is much more accurate than IP address splitting because a cookie can remain in place with an application whereas an IP address often drops as an individual user roams. Google estimates that precision for traffic routing on GCP can be as close as 0.1 percent for a target split with cookie splitting.

Like IP address splitting, cookie splitting has a few limitations. A mobile or desktop app must also manage the GOOGAPPUID cookies. Assuming a Set-Cookie response is used, the app must store and include the cookie with each follow-up request. Browser-based apps take care of cookie management automatically, as the cookie is placed in the content header, allowing for the session to remain stable. A second shortcoming is the extra work it takes to split cookie-based traffic. A cookie requires a request to be sent from inside the GCP infrastructure. That means you need to forward the request each time you are inside the bounds of GCP from one app to another app. It is not recommended that a request be made outside of a given internal user.

Chapter Review

App Engine is GCP's Platform as a Service offering. It offers developers the ability to create and deploy applications in specific programming languages. App Engine applications are deployable in a standard or flexible environment. Standard is best when traffic activity and demand will have low latency, resulting in little to no cost for deployment. Flexible environments are containerized, sharing many of the same attributes as Compute Engine and Kubernetes Engine. Weighing what environment is best suited for the deployment of an app often comes down to performance, scale, and cost requirements. Architecturally speaking, App Engine deployments consist of services, versions, and instances. Depending on the depth and capabilities of your application, it is possible to run multiple versions of an application concurrently. Traffic splitting helps manage application performance. The three options for traffic management are address by IP, HTTP cookie, and random assignment. Almost all configuration activities for App Engine take place in the app.yaml file. Parameters that you need to concern yourself with for the exam include language assignment and scaling exclusively.

Questions

1. You are trying to describe to a first-time app developer the hierarchy within an App Engine app. Which of the following is best suited to handle the developer's bug control issues during the development process?

    A. Application

    B. Version

    C. Service

    D. Instance

2. John needs to deploy an update to his Python app. He has been asked to enable `automatic_scaling`. What file would John need to modify in order to deploy this change?

    A. main.py

    B. main_test.py

    C. app.yaml

    D. app.config

3. Your team recently launched a new online microservice for your corporate intranet. Before deploying the service companywide, you would like for a small subset of users to test the service. In order to ensure the microservice works, how would the development team go about deploying the microservice without fully exposing it to the entire company?

    A. `gcloud app deploy set-traffic --no-promote`

    B. `gcloud app services set-traffic --split-by`

    C. `gcloud app services set-traffic --migrate`

    D. `gcloud app services set-traffic --block`

4. You are trying to determine the best development environment to implement your salary calculator that will be accessible 10–15 times per month by the human resources department at your company. The calculator will often be used in waves. What kind of environment is best suited for this type of application?

    A. Standard environment

    B. Flexible environment

    C. Compute Engine

    D. Kubernetes Engine

5. The app.yaml file needs to be modified to ensure that there is a minimum number of instances that run at all times and are able to serve traffic. Which parameter should be included in the app.yaml file?

   A. min_instances

   B. max_instances

   C. min_idle_instances

   D. max_idle_instances

6. What are the three modes of scaling in App Engine?

   A. Automatic, basic, and dynamic

   B. Automatic, basic, and manual

   C. Automatic, dynamic, and resident

   D. Automatic, basic, and resident

7. You are trying to decide a method to split traffic for your microservice application. The application is predominantly used on smartphones and tablet computers. What method would best serve users who actively roam?

   A. IP splitting

   B. Random

   C. HTTP cookie splitting

   D. Mitigating

8. Which of the following is not a method to view the status of a component in App Engine from Google Cloud Console?

   A. Settings

   B. Services

   C. Instances

   D. Versions

9. A team at DynaLearning just deployed their new microlearning app. They want to send out an e-mail to the North America team informing them that their new application is up and running. What URL would they send out in a companywide e-mail?

   A. https://edynalearn.uc.r.appspot.com/

   B. https://edynalearn.ew.r.appspot.com/

   C. https://edynalearn.r.appspot.com/

   D. https://edynalearn.usa.appspot.com/

10. What step should a cloud engineer take before deploying an app.yaml file assuming the Python Extension is already installed?

    A. They should run `cat app.yaml`.

    B. They should run `gcloud components list`.

    C. They should run `gcloud components describe`.

    D. They should run `gcloud components install app-engine-python`.

11. You have a PHP application that you would like to host in GCP. It will have consistent traffic flow at all times. The administrators want to take a hands-off approach on system maintenance. What GCP product approach would best suit this application?

    A. Standard environment

    B. Flexible environment

    C. Compute Engine

    D. Kubernetes Engine

12. Which of the following programming languages is not supported in the standard environment?

    A. .NET

    B. Java

    C. Python

    D. PHP

13. An App Engine microservice is recently deployed at ABC Health Corp. The development team has decided it needs to split traffic for its users. Physicians need dedicated access to the application, while patients will be given access based on availability. What would the team at ABC Health need to do if they decided to use IP splitting for traffic management?

    A. Migrate all traffic to the physician app instance.

    B. Apply GOOGAPPUID in the header.

    C. Get a static IP address.

    D. There are no special requirements.

14. `idle_timeout` and `max_instances` are the only two parameters available for what type of scaling?

    A. Dynamic scaling

    B. Manual scaling

    C. Resident scaling

    D. Basic scaling

15. Why would one choose App Engine over Compute Engine?

    A. It allows for GCP to handle system maintenance on a weekly basis for VM instances for those environments that experience use patterns.

    B. Short-duration and preemptible VMs are in line with App Engine usage objectives.

    C. Sustained and committed pricing is an advantage.

    D. All of the above are reasons to choose App Engine.

Answers

1. **B.** Versions help developers manage bug development and rollbacks within the control life cycle. It is also beneficial for migration and traffic splitting. Applications are the top-level folder. Instances are the output once a version is compiled and rolled out. Services contain different components within a version.

2. **C.** app.yaml is the configuration file in the Python deployment that contains the configurations. The .py files are the application code files. app.config is a fictious file.

3. **A.** `--no-promote` hides visible traffic from the public. `--split-by` redistributes traffic. `--migrate` shifts traffic from once instance to another. `--block` is a fictious parameter.

 4. **A.** Standard environments support low-level, infrequent usage by very small user populations. Since this application is low to no cost but will have occasional traffic, it fits the scope of a standard application (sandbox-type environment). The application seems to be too small and will not require the resources for a flexible environment or GKE instance. Unless the application intent was for one-time or short duration use (preemptible VM), Compute Engine is also not an advantageous option.

5. **C.** The minimum number of instances to keep running and capable of serving traffic is only covered by the parameter `min_idle_instances`. The number of instances for App Engine to create for a given module version is `min_instances`. Both `max`-based variables cover the upper limits, not the minimum number of instances.

6. **B.** Dynamic and resident are two instance types, not modes of scaling. Any mention made of dynamic or resident make the answer incorrect. Therefore, by process of elimination, only answer B is accurate for scaling: automatic, basic, and manual.

7. **C.** HTTP cookie splitting is the only option that will hold a session consistent for a mobile or smartphone device. Google indicates that HTTP cookies have the most precision, assuming the cookie is called out in the header and remains intact. IP splitting is dynamic. When a user changes location, there is a change in IP address because the device often connects to different networks. It is often

an unreliable way of splitting traffic for mobility solutions. Random splitting is a way to balance traffic, but it cannot provide the most definitive way to ensure traffic reliability. Mitigation is not a traffic-splitting option. It is a technique to move traffic from one instance to another.

8. **A.** Settings only allow you to disable an App Engine instance. They do not allow you view the status of a component. All other options allow for the viewing of component status in App Engine.

9. **A.** Only uc is an accurate regional ID within North America (us-central). Answer B (ew) is for European West. Answer C does not contain a region, and answer D is an invalid region.

10. **D.** Even though the Python extension is already in place, best practices suggest you make sure that the latest version is available. Answer A indicates a post-process extension deployment action. Answers B and C evaluate and describe the components available. They do not; however, update the actual extensions to the latest version.

11. **B.** Predictable, consistent traffic with a low-touch maintenance approach describes a flexible environment. Standard environment and Compute Engine require a system administrator to support the environments (patch and security management). Kubernetes Engine, which supports a hands-off approach, is for more robust, larger-scale workloads. The description does not meet the business need.

12. **A.** .NET is only supported in a flexible environment. All other languages are supported in the standard environment.

13. **C.** The only way to ensure that the doctors will be able to maintain a consistent traffic flow is if a static IP address is assigned to the physician-based portion of the application. A dynamic IP address will result in access problems for the physicians. Migrating all traffic to the physician app is only good if the address remains static. Applying the cookie in the header is an appropriate tactic for HTTP cookie or random traffic splitting only. Answer D is not applicable.

14. **D.** Basic scaling only uses the `idle_timeout` and `max_instances` parameter types. Manual scaling can utilize more than just these parameters. There is no such thing as dynamic and resident scaling. These are two App Engine instance types.

15. **A.** Flexible environments leverage Docker-based containers. Google runs weekly maintenance on these environments and allows for such environments to be "low touch" when traffic is predictable and has a known use pattern. Answer B is incorrect because preemptible VMs are appropriate for Compute Engine, not App Engine. With answer C, one can leverage sustained and committed pricing as an advantage; however, this, too, is a Compute Engine principle that does not fully resonate with App Engine. Answer D is not applicable because answers B and C are incorrect.

Cloud Functions and Cloud Run

In this chapter you will learn to

- Determine when to use Cloud Functions and Cloud Run for Google Cloud Platform (GCP)
- Deploy and implement Cloud Functions and Cloud Run resources
- Determine best practices for traffic splitting, scaling, and versioning

Serverless Compute Options

Serverless computing allows a developer to focus on development activities, such as writing code, instead of having to worry about infrastructure and system maintenance. Some of the benefits serverless computing offers are zero server management, autoscaling, pay-as-you-go resource usage, and on-demand resource provisioning. You should consider using serverless computing solutions for systems that offer stateless HTTP applications, web and mobile applications, IoT and sensor-based applications, data processing solutions, and chatbots. With GCP, three platform offerings support serverless computing: App Engine, Cloud Functions, and Cloud Run. Each of the serverless compute options in the GCP portfolio has unique features. The differences between the three are defined as follows:

- **App Engine** When you are looking to build a serverless application meant for use with a web or API-based backend, App Engine is a solid choice. App Engine supports key development languages without the need to worry about infrastructure support.

- **Cloud Functions** Solutions that are event-driven and can easily extend to Google and third-party services best fit in this category. Applications that scale quickly best fit this description, too.

- **Cloud Run** If you require a serverless compute platform that requires an application run in stateless containers, you are likely to find that Cloud Run is the best choice for your deployment. Cloud Run is fully managed, but also the pricing is based on consumption exclusively. Anthos, the GKE serverless container option built on Knative, an open source platform, is available for Cloud Run. Anthos allows for a mixed architecture using on-premises and cloud consumption.

event → Trigger → function : data pass to event f(x)

In Chapter 5, you explored the capabilities of App Engine. This chapter focuses on serverless computing options that are not exclusive to web and API-based backends.

Cloud Functions

Cloud Functions are serverless. A big difference between App Engine and Cloud Functions is that App Engine supports the use of many services in a single application. Cloud Functions support individualized services. Each service is managed and operated independently from the other services. When you have an application that must communicate with multiple application services, such as a web application or one that leverages APIs, App Engine is a suitable choice. The inter-relationship among these services allows for an application to be treated as a managed entity.

If your compute requirements are not associated with multiple services, Cloud Functions should be considered. For example, if you are looking to save or extract data from a database, post a file to a specific storage location, or validate data in order to meet a business requirement, the use of Cloud Functions is likely more appropriate. Cloud Functions enable developers to focus on the activity itself. A developer would not need to worry about activities such as extraction, transformation, and load (ETL) with Cloud Functions in terms of communication among other services. The goal is specific to a single service. Cloud Functions time out after one minute, although the timeout can be extended up to nine minutes in total.

Events, Triggers, and Functions

Events occur when a particular action initiates within the Google Cloud Platform. Examples might include a message being written to the Pub/Sub message queue and documents being pushed to a storage repository. Actions are associated with a given event. GCP supports events in five categories: Cloud Storage, Cloud Pub/Sub, HTTP, Firebase, and Monitoring Logging. Table 6-1 illustrates the event categories and associated activities. Most events require some form of response. A *trigger* is the result of an event response, whereas a *function* is the response to the trigger. A function is when a data argument is passed to a given event.

EXAM TIP Terminology can get confusing at times. Make sure that you know the difference between an event, trigger, and function, as these concepts often come up on the exam within the same question.

Event Category	Action
Cloud Storage	Upload, delete, archive files
Cloud Pub/Sub	Message (topic) published from a queue
HTTP	POST, GET, DELETE, PUT, and OPTION calls
Firebase	Trigger-based activities associated with the Firebase database
Monitoring Logging	Produces a result because of a trigger

Table 6-1 Cloud Functions Event Categories and Actions

Runtime Environments

Functions operate independently in their own environment. When a function is invoked, it runs in a separate instance from other function calls. Unlike in App Engine, where data is shared among application instances, once a function is invoked, it operates on its own. If you need to keep track of the data associated with the events processed, you should use a database or maintain a writable file in Cloud Storage. Currently, GCP supports three runtime environments: Node.js, Python, and Go.

 TIP Building serverless resources can become expensive if you leave the resources in use. You are still required to pay for storage capacity, bandwidth, and any ancillary system activity. Unless you intend to use the resource that you create for regular use, consider creating a new project instead of using an existing project. Once the use of the serverless resource is complete, you can dispose of the resources associated with a project.

In the following exercise, you will learn how to leverage a Cloud Function in the Cloud Pub/Sub category. Of all the categories, Cloud Pub/Sub is associated most often with Cloud Functions.

Exercise 6-1: Executing a Basic Cloud Function

Before you start creating a Cloud Function, make sure you have the Cloud Functions API and Cloud Pub/Sub API enabled in Google Cloud Console. The next steps can be completed using either the Cloud Console or the Cloud Shell/Cloud SDK. This exercise will use the Cloud Shell.

1. Update the components available by entering the following command:

```
gcloud components update
```

2. Once the command is complete, establish your development environment:

```
git clone https://github.com/GoogleCloudPlatform/nodejs-docs-samples.git
```

This example uses the Node.js file:

```
exports.helloPubSub = (data, context) => {
  const pubSubMessage = data;
  const name = pubSubMessage.data
    ? Buffer.from(pubSubMessage.data, 'base64').toString()
    : 'World';

  console.log(`Hello, ${name}!`);
};
```

3. Deploy the helloPubSub runtime. You should enter a name for the Pub/Sub message you would like to express in <YOUR_TOPIC >.

```
gcloud functions deploy helloPubSub --runtime nodejs8 --trigger-topic
<YOUR_TOPIC_NAME>
```

NOTE Node.js version 8 is the current standard. Future iterations are available in beta.

4. After deploying the event, you will want to try to trigger it:

```
gcloud pubsub topics publish <Your Topic> --message <YOUR_NAME>
```

In the example, you would enter:

```
gcloud pubsub topics publish pubsubexample --message jack@dynalearning.com
```

5. Check to make sure the execution is complete:

```
gcloud functions logs read --limit 10
```

6. Assuming you do not want to keep the instance and be charged for use of Cloud Functions and Pub/Sub, enter the following command line to delete these events, triggers, and functions from the system:

```
gcloud functions delete helloPubSub
```

This exercise demonstrates how you can load an application from GitHub and deploy it using Node.js. The application, once deployed, allows you to submit two parameters: Project ID and Your Name. In the example, you only provided one. The event captures the data, and the trigger is the publishing of the message. In this case, the output is Hello, jack@dynalearning.com. The function also allows for the log to produce the first 10 entries stored in the system. Once this exercise is complete, you delete the application.

Whether the code executed is intended for Cloud Storage, HTTP, Cloud Pub/Sub, or another category, the deployment process is the same except for the category parameter.

Cloud Run

Cloud Run is a serverless compute platform that is fully managed by Google Cloud. The difference between Cloud Run, App Engine, and Cloud Functions is that the Cloud Run platform can scale stateless containers, with emphasis on Kubernetes Engine. Because Cloud Run is serverless and abstracts all infrastructure responsibilities, you do not need to worry about application backend support.

Cloud Run is available in two variations. Cloud Run native fully embraces the Google Cloud Platform exclusively. Cloud Run for Anthos supports both Google Cloud and on-premises environment connectivity using Google Kubernetes Engine. Cloud Run is built on an open source application standard, Knative, which allows you to create portable applications.

Exercise 6-2: Deploying an Application in a Container Using Cloud Run

In order to deploy an app using Cloud Run, make sure you have the Cloud Build, Container Registry, and Cloud Run API enabled using Google Cloud Console. The next steps can be completed using either Cloud Console or Cloud Shell/Cloud SDK. This exercise will use Cloud Shell.

1. You first want to write the sample application code. Using the out-of-the-box script available in Google Cloud Platform for Python, a prerequisite for writing the application is creating the necessary directories. Therefore, enter the following into Cloud Shell:

```
mkdir helloworld-python
cd helloworld-python
```

2. You are now ready to create a basic application. You start by creating the data file that will house the script. To create the file, enter the following:

```
docs/serving/samples/hello-world/helloworld-python/app.py
```

The following is the content you would enter into the .py file:

```python
import os

from flask import Flask

app = Flask(__name__)

@app.route('/')
def hello_world():
    target = os.environ.get('TARGET', 'World')
    return 'Hello {}!\n'.format(target)

if __name__ == "__main__":
    app.run(debug=True,host='0.0.0.0',port=int(os.environ.get('PORT',
8080)))
);
};
```

Notice the use of the PORT environment variable. The code responds to requests from the "Hello World" greeting. HTTP handling is done by an existing web server in the container. In this example, the Gunicorn server (https://gunicorn .org/) is utilized because GCP leverages Flask, a Full Stack Python web development framework. If you invoke the application locally, the output is a basic web server that listens to activity on the port.

3. At this point, your application can be containerized. Using a Python Dockerfile, you start a Gunicorn web server that listens to the portal environment variable. Enter the following on the command line to open the Python Dockerfile:

```
docs/serving/samples/hello-world/helloworld-python/Dockerfile
```

4. Enter the following code to prepare the application for deployment into the container:

```
# Use the official Python image from GitHub.
# https://hub.docker.com/_/python
FROM python:3.7-slim

# Copy code that is specific to the local instance into the file.

ENV APP_HOME /app
WORKDIR $APP_HOME
COPY . ./

# Install all production dependencies for the application to work in the
container

RUN pip install Flask gunicorn

# Run the web service upon the container startup. In this
# example, we utilize two worker processes and 6 threads
# per processor. For environments with additional CPU
# cores, you would increase the number of workers to be
# equal to the cores available. This example assumes two
# available cores.

CMD exec gunicorn --bind :$PORT --workers 2 --threads 6 --timeout 0
app:app
```

5. After deploying the script, you may want to add a file. Add the .dockerignore file to exclude files from a container image. To exclude all files from being uploaded to Cloud Build, consider adding a .gcloudignore file.

```
docs/serving/samples/hello-world/helloworld-python/.dockerignore
# In the file you would enter the following items
Dockerfile
README.md
*.pyc
*.pyo
*.pyd
__pycache__
```

6. Now that all parameters are in place, you should build the instances using Cloud Build. Here is the command to enter:

```
gcloud builds submit --tag gcr.io/<project-id>/<application name>
```

On the command line, you need to replace <project-id> with your project's name and <application name> with the name of the application you're building.

7. Your application is built. The last step is to deploy to Cloud Run. To deploy, enter the following command line:

```
gcloud run deploy --image gcr.io/<project-id>/<application name>
--platform managed
```

8. During the deployment, you will be asked a few questions. The default response for each question follows:

- The service name is the application name. In the sample script, it would be helloworld.

- Select the region of your choice for the second prompt. Remember, these are regions, not zones. A sample region is us-east1.
- Enter Y in the command line to allow unauthenticated invocation.

Your application is now deployed to Cloud Run.

 TIP As with Cloud Functions, you will still be charged for storage capacity even when your application is idle within the Container Registry. Should you decide that your application is no longer needed, it is strongly recommended that you delete the build using Google Cloud Console under the Cloud Run section. You do not want to incur any unexpected charges when you are no longer running a service.

Cloud Run for Anthos

If on-premises and container-based support are necessary to manage your serverless application, Cloud Run for Anthos is the best choice for you to consider implementing. Reasons why a developer would choose Cloud Run for Anthos over Cloud Run include the following:

- Simplified development environment
- Operational use of Google Kubernetes Environment
- Serverless capabilities regardless of geography
- Extended autoscaling capability
- Allows for any runtime environment
- Supports monitoring and workflows
- Leverages container workflows and standard APIs, including Container Registry, Cloud Build, and Docker
- Can utilize a custom domain for an application
- Built on Knative, an open source platform allowing for application portability
- Use of GPU/TPU-based compute capacity for larger deployments

The list of features is quite extensive, but it comes down to availability of enterprise features for on-premises and cloud-native capabilities.

Deploying Cloud Events

Cloud Events can be deployed using Cloud Console, Cloud Shell, or Cloud SDK. To fully utilize Cloud Functions, you must enable the Cloud Functions API or the Cloud Run API. If you decide to deploy an instance using Cloud Console, go to the navigation area and locate Cloud Functions under the Compute section (see Figure 6-1).

Figure 6-1
Cloud Functions
and Cloud Run
in Cloud Console
Navigation

Cloud Events and Cloud Storage

Limited knowledge is required for managing Cloud Events using Cloud Storage. In later chapters, you will learn more about the types of storage to utilize. All files are stored in Cloud Storage, which utilizes buckets to add, update, delete, and archive files. You can manage all facets of the Cloud Functions life cycle with events using Cloud Storage.

EXAM TIP   You need to understand about Cloud buckets and object storage as a cloud engineer. You will learn more about object storage in Chapter 7. Know that Cloud buckets are heavily used for creating many dynamic file types throughout GCP.

Cloud Functions Deployment Using Cloud Console

To create a Cloud Function, you first need to enable the Cloud Functions API. Once it's enabled, select the Cloud Functions menu option under Compute. You are prompted to initiate the process of creating a Cloud Function.

Once the Cloud Function is activated, a screen will appear that allows you to define the necessary parameters to create the Cloud Function, as shown in Figure 6-2.

You are asked to provide the following information:

- Function name
- Memory allocation
- Trigger type
- Source code location
- Preferred runtime
- Targeted function to execute
- Environmental variables

Figure 6-2
Creating a Cloud
Function using
Cloud Console
for Storage
Events

You must fill out each field on the page to create and enable the Cloud Function. Of note, you can enter the function code as part of the in-line editor. If you choose to upload the code using a file format, make sure the upload matches the runtime environment selected. Upon Cloud Function creation, it will appear on the Cloud Functions dashboard page, as seen in Figure 6-3.

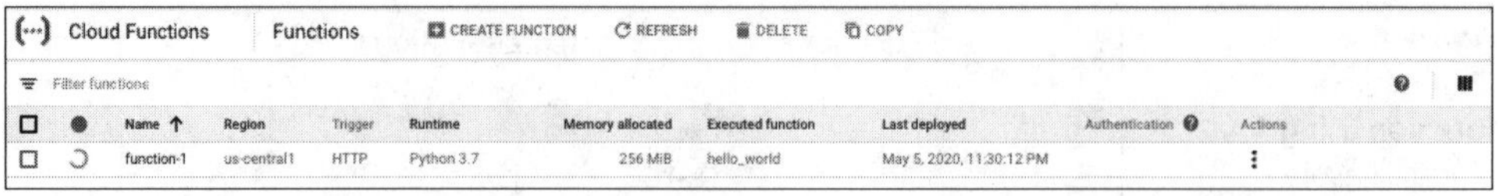

Figure 6-3   Cloud Functions dashboard example

Cloud Functions Deployment Using Cloud Shell and SDK for Storage Events

Building Cloud Functions using command-line tools requires the latest components to be enabled, including making sure all commands and libraries are installed. As previously demonstrated in Exercise 6-1, here is the command to ensure your data is up to date:

```
gcloud components update
```

Runtime environments will be updated if you are told that an update is required, as shown in Figure 6-4. Should you have the latest updates, you are informed that in Cloud Shell or Cloud SDK, all components are up to date. GCP is continually updating the runtime environments; therefore, you may need to install an update if identified. The command for this is

```
gcloud components install <version>
```

Deciding what version of the components you want to install and ensuring it is updated can be completed using the following command:

```
gcloud version
```

The output of all available components appears in Figure 6-5.

For this example, you will install the following:

```
gcloud components install beta
```

Figure 6-4
An update to
the runtime
environment is
needed.

```
Your current Cloud SDK version is: 290.0.1
You will be upgraded to version: 291.0.0

┌─────────────────────────────────────────────────────┐
│          These components will be updated.          │
├──────────────────────────────┬────────────┬─────────┤
│            Name              │  Version   │  Size   │
├──────────────────────────────┼────────────┼─────────┤
│ BigQuery Command Line Tool   │    2.0.57  │ < 1 MiB │
│ Cloud SDK Core Libraries     │ 2020.05.01 │ 14.5 MiB│
│ Cloud Storage Command Line Tool │  4.50   │  3.5 MiB│
│ gcloud app Java Extensions   │    1.9.80  │ 62.4 MiB│
│ gcloud cli dependencies      │ 2020.05.01 │  3.4 MiB│
│ kubectl                      │ 2020.05.01 │ < 1 MiB │
│ kubectl                      │   1.15.11  │ 72.2 MiB│
└──────────────────────────────┴────────────┴─────────┘
```

Figure 6-5
List of updated
components

```
jack@cloudshell:~ (edynalearn)$ gcloud version
Google Cloud SDK 291.0.0
alpha 2019.05.17
app-engine-go
app-engine-java 1.9.80
app-engine-php " "
app-engine-python 1.9.90
app-engine-python-extras 1.9.90
beta 2019.05.17
bq 2.0.57
cbt
cloud-build-local
cloud-datastore-emulator 2.1.0
cloud_sql_proxy
core 2020.05.01
datalab 20190610
docker-credential-gcr
gsutil 4.50
kind
kubectl 2020.05.01
pubsub-emulator 2019.09.27
skaffold
```

Once these prerequisites are covered, you will want to deploy your function. Recognize that using a function is not limited to just the command `gcloud deploy`. You must include other parameters to fully qualify the function and save the items correctly in storage. The parameters you can pass are detailed in Table 6-2.

Cloud Events and Cloud Pub/Sub

Cloud Pub/Sub triggers a message based on the conditions set forth by a function. An event produces the triggered action, named topic, by which there is an expected reaction. Cloud Pub/Sub can be deployed using Cloud Console, Cloud Shell, or Cloud SDK.

Cloud Events and Cloud Pub/Sub Using Cloud Console

There are several ways in which you can go about creating a Pub/Sub event using a Cloud Function within Cloud Console. The quickest way is to complete all activities from the Cloud Functions interface, like so:

1. Select the Cloud Functions menu.

2. You'll then be prompted to enter the name and the required memory allocation.

Parameter	Purpose
`--runtime`	Identifies the runtime environment.
`--trigger-events`	The trigger type that will be used to execute the event. There are four trigger options: `finalize`, `delete`, `metaupdate`, and `archive`. The structure for passing the executable is as follows: `gcloud.storage.object.<trigger>`
`--trigger-resource`	Provides the name of the bucket associated with the trigger.

Table 6-2   Cloud Functions Installation Parameters

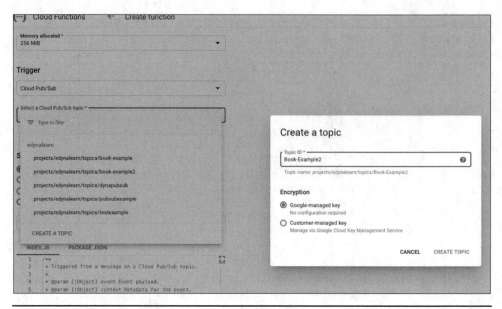

Figure 6-6   Creating a new topic for a Cloud Function using Cloud Console

3. Select the Pub/Sub trigger.

4. If you already have a Pub/Sub trigger established, select the trigger. Otherwise, create a new trigger.

5. To create a new Pub/Sub trigger, you need to create a topic. Enter the topic name, as shown in Figure 6-6.

6. Fill in the remaining fields by selecting the runtime and parameters necessary for your Cloud Function.

7. Click Create.

8. Once your Pub/Sub event is created, verify that it works by going to the dashboard and selecting the drop-down menu that allows you to test the function (see Figure 6-7).

Figure 6-7   Test a Pub/Sub Cloud Function using Cloud Console

Cloud Events and Cloud Pub/Sub Using Cloud Shell or Cloud SDK

Like in the previous section on Cloud Storage, you are strongly encouraged to make sure all components are updated and installed properly before deploying a function using Cloud Pub/Sub.

You use `gcloud functions`, similar to other command lines, to deploy the Pub/Sub function. For Pub/Sub, the number of parameters you must attach to the command is limited. Requirements include the name of the runtime environment as well as the name of the function and the name of the topic triggering the function. The command line appears similar to the following:

```
gcloud functions deploy <name of function> --runtime <enter runtime name>
--trigger-topic <name of topic>
```

Here are the three passed parameters you must provide data for:

- Name of function
- Name of runtime environment
- Name of topic

If all three parameters are included, a Pub/Sub topic will trigger as expected.

Pub/Sub and Object Change Notification Events

The purpose of object change notification events is to notify an application when an object's state has changed. Before Pub/Sub, the use of this legacy option was available to pass events to Cloud Storage buckets. Generally, Pub/Sub is the preferred approach, as it is easier to use, more flexible, and provides more capability than object change notifications.

Traffic Management

Cloud Functions traffic management is handled under the Network Settings section when you create a new Cloud Function. You have two choices:

- **Route only requests to private IPs through the VPC connector**   This is the default option. Only requests to RFC 1918 IP addresses are routed to a VPC network. The remaining requests are sent to the Internet.

- **Route all traffic through the VPC connector**   All outbound requests for the function are sent to the VPC network.

Cloud Run has several traffic management alternatives. The first way is to specify which revisions should receive traffic and at what percentage. The second method allows you to roll back to a previous revision, ultimately enabling the rollout of the revision. The third method is to split traffic among multiple revisions. The final method is to send all traffic to the newest revision.

The quickest and most efficient way to make these modifications, regardless of approach, is from the Cloud Functions or Cloud Run dashboard using Google Cloud Console.

Scaling and Versioning

Scaling capabilities are different between Cloud Functions and Cloud Run. With Cloud Functions, the `max_instances` parameter defines the degree to which your function can scale in response to an incoming request. If your application must scale, you do so by creating new instances for each of your functions since an instance can only handle a single request at a time. Many requests will result in a performance spike, creating many instances. For most applications, this is acceptable. However, there are instances where a certain number of connections may cause performance issues. Such is the case when you are using a database with a Cloud Function.

Cloud Run, on the other hand, uses revisions to automatically scale to the number of container instances necessary for the incoming requests. Three determinants should be considered when scaling with Cloud Run: CPU process capacity, concurrency settings, and maximum containers established. When thinking about budgetary constraints, you are strongly encouraged to limit the number of containers, as it can become costly to run concurrent open connections.

Choosing App Engine, Cloud Functions, or Cloud Run

Choosing between App Engine, Cloud Functions, Cloud Run, and Cloud Run for Anthos can be decided using nine technical areas. Figure 6-8 illustrates how you would go about choosing either App Engine, Cloud Functions, or Cloud Run using a flowchart approach that best serves organizational needs.

From a technical point of view, there are nine metrics to consider, each with specific capabilities for the type of application that is deployed:

- **Deployment type**   Delivery method to deploy your stateless application.
- **Scaling**   Identifies if scaling is possible, and if so, what method of scaling is enabled. Only Cloud Run for Anthos autoscales differently from a standard stateless application.
- **Runtime environment support**   Programmatic language support to deploy an application on Google Cloud Platform. Whereas Cloud Run and Cloud Run for Anthos support virtually all programmatic runtimes, App Engine and Cloud Functions have limitations.
- **Access controls**   Approaches to handle security and identity management for a stateless application using GCP. Each stateless application handles access control differently.
- **HTTP/gRPC**   Cloud Endpoints support for protocol transcoding that allows for access to your gRPC (Google RPC remote procedure calls) API via HTTP/JSON. Only Cloud Run with Anthos handles Cloud Endpoints management because of the mixed cloud and on-premises topology requirements.

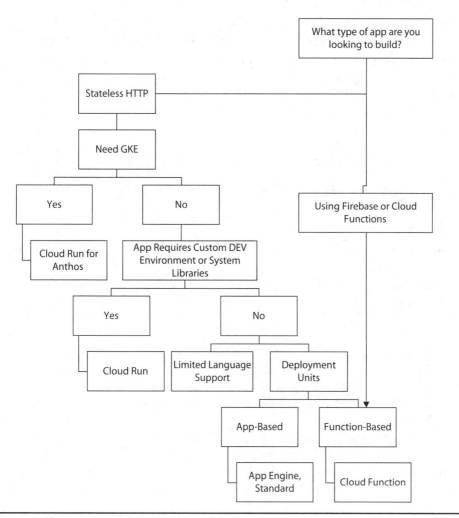

Figure 6-8   Choosing between App Engine, Cloud Function, and Cloud Run

- **Custom domains**   Allows you to map to your domain name versus the
  GCP-branded domain that hosts the application. Standalone and container-
  based applications allow for custom domains. The Cloud Functions platform
  does not support custom domains.

- **GPU/TPU support**   Extends CPU capability using either graphics processing
  units (GPUs) or tensor processing units (TPUs) for extended memory and compute
  capacity. Only Cloud Run for Anthos extends CPU supports with GPU/TPU.

	App Engine	Cloud Functions	Cloud Run	Cloud Run for Anthos
Deployment type	App	Function	Container	Container
Scaling	Yes	Yes	Yes	Only using Pods
Runtime environment support	Java Node.js Python Go PHP	Node.js Python Go	All available	All available
Access controls	OAuth 2.0 CICP Firebase authentication Google Sign-in Users API	IAM permissions	IAM permissions CICP Google Sign-in Firebase authentication	Cluster-only VPC-only
HTTP/gRPC	No	No	No	Yes
Custom domains	Yes	No	Yes	Yes
GPU/TPU support	No	No	No	Yes
Timeout (minutes)	1	9	15	15
VPC networking	Yes	Yes	No	Yes

Table 6-3   Comparing Stateless Application Types

- **Timeout (minutes)**   The number of minutes before an application will quit if there is no activity. App Engine times out after one minute. Cloud Functions will time out after nine minutes. Cloud Run and Cloud Run for Anthos time out after 15 minutes.

- **VPC networking**   On-demand pool of shared computing resources available within a public cloud that allows isolation among organizations and their instances. All stateless applications except for Cloud Run allow for this capability. GCP does not have VPC networking available in general availability at this time.

Table 6-3 provides a technical comparison of the features that distinguish the four stateless application environment types.

Chapter Review

The chapter begins with you learning about the different options available in GCP with serverless computing. You can select from App Engine, Cloud Functions, Cloud Run, and Cloud Run for Anthos. App Engine is best suited for those looking for a serverless computing option that enables web application or API-based backend support. Cloud Functions are ideal for the event-, trigger-, and function-based delivery of applications in a serverless setting. Cloud Run, which also includes the use of Anthos, leverages containers to deliver serverless applications to users.

The next two sections of the chapter addressed deployment approaches for Cloud Functions and Cloud Run using Cloud Console, Cloud Shell, and Cloud SDK.

Each deployment method allows for the use of the most popular programming languages, including Python, Node.js, and Go. For each deployment option, the use of events, triggers, and functions is allowed. Every deployment option has a specific set of parameters that can be used for events associated with Cloud Storage, Cloud Pub/Sub, and traffic management activities. Finally, throughout the chapter, you learned various command-line functions that can be used for Cloud Shell or Cloud SDK to work with Cloud Functions and Cloud Run for creating events, triggers, and functions in support of scaling, managing traffic, and versioning stateless applications.

Questions

1. You have been tasked with deploying a serverless web-based application that integrates a number of third-party APIs. The APIs are not hosted by your team. Rather, they are hosted by financial institutions and content aggregators. Which serverless platform would be the best option to deploy the web-based application?

   A. App Engine   *collection of ransomwer*

   B. Cloud Functions

   C. Cloud Run

   D. Cloud Run for Anthos

2. An organization is looking to containerize its application. The team using the application is spread out across three continents. In order to optimize application performance, the IT administrators are evaluating the best approach to handle distributed containerization that also requires the use of some on-premises infrastructure resources. Which environment is best suited for the deployable stateless application?

   A. App Engine

   B. Cloud Functions

   C. Cloud Run

   D. Cloud Run for Anthos

3. The IT administrators at your organization are trying to troubleshoot specific system performance errors with their recently deployed stateless application. They've noticed that the application—a financial transaction solution that ingests and reviews tens of thousands of records a minute—continues to perform poorly at peak periods during the day. What would you recommend to the IT administrators?

   A. Migrate the solution to Cloud Run for Anthos and apply GPU/TPU capacity.

   B. Migrate the solution to Cloud Run and increase the timeout to the maximum threshold available.

   C. Migrate the solution to Cloud Run for Anthos and apply VPC networking.

   D. Migrate the solution to Cloud Run and switch to another programming language that has a smaller footprint.

4. Which of the following is not a true statement about event types?

   A. There are five event type categories.

   B. Events are action based, such as a file being uploaded or a message being queued.

   C. Firebase events occur based on a function call.

   D. Triggers are a method to respond to an event.

5. The DynaLearning team recently built a stateless application for payment processing. The developers have noticed that not all transactions are recognized, causing significant concern about system accuracy and reliability. What would you recommend the cloud administrator do to correct the loss of transactions?

   A. Utilize a custom domain.

   B. Use a database to record transactions of function activity.

   C. Switch the application from a Cloud Functions environment to an alternative option.

   D. Increase the timeout of the stateless application.

6. Which of the following runtimes are supported for both Cloud Functions and Cloud Run?

   A. Node.js, Python, Java

   B. Node.js, Python, Go, PHP

   C. Node.js, Python, Go

   D. All runtimes are supported for Cloud Functions and Cloud Run.

7. Which of the following environment types offers the longest timeout option?

   A. App Engine standard environment

   B. Cloud Functions

   C. Cloud Run

   D. App Engine flexible environment

8. You are looking to build your container using Cloud Build, which allows you to deploy your container named LMS-1 to Cloud Run. Which of the following statements will allow you to execute a container build for the eDynaLearn Project?

   A. `gcloud builds submit --tag gcr.io/LMS-1/edynalearn`

   B. `gcloud run deploy --image gcr.io/LMS-1/edynalearn`

   C. `gcloud run deploy --image gcr.io/edynalearn/LMS-1`

   D. `gcloud builds submit --tag gcr.io/edynalearn/LMS-1`

9. Under what conditions are you still charged to utilize Cloud Run when a project is not active?

   A. When the image is stored in the Container Registry after the deployment

   B. When you delete the image or your cloud project

   C. When you delete all of the resources in a project

   D. All of the above will result in no additional charge.

10. Which API(s) are required to build and deploy a Cloud Run or Cloud Run for Anthos instance?

    A. Cloud Build and Container Registry

    B. Cloud Build and Cloud Monitoring

    C. Container Registry and Cloud Monitoring

    D. Cloud Run, Container Registry, and Cloud Build

    Cloud Run
    Container Registry
    Cloud Build

11. When you're trying to autoscale an instance in Cloud Run, a revision is automatically scaled to handle the number of container instances. Which of the following is not a condition for autoscaling?

    A. Amount of CPU needed to process a request

    B. Concurrency setting   *storage doesnot impact autoscaling*

    C. Type of storage used

    D. Number of container instance settings

12. What is the key difference between Cloud Run and Cloud Run for Anthos? *GKE*

    A. Cloud Run and Cloud Run for Anthos have different timeout parameters.

    B. Cloud Run for Anthos supports GKE, whereas Cloud Run does not require GKE support in a fully managed setting.

    C. Cloud Run and Cloud Run for Anthos require the use of different types of programming language development environments.

    D. Cloud Run does not support the use of custom domains, whereas Cloud Run for Anthos does support the use of custom domains.

13. Why might you choose not to use Cloud Run for traffic management?

    A. Cloud Run allows you to split traffic on a percentage basis.

    B. Cloud Run uses random traffic management as the default methodology.

    C. Cloud Run allows you to maintain multiple configurations for a single route, or reference multiple versions during a rollout and *n*-way split.

    D. Cloud Run allows you to assign traffic routes to addressable domains or any backing revision.

14. You are looking to deploy a stateless application. The application does not require the use of Kubernetes. The application requires the use of special libraries and a Java Runtime Environment. Which of the following options would best serve the team using Google best practices?

  A. Cloud Run

  B. Cloud Functions

  C. Cloud Run for Anthos

  D. App Engine standard environment

Answers

1. A. App Engine is appropriate for web- and API-based applications. Cloud Functions are appropriate for event-driven applications that also use third-party sources. However, in this case, the question does not discuss events, triggers, or functions. Cloud Run and Cloud Run for Anthos are intended for apps within containers or GKE.

2. D. Only Cloud Run supports containerization which eliminates all answers except for C and D. The difference between Cloud Run and Cloud Run for Anthos is the support for on-premises integration. Only the Anthos option supports a hybrid container approach.

3. A. Cloud Run alone does not allow for GPU/TPU support, which is the type of compute and memory performance optimization recommended in this question. Using Anthos does allow for GPU/TPU support. Nowhere in the question is there a recommendation on networking issues; this is a compute and memory-consumption issue.

4. C. Events occur based on triggers, not a function call. The remaining answer options are all correct statements.

5. B. If there is transactional activity associated with an event, trigger, or function, you should use a database to keep a record of your transactions. This is the only way to maintain a history without losing any data. Custom domains are not available for Cloud Functions, only App Engine and Cloud Run–based stateless environments. Switching to another environment does not solve the transactional activity capture issue, as there is still no living record of events and trigger-based activity. Increasing the timeout of the stateless application will not solve the problem.

6. C. Node.js, Python, and Go are available for both Cloud Functions and Cloud Run development environments. Java and PHP vary depending on environment. By default, answer D is incorrect because there are limits to the environments based on language.

7. C. Cloud Run and Cloud Run for Anthos offer a timeout of up to 15 minutes. App Engine offers a one-minute timeout. Cloud Functions offer a nine-minute timeout.

8. **D.** The difference among the four command lines has to do with two focal areas: the location of the project and application and the step in the process. You are being asked to build the containerized app, not deploy it. The command for deploying is `gcloud run deploy`. The command for building is `gcloud builds submit`. By elimination, that only leaves one choice based on the parameters of building a container and properly ordering the project and application.

9. **A.** Keeping one or more images in the Container Registry after a run will likely prompt additional utilization charges. On the other hand, deleting a project and all of the resources entirely will immediately result in no further charges. Therefore, answers B and C are incorrect. Also, given that answers B and C have been eliminated, answer D is therefore incorrect.

10. **D.** Building an instance of Cloud Run for Anthos requires the initiation of three APIs: Cloud Run, Container Registry, and Cloud Build. The Cloud Monitoring API is not required. Only answer D covers all three prerequisites.

11. **C.** The type of storage does not impact autoscaling configurations. All other parameters are influential in scaling.

12. **B.** Cloud Run for Anthos provides a flexible serverless development on GKE. Cloud Run is available as a fully managed serverless platform without requiring Kubernetes. Timeout parameters, development environments, and custom domain support are the same for both Cloud Run and Cloud Run for Anthos, making answers A, C, and D incorrect.

13. **B.** Random traffic management is not the most reliable solution suggested for Cloud Run. The other three options are all available alternatives for Cloud Run traffic splitting.

14. **A.** An application that requires environment support for Java and requires the use of special libraries is best suited for Cloud Run over App Engine or Cloud Functions. Since Cloud Run supports the use of special libraries and all programming language environments, it is the only answer choice that is feasible. The question explicitly states GKE is not necessary, thus eliminating Cloud Run for Anthos. The remaining two options do not fit the requirements because there are specific programming language support requirements and library requirements, which App Engine and Cloud Functions do not support.

Storage and Database Management

In this chapter you will learn to

- Understand the different planning strategies for storage in GCP
- Explain how to deploy and manage object, relational, and NoSQL storage
- Describe approaches for loading data in object, relational, and NoSQL storage

As a cloud engineer, you can select from many storage options using Google Cloud Platform (GPC). Exactly which one is the right choice is often a matter of knowing the business need. You are required to know how to utilize various storage facilities, including object and database capabilities, to support your querying and storage management needs. This chapter addresses all types of storage, including an overview of the various database platforms GCP supports. As you read the chapter, keep in mind three metrics that can help you select the best storage option: access time, data model, and performance requirements.

Storage Options in GCP

Access time is instrumental in selecting your storage option when using GCP. Fast transactional activity requires one type of storage. On the other hand, infrequently accessed data can use an alternative. When deciding which option best suits the business need, you should factor in speed, persistence, and redundancy. Storage speed can be extremely fast, as fast as nanoseconds, assuming the use of certain CPU and cache configurations. Persistence is dependent on storage volatility needs. Cache offers the best latency, assuming the system does not power down or there is no operational disruption. However, upon a system reboot, all data is erased. That is why using traditional storage formats, including hard disks, offers more reliability for long-term data retention. The downside is that a disk has a higher likelihood of failure over time. Redundancy, the ability to replicate data across disks, zones, and even regions, is critical across any cloud platform, including GCP. By making copies of the data, you ensure that the data is preserved in case one storage instance suddenly fails.

 TIP Storage redundancy protects critical infrastructure. Here are three things you should consider as you address storage needs: First, consider data replication requirements. Second, consider that GCP offers replication across availability zones, even if you are in the same region. Third, if storing in a single region poses a risk for disaster recovery, you should consider multiregional replication.

Persistent Storage

Persistent disks are a type of block storage available on Google Cloud Platform. You can attach a persistent disk to a virtual machine instance within Google Compute Engine or Google Kubernetes Engine. If you are looking to create a file system on a disk, a persistent disk is an appropriate selection because it offers block storage capabilities.

Persistent disks do not directly attach to a server. Rather, they attach to the server hosting the network-accessible virtual machine. With a VM, if you attach a disk locally and then shut down, data stored on a persistent disk is lost when a virtual machine is terminated. However, the data on the disk itself remains when an instance is terminated. Persistent disks are independent of a virtual machine instance, whereas a locally attached SSD is not independent.

Two types of persistent disks are available: solid-state drive (SSD) and hard disk drive (HDD). You select an SSD when you require high throughput and consistent performance across an environment. HDDs have longer latencies and cost less. An HDD is the preferred choice for large data ingest, when you are performing a batch operation, and you require less sensitivity to data variability. Table 7-1 illustrates the difference among the various persistent storage types as well as local SSD options.

The input/output operations per second (IOPS) increase dramatically when you compare HDD to SSD-based persistent disks. Throughput is variable, although again, SSD is often much faster and reliable in comparison to HDD. For a locally attached SSD, performance exceeds any other form of persistent disk. The downside is the loss of data after a virtual machine reboot with a locally attached SSD.

Persistent disks allow for several features. First, if you mount a persistent disk on multiple virtual machines, it provides multistorage capacity. Second, snapshots, when leveraging persistent disks, can be created quickly, supporting quick virtual machine distribution. If you intend to use a snapshot mounted to a single virtual machine instance, read/write operations are often permissible. Other considerations include size, encryption options, zone/regionality, and type of instance you are looking to create. Based on your organization need, you will find that one storage type may better suit your needs.

Storage Type	Zonal Standard Persistent Disk	Regional Standard Persistent Disk	Zonal SSD Persistent Disk	Regional SSD Persistent Disk	Local SSD
	Efficient and reliable block storage	Efficient, reliable block storage that has synchronous replication capabilities across two zones in a region	Fast and reliable block storage	Fast, reliable block storage that has synchronous replication capabilities across two zones in a region	High performance block storage
Read IOPS per GB	0.75	0.75	30	30	—
Write IOPS per GB	1.75	1.5	30	30	—
Read IOPS per Instance	7500	3000	15,000–100,000	15,000–100,000	900,000
Write IOPS per Instance	15,000	15,000	15,000–30,000	15,000–30,000	800,000
Read Throughput per GB	0.12	0.12	0.48	0.48	—
Write Throughput per GB	0.12	0.12	0.48	0.48	—
Read Throughput per Instance	240–1200	240	240–1200	240–1200	9360
Write Throughput per Instance	76–400	38–200	204–800	102–400	4680
Minimum Capacity	10GB	200GB	10GB	10GB	375GB
Maximum Capacity	64TB	64TB	64TB	64TB	375GB
Capacity Increment	1GB	1GB	1GB	1GB	375GB
Max Capacity per Instance	257TB	257GB	257GB	257GB	3TB
Scope of Access	Zone	Zone	Zone	Zone	Instance
Redundancy	Zonal	Multizonal	Zone	Zone	N/A
Encryption at Rest	Yes	Yes	Yes	Yes	Yes
Custom Encryption Keys	Yes	Yes	Yes	Yes	No
Machine Types Supported	All	All	Most	Most	Most

Table 7-1   Persistent and Local SSD Storage Options

Configuring a Persistent Disk

The easiest way to create a persistent disk is to do so using the Cloud Console. You may want to learn how to create a disk using the SDK; however, the passing of all the parameters can be quite cumbersome. To create a new persistent disk, follow these steps:

1. Go to Compute Engine menu and select Disks.

2. If you have never created a disk before, you are prompted with the screen "Create a disk," as seen in Figure 7-1.

3. Enter the following details:
   - Name
   - Description (optional)
   - Type of disk
   - Replicate disks within a region
   - Region/zone
   - Snapshot schedule
   - Source type (blank disk, image, or snapshot)
   - Size (GB)
   - Estimated performance
   - Encryption (Google-managed key, customer-managed key, or customer-supplied key)
   - Labels (optional)

4. Click Create.

Here are some items to consider when you create a new disk:

- The type of disk choice is either standard persistent or SSD persistent. Your costs are dramatically higher with SSD persistent, but the performance change is significant.

- You select the option for replicating disks within a region if you want to make a backup of a disk within a given region.

- When selecting the region/zone, make sure you select the location closest to the majority of users. If no one region is appropriate, pick a central location.

- A snapshot schedule is not required; however, if you do require one, it results in an additional storage charge as time goes on.

- The source type is the basis of how you intend to use the initial disk you are creating. A blank disk has nothing on it, whereas an image or snapshot takes data from an existing instance to create the new disk.

- Encryption can be handled using a Google-managed key. Alternately, if you have your own set of encryption keys, you should select the option Customer-managed Key.

Figure 7-1
Disk creation
interface under
Compute Engine

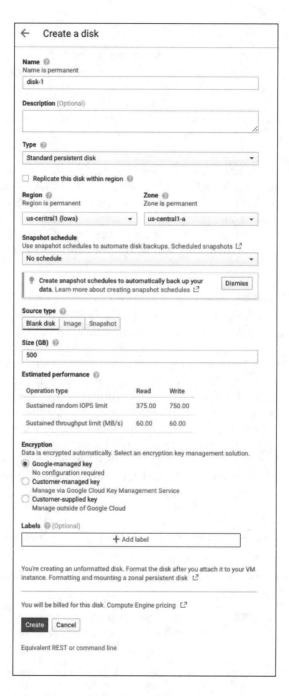

Using a customer-managed key requires that you, the customer, specify the name of the keys created in the Cloud Key Management Service.

- Although labels are optional, you are strongly encouraged to create them to help you manage your collection of disks as you build out more instances over time.

Cache

The fastest low-latency type of memory available in GCP is cache. When you are looking for an in-memory data storage solution to provide your applications with quick data access, cache is a formidable option. While the speed and latency are two critical reasons to use cache, limitations include capacity and long-term retention options. If you are looking to process data quickly and know the handling of data is short term, cache benefits may outweigh any shortcomings.

 TIP   Caching can be leveraged as more than just an memory-based storage solution. With GCP, it is often utilized as a way to improve application performance for data lookups. Instead of having to retrieve data repeatedly, a cache solution allows for in-memory utilization to help expedite common lookup requirements of accessible data objects. If cache is not utilized, an application may experience performance degradation.

Memorystore

If you are looking for storage that can hold user session data, maintain short-lived web and mobile applications data, or handle gaming data at speed and scale, Cloud Memorystore is the storage option to consider. *Cloud Memorystore* is a managed Redis service, which is an open source cache solution. Memorystore offers a fully managed in-memory data store with features such as scalability, a well-built security posture, and high availability, all managed by Google. Applications that utilize Memorystore can gain submillisecond data access. Given that Cloud Memorystore is compatible with Redis and Memcache open source protocol, migration and no-touch coding changes are feasible. Assuming you create instances that run Redis, Cloud Memorystore allows for configurable memory up to 300GB regionally as well as high availability, which supports redundancy.

Cloud Memorystore supports applications running in Compute Engine, Kubernetes Engine, and App Engine. Depending on the application need, your configuration varies upon accessing the Memorystore form. When you access the menu, you have two choices:

- **Redis**   In-memory data structure store that can be used as a database, cache, and message broker
- **Memcached**   In-memory key-value store intended exclusively for caching data

 EXAM TIP   For the purposes of the exam, you need to be familiar with Redis, given the number of possible use cases available.

Redis instance creation, as shown in Figure 7-2, requires you provide the following data points:

- Instance ID
- Display name

Figure 7-2
Interface to
set up a Redis
instance

- Tier (Basic for no high-availability or Standard for high-availability)
- Location (Region/Zone)
- Capacity (up to 300GB)
- Version (3.2, 4.0, or 5.0)
- Configuration value
- Authorized network (including IP address assignment)

Once you fill out the entire form, click Create. You are able to assign your Compute Engine, Kubernètes Engine, or App Engine from this form interface.

Object Storage

Object storage is a strategy to manage and manipulate data storage as a distinct unit, called an object. Each object can be stored in a single storage unit instead of being embedded into files or folders. Object storage combines data elements that consist of files, integrate relevant metadata to the files, and apply custom identifiers so that each item is unique. Unlike in a file storage topology, object storage retains comprehensive metadata attributes within a file. Objects are placed in a flat space, referred to as a storage pool. Creating a storage pool allows for in-depth analysis when combined with regular use of metadata.

The advantage of using object storage is considerable. You get greater visibility into data life cycles when combining object storage with the power of data analytics. Storage scalability is virtually limitless compared to persistent disks usage. Data retrieval, due to the usage of metadata and categorization structures, can be much faster. Finally, resource utilization is optimized because object storage does not have to follow a hierarchy, which is the case with block or file storage.

Cloud Storage

Cloud Storage is a type of object storage. You would consider using Cloud Storage when you require extensive storage capacity, and the ability to share that capacity, for your workloads. Files stored in the Cloud Storage system are treated as an atomic unit. You cannot manipulate or conduct an activity on just part of a file. You can operate at the object level, though, to complete specific tasks such as creating, editing, or deleting the object. With Cloud Storage, you cannot manipulate a file partially; it is all or nothing. Cloud Storage does not offer a method to overwrite part of a file. It also lacks support for concurrency and locking. Several users can access only one copy of a file. The last file written to the object store is the one that persists in the system. Keep in mind that Cloud Storage is useful for storing large volumes of data, particularly unstructured data sets.

The logical unit for storing data in Cloud Storage is called a *bucket,* which is a resource inside a project. Buckets maintain a global *namespace*, which means that when you call a bucket, it can be unique across all projects, not just a single project. Because object storage does not maintain a file system, a bucket is the equivalent to a directory for organizing objects into groups. The difference, though, is that buckets do not allow for subdirectories or subbuckets. Everything is at a single level. If you are looking for a file system–like architecture for your object storage, Google does support an open source project called Cloud Storage FUSE, which treats a bucket as a file system on a limited number of operating systems.

Object Storage Classes *Nearline (1mo.⁺), coldline (3mo.⁺), Archive(1yr)*

Your Cloud Storage bucket is tied to a location. That means all items stored in a bucket can be found in one or more locations, depending if you pay for features such as disaster recovery, backup, and system redundancy. Data being stored in a single region is referred to as *regional,* whereas buckets stored across several regions are referred to as *multiregional.* Both of these storage types can be grouped together under a single category called Standard storage.

There are notable differences between regional and multiregional buckets. The two notable differences are price and redundancy. Multiregional object storage is used when there is a requirement for storage across multiple regions. Redundancy and disaster recovery options are in place in case of failure at one or more zones. Multiregional storage is more expensive than regional storage. Regional storage is location specific, which means that all items are stored in a single geography. You can have multiple disks in the same geography; however, this does not constitute true redundancy or disaster recovery. Regional storage is less expensive than multiregional storage. One thing to consider is where the user is located. If your teams are dispersed among many geographies, multiregional storage is a more appropriate for achieving performance benchmarks. Data synchronization and near-constant availability are also ensured with multiregional storage.

Organizations do not require that their data be readily available at all times in some instances. One example includes when medical, bank, and insurance records must be kept in storage a minimum of three to seven years for compliance reasons. If you do not require access to such data often, having an archival system available to store data for infrequent access is preferred. Likewise, a system that offers file backup for disaster recovery where access is needed less than once a year is also formidable. Google offers nearline and coldline storage for such data requirements.

Nearline and coldline storage are good options when your data is accessed infrequently. *Nearline* is intended for access to files less than once a month. *Coldline* is priced for those who store data with the intent they will access files with even less frequency. The time horizon for access is often greater than 90 days. There is a tendency to use coldline for storage for longer duration use cases, including archiving when the amount of time to store data is uncertain. Finally, the *archive storage* class is available for situations where the frequency of data access is greater than one year. Depending on what storage option you select, the price, service level agreement (SLA) standard, and retrieval will vary. Additional charges may accrue for network and operational access within a geographical location or across continents. Table 7-2 illustrates the difference among the storage classes.

EXAM TIP   You do not need to know the pricing details for the storage classes for the exam.

Storage Class	Name for API Using `gsutil`	Min. Storage Duration	Availability	Cost (per GB/ per Month)
Standard	STANDARD	N/A	>99.99 percent in multiregions and dual regions. 99.99 percent in regions.	$0.026
Nearline	NEARLINE	30	99.95 percent in multiregions and dual regions. 99.9 percent in regions.	$0.016
Coldline	COLDLINE	90	99.95 percent in multiregions and dual regions. 99.9 percent in regions.	$0.007
Archive	ARCHIVE	365	99.95 percent in multiregions and dual regions. 99.9 percent in regions.	$0.004

Table 7-2 Differences Among Storage Classes for Price and Uptime

Storage Versioning and Object Lifecycle Management

Buckets created for Cloud Storage allow for version control of objects. Each time an object changes, be it deleted or overwritten, the previous version is archived as a version. This assumes that versioning is enabled for buckets. Versioning is helpful when you need to keep a historical record of all objects without risking the accidental deletion of changes.

Object Lifecycle Management allows you to configure rules for current and future objects in a bucket. When you apply a configuration and the object meets the criteria for a given rule, Cloud Storage automatically triggers an action on a given object. Here are two examples where Object Lifecycle Management might be useful:

- Downgrading a storage class of objects older than 90 days to coldline storage
- Deleting objects created before December 31, 2015

An Object Lifecycle Management configuration contains a set of rules, and these rules can contain several conditions. However, if you present multiple conditions in a rule, all conditions must be met. When you present a rule that contains the same action, only when a rule matches the action will a condition be triggered. That is why a rule should only include one action. If you do apply multiple Object Lifecycle Management rules to a given condition to satisfy conditions for a single object, Cloud Storage only triggers the action associated with one rule at a time under one of two conditions:

- `Delete` supersedes any `SetStorageClass` action.
- The `SetStorageClass` action switches the object to the storage class, where the lowest at-rest storage price available takes precedence.

Once an action commits, the object is re-evaluated to see if additional conditions must be met. Conditions evaluated as part of Object Lifecycle Management rules include Age,

`CreatedBefore`, `IsLive`, `MatchesStorageClass`, and `NumberOfNewerVersions`. Adding all conditions is optional, but you must add at least one condition to a ruleset. Not adding a condition results in an invalid Object Lifecycle Management configuration and produces a 400 Bad Request response visible to the end user.

Configuring Cloud Storage

You may need to create a bucket for your project. The most convenient way to complete this activity is from the Cloud Console. Go to the Cloud Console menu and select Storage. On the page that appears, click the Create Bucket button to create a new Cloud Storage bucket. You then see an interface similar to Figure 7-3. Fill in the fields by answering the following guided questions in the center of the page:

- **Name your bucket**   Provide a globally unique identifier. Enter the name of the bucket in this field.

- **Choose where to store your data**   Following the guidance from the previous section, select if you would like your bucket in a single region, dual region, or multiregion. Multiregion results in the most expensive footprint because of redundancy across geographies. You also select the data center location(s) where you want a bucket located. For example, if based in the US, you might select us-central1.

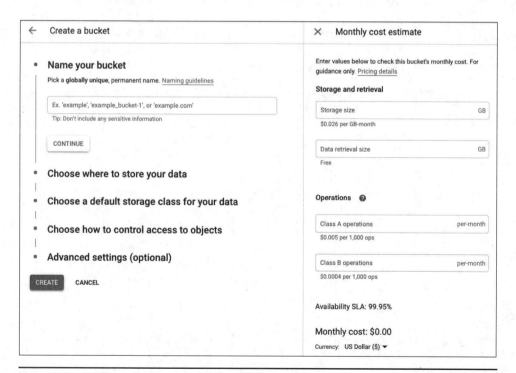

Figure 7-3   Configuration interface for Cloud Storage buckets under the Storage menu

- **Choose a default storage class for your data** You select the type of storage that is required. The choices are Standard, Nearline, Coldline, and Archive. The list goes from most expensive to least expensive due to the retention requirements.

- **Choose how to control access to objects** Select from fine-grained (individual object access) or uniform access (across all objects).

- **Advanced settings** Some of the advanced settings you can configure include

  - **Encryption** Either Google can manage the bucket encryption using Google-managed keys or you can provide your encryption via Cloud Key Management Service using customer-managed keys.

  - **Retention policy** If objects require system retention, check this box. You specify how long the retention period needs to be in seconds, days, months, or years.

  - **Labels** Adding descriptors for your bucket is always beneficial to help group related objects together within Google Cloud Platform.

Notice on the right side of the interface that the price changes, as shown in Figure 7-4, assuming you are entering the values into the calculator.

Figure 7-4
Storage cost
calculator for
applying bucket
parameters

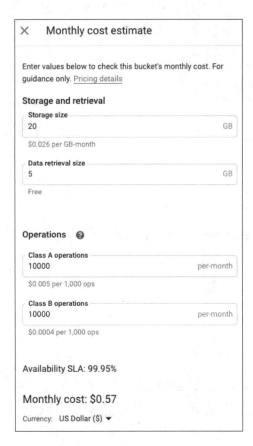

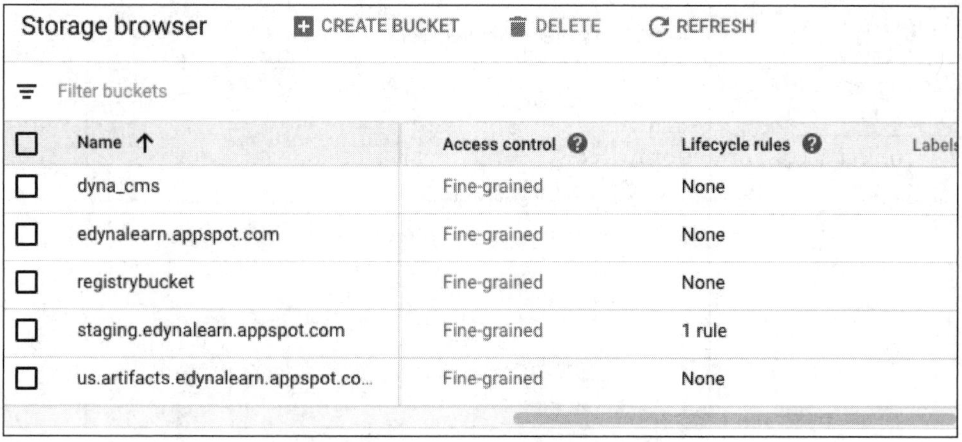

	Name ↑	Access control ❓	Lifecycle rules ❓	Labels
Storage browser	➕ CREATE BUCKET	🗑 DELETE	↻ REFRESH	
☰	Filter buckets			
☐	dyna_cms	Fine-grained	None	
☐	edynalearn.appspot.com	Fine-grained	None	
☐	registrybucket	Fine-grained	None	
☐	staging.edynalearn.appspot.com	Fine-grained	1 rule	
☐	us.artifacts.edynalearn.appspot.co...	Fine-grained	None	

Figure 7-5   Browser interface for accessing lifecycle rules

Once you have created a new bucket, you may decide to establish Object Lifecycle Management rules. To create rulesets, go to the browser window and scroll to the right among your list of buckets until you find the Lifecycle Rules column. Click the link for the row you want to modify (see Figure 7-5).

Once you click the link, a form appears that enables you to view or add Object Lifecycle Management rules. To add an Object Lifecycle Management rule, click Add Rule. The next page allows you to create the ruleset for the Object Lifecycle Management rule (see Figure 7-6). You can select from one of five conditions:

- Age
- Creation date
- Storage class
- Newer version
- Live state

For each option selected, you input a parameter and an action.

Once you fill in all the requirements, click Save. In Figure 7-7, you see an Object Lifecycle Management rule that states that an object 15 days or older should be deleted.

Figure 7-6
Object Lifecycle
Management rule
creation form

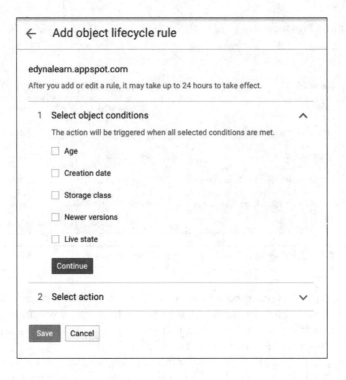

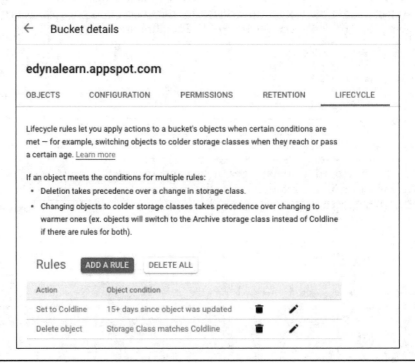

Figure 7-7   Example of an Object Lifecycle Management rule

Data Model Options

Google Cloud Platform has three broad categories of storage: object, relational, and nonrelational. The database platforms vary in size, scale, and capability. Nonrelational databases consist of platforms that support NoSQL as well as alternative solutions developed by Google, such as Cloud Firestore and Firebase. These two platforms are mobile NoSQL solutions.

Object: Cloud Storage Solutions

Any file found in an object storage model constitutes an atomic object. A Cloud Storage solution is an example of an object storage type. You cannot erase or modify a part of an object. A change requires a complete modification to an object on a server and all associated storage systems. Organizations use object storage for large-volume data ingest as well as when security requirements are not substantiated. Object storage is a solid choice for data intended for archival purposes or large datasets used for training. Data stored for several years to meet regulatory and compliance objectives, but seldom accessed, falls into this category.

Managing Cloud Storage

When you initially set up your Cloud Storage, you make assumptions at that given point in time. Conditions change, which results in modifications to a Cloud Storage bucket configuration. Table 7-3 provides a series of gsutil commands you should be aware of that are often used in managing Cloud Storage. Here is the syntax for accessing resources:

```
gs://<bucket name>/<object name>
```

Command	Definition
gsutil cp	Copy documents to/from bucket
gsutil iam ch -d user	Remove user access from bucket
gsutil iam ch user	Give user access to bucket
gsutil mb	Make a bucket
gsutil mv	Move a bucket
gsutil ls	List items in bucket
gsutil ls -l	List all items in bucket
gsutil rewrite -s	Rewrite the storage class
gsutil rm	Remove an object in storage
gsutil rm -r	Delete bucket and all contents inside
gsutil rsync -d -m /data	Used to sync the content of two buckets/directories

Table 7-3 gsutil Commands for Cloud Storage

Here are a few examples:

- The command to move a bucket:

  ```
  gsutil mv gs://<bucket name>/<old object name> gs://<bucket name>/<new
  object name>
  ```

- The command to copy objects from one bucket to another:

  ```
  gsutil cp gs://<old bucket name>/<original object name> gs://<new bucket
  name>/<intended object name>
  ```

- The command to change the storage class and the bucket path/directory:

  ```
  gsutil rewrite -s <storage class> gs://<path to object >
  ```

If you prefer to use Cloud Console instead of the command-line editor, you can find the Storage option under the Storage Header in the navigation area. Once you click the menu, select any of your existing buckets. The next step is to click Edit. Using the form, you can complete changes similar to the command-line activities listed in Table 7-3.

Relational Storage Solutions

The relational database dates back to the 1970s as a tool to record transactions in the enterprise. Data is clearly defined and stored in a series of tables. Each *table* has a relationship because there are one or more fields that are connected by either primary or foreign keys. A *primary* key ensures a data relationship is specific and unique to a column, whereas a *foreign* key is meant to provide a link between data in two or more tables among a column or group of columns. The mapping of the relationships forms a *schema,* which requires a clear definition so that a user can query for data using the SQL programming language. A user who commits a transaction searches for specific data such as product SKU, customer name, or telephone number. The user will either find the data or not, based on the operators used in the query. Similarly, if the user intends to add or delete data in the system, the transactions must be recognized; otherwise, a rollback to a previous version occurs to meet data requirements.

Google Cloud Platform offers three relational database types: Cloud SQL, Cloud Spanner, and BigQuery. Table 7-4 explains when you would use each of these database types.

Database	Purpose	Intended For
Cloud SQL	A managed database service for relational usage, including MySQL, PostgreSQL, and SQL Server. Intended for databases that require minimum horizontal scaling. Architecture by design is for adding more memory and CPU capacity instead of adding servers to a cluster.	Web applications, business intelligence, e-commerce
Cloud Spanner	Large relational data ingest with global distribution. Need for consistency, transactional integrity, and redundancy at scale and speed. Significantly more expensive than Cloud SQL.	Large enterprise applications such as financial applications, ERP, HRM
BigQuery	Intended for data warehousing and big data analytics appliances exclusively. Ingest rate tends to be tens of thousands to millions of rows per minute. Can hold petabytes of data. Also holds the greatest number of columns and rows.	Data warehousing

Table 7-4 Comparison of Relational Storage Options

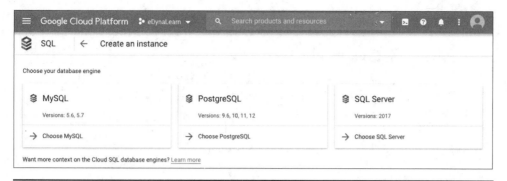

Figure 7-8 Cloud SQL database options interface

Configuration: Cloud SQL

Creating a Cloud SQL database is fairly simple. You can pick one of three options: MySQL, PostgreSQL, or SQL Server (see Figure 7-8). To create an instance, go to the Cloud Console and locate SQL under the Storage menu. For all instances, you will be asked at a minimum to provide an instance name, a strong password, a region/zone in which to store the database, and a database version. For SQL Server, there are several other parameters you must provide to create a database successfully.

Configuration: Cloud Spanner

For a robust, global-scale, transaction-oriented database, Cloud Spanner is a formidable option to consider. Creating a Spanner instance can be completed in just a few steps:

1. Go to the Storage menu and locate Spanner.

2. If you have not enabled the API, do so; otherwise, proceed to the next step.

3. Select Create Instance.

4. Enter the following parameters:

   - Instance name
   - Instance ID
   - Configuration (Region/Multiregion)
   - Number of nodes

You need to select the region from the region/multiregion drop-down menu. The geography correlates to the price and uptime, as does the number of nodes you input in the box. In Figure 7-9, instance examplespanner has a regional location in us-east1 (South Carolina).

Two nodes are selected. The base price of a single node runs around 90 cents per hour in the United States, so the estimated hourly cost is $1.80, with a projected $1,296.00 per-month cost. The most expensive node is nam-eur-asia1 for $9.00 per hour, with a

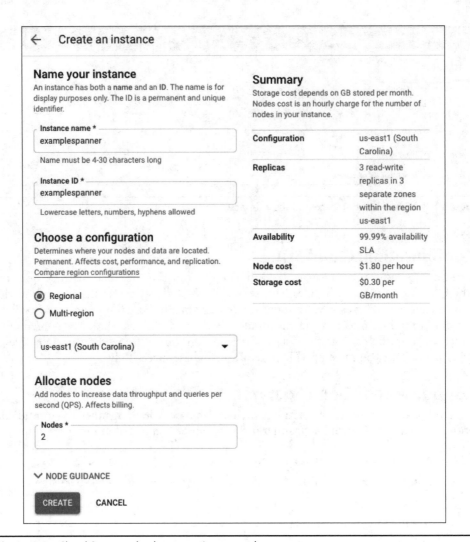

Figure 7-9   Cloud Spanner database creation example

multiregional node configuration. To understand how the calculation was derived, $1.80 estimated hourly cost × 24 hours × 30 days equals $1,296.00.

Configuration: BigQuery

BigQuery is a platform to analyze big data sets found in data warehouses. The platform provides storage, query capability, statistical analysis, and deep learning tools to evaluate relational data ingested at speed and scale. BigQuery is accessible from the Console menu under Big Data. You do not have to configure BigQuery itself; you simply need to point to your dataset.

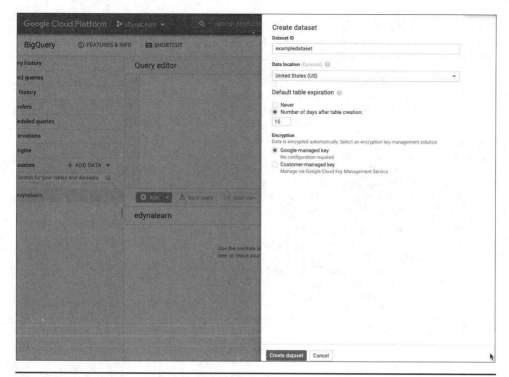

Figure 7-10   BigQuery dataset creation

To initiate the creation or identification of a dataset, select the name of your project on the left. Then, on the right, click Create Dataset (see Figure 7-10). You will need to enter the following parameters:

- **Dataset ID**   The name of your data
- **Data location**   The region in which to store your dataset
- **Default table expiration**   The period of time after which the data will expire
- **Encryption**   The type of encryption

Once this is complete, click Create.

Nonrelational Storage Solutions

NoSQL databases are appropriate for those organizations looking for speed, flexibility, and scale in comparison to the traditional tabular relational database. The data structure in a NoSQL database can be based on one of several designs: key–value, wide column, graph, or document. This data structure differs from that of a relational database design. Whereas a SQL database places constraints on data types and enforces consistency, a NoSQL database

Type	Purpose	Intended For
Cloud Datastore	Nonstructured datasets that maintain nonanalytic, nonrelational storage requirements. Will have varying characteristics or properties associated with a given document. Does not have a fixed schema, although a pattern does exist to organize document data in a system.	Catalog data, use profile data, gaming profiles, and application-oriented profiling data
Cloud Firestore	A managed NoSQL database that leverages a document data model. Supports storing, synchronizing, and querying data in distributed applications at near-real-time capacity. Offers transactional and multiregional replication support.	Mobile, web, and IoT apps at global scale
Bigtable	A wide-column NoSQL database where all rows do not need to map to a column to create a fixed schema. Storage capacity is designed for petabyte scale. Bigtable offers consistent sub-latency, replication, high availability, durability, and resilience in the event of any zonal failures.	Advertising technology (AdTech), financial technology (FinTech), and IoT

Table 7-5   Comparison of NoSQL Storage Options

does away with most of these requirements to optimize performance. NoSQL databases such as Cloud Datastore, Cloud Firestore, and Bigtable are available GCP options when an organization must store a large amount of data—particularly unstructured data. Table 7-5 provides an overview of the key features among each NoSQL platform.

Configuration: Cloud Datastore

Cloud Datastore is a NoSQL database that organizes data into structures called *documents,* which consist of key–value pairs. Each key–value pair in a document datastore is called an *entity.* Similar to a relational database, there is no requirement to have the same properties across all entities. Of all the NoSQL databases, Cloud Datastore shares two commonalities, unlike other solutions: transactional support and index querying. Like all NoSQL databases, though, you do not require a fixed schema. Follow these steps to create a new datastore:

1. In the Storage menu in Cloud Console, select Datastore.

2. Once the next page opens, select Create Entity.

3. Once the interface to create an entity is open, fill in the following fields:

   - **Namespace:** A method to group entities
   - **Kind:** Describes the document or schema

- **Key Identifier:** Can either be autogenerated or custom
- **Properties**
    - **Type:** Field type may include text, number, date, or currency
    - **Value:** Number of characters limited in the field

An example of the form is shown in Figure 7-11.

Figure 7-11
Entity creation
form

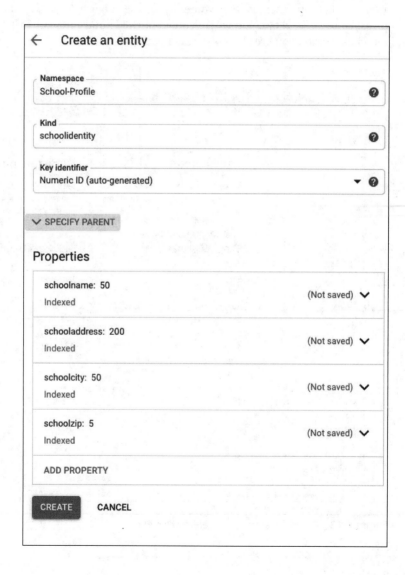

Configuration: Cloud Firestore

Cloud Firestore is a newer version of Cloud Datastore. If you have already created an instance of Datastore in a project, you are asked if you want to convert the existing database to Native mode. There are two differences between Native mode and Datastore mode. First, the max writes per second is 10,000 for Native mode. Second, the user can experience real-time updates as well as access mobile/web client libraries with offline data persistence. That is not the case with Datastore mode. If you decide this is the path forward, click the Select Native Mode button (see Figure 7-12). On the next screen, you are asked to select the region where you want the Cloud Firestore instance hosted. Once you click Create, you are able to start collecting data.

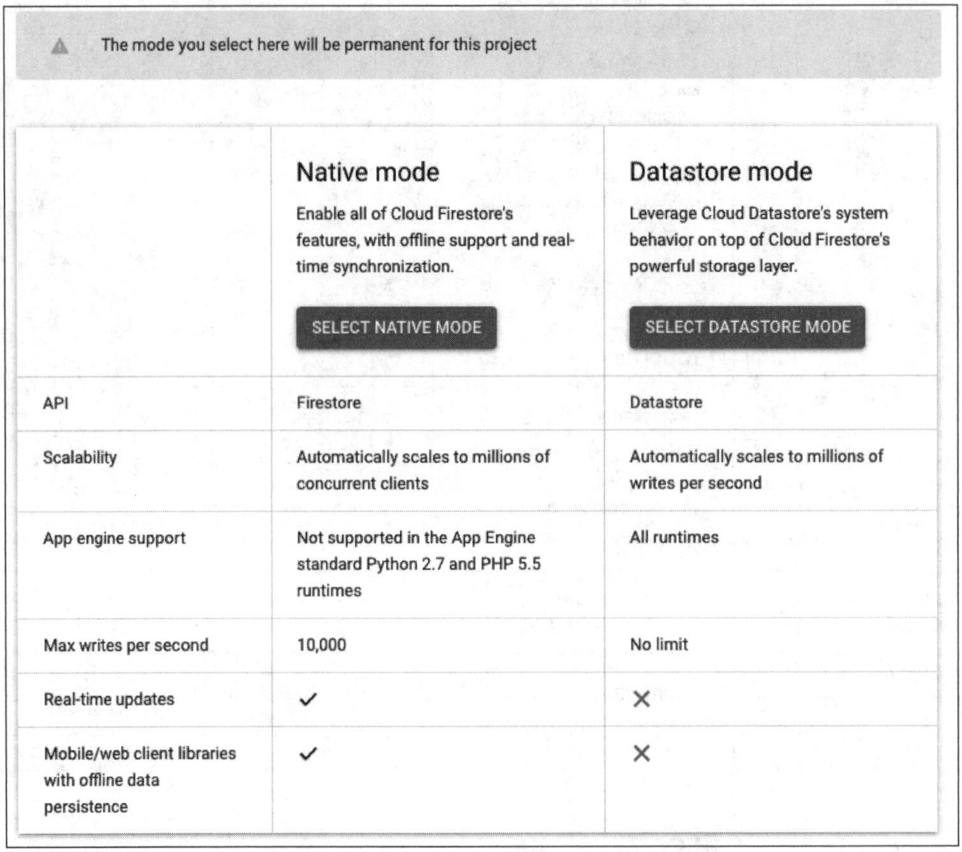

⚠ The mode you select here will be permanent for this project		
	Native mode Enable all of Cloud Firestore's features, with offline support and real-time synchronization. SELECT NATIVE MODE	**Datastore mode** Leverage Cloud Datastore's system behavior on top of Cloud Firestore's powerful storage layer. SELECT DATASTORE MODE
API	Firestore	Datastore
Scalability	Automatically scales to millions of concurrent clients	Automatically scales to millions of writes per second
App engine support	Not supported in the App Engine standard Python 2.7 and PHP 5.5 runtimes	All runtimes
Max writes per second	10,000	No limit
Real-time updates	✓	✗
Mobile/web client libraries with offline data persistence	✓	✗

Figure 7-12 Cloud Firestore mode selection screen

Configuration: Bigtable

Bigtable is a fully managed, wide-column NoSQL database. Bigtable offers low latency and replication for high availability. To create a new instance, go to the Storage menu and select Bigtable. Once the form opens up, select Create Instance. You are asked to provide an instance name. The instance ID is automatically populated. Select the type of storage. Depending on the type of storage, your price changes. Similarly, the region and cluster selected also reflect in a change of price on the right side of the page. Once you have configured all parameters to your liking, click Create.

Notice the price per month given your specific conditions on the right side changes (see Figure 7-13) This varies depending on the storage selected, the region, the number of nodes, and the clusters.

Figure 7-13 Bigtable creation form

Deploying and Managing Data

Creating and configuring different types of storage is a prerequisite for the Associate Cloud Engineer exam. A second prerequisite is knowing how to deploy, manage, and store data in various types of storage solutions. Some options allow for both Cloud Console and the command line, while others use the command line exclusively. This section addresses how to configure object, relational, and NoSQL databases against the expected requirements for the exam.

Cloud SQL Deployment and Management

For the exam, Google expects you to know how to create a database instance, connect an instance, load data into a database, query a database, and back up a database using Cloud SQL.

Creating a SQL Database Instance

The first thing you need to do is create an initial database instance (for this example, we'll name the instance schoolroster). You are then asked to create a password for this database instance. Next, select a region/zone. Finally, click Create. After a few minutes, your database instance is created (see Figure 7-14).

Connecting an Instance

Once the database is created, go to Cloud Shell and enter the following:

```
gcloud sql connect schoolroster
```

You are told that the IP address must be whitelisted. This is a security measure that allows you access to the database, assuming you have the appropriate username and password for read/write permissions. Once granted permission, you are prompted to enter additional queries in the system. You can now create tables and enter data into the database.

Creating, Loading, and Querying Data

Even though you are using Cloud Shell, the command line that you just executed allowed you to enter into MySQL, the specific database command-line environment for Cloud SQL.

In order for you to use a database, create a table, load data into the table, and then query a database, a series of actions must occur using the MySQL command-line utility.

To create the database instance, enter the following on the command line:

```
Create Database studentroster1; Use studentroster1;
```

Once the database is created, you are now ready to create the table. You need to qualify each field with its field type, as shown next. To create a table, you must establish a connection to the database beforehand.

```
CREATE TABLE students (fullname VARCHAR(255), zipcode INT,
student_id INT NOT NULL AUTO_INCREMENT, PRIMARY KEY (student_id));
```

Figure 7-14
Cloud SQL
instance creation
complete

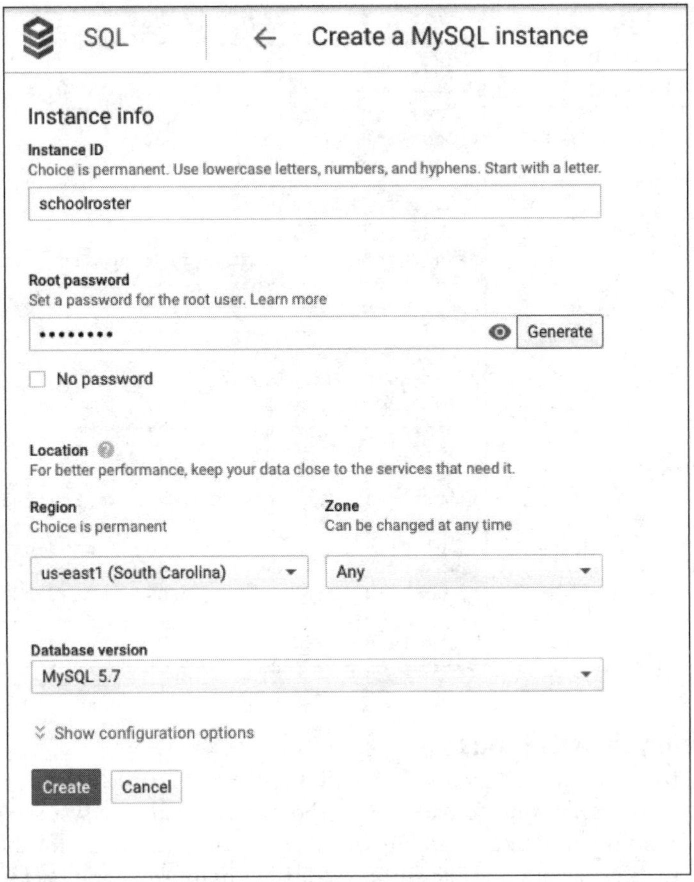

Once you have created a table, you can now start entering data into it. Here is a sample entry:

```
INSERT INTO students (fullname, zipcode) VALUES ('George Washington', 20001);
INSERT INTO students (fullname, zipcode) VALUES ('John Adams', 20002);
```

To query the dataset that you just inserted into the table, you can try a few queries, such as the following:

```
Select* from students;
Select fullname, zipcode from students;
Select * from students where student_id =1;
```

Figure 7-15 provides an example of these queries.

Figure 7-15
Cloud SQL query
output examples

```
mysql> select * from students;
+--------------------+----------+------------+
| fullname           | zipcode  | student_id |
+--------------------+----------+------------+
| George Washington  |   20001  |          1 |
| George Washington  |   20001  |          2 |
| John Adams         |   20001  |          3 |
+--------------------+----------+------------+
3 rows in set (0.04 sec)

mysql> select fullname, zipcode from students;
+--------------------+----------+
| fullname           | zipcode  |
+--------------------+----------+
| George Washington  |   20001  |
| George Washington  |   20001  |
| John Adams         |   20001  |
+--------------------+----------+
3 rows in set (0.04 sec)

mysql> select * from students where student_id =1;
+--------------------+----------+------------+
| fullname           | zipcode  | student_id |
+--------------------+----------+------------+
| George Washington  |   20001  |          1 |
+--------------------+----------+------------+
1 row in set (0.04 sec)
```

Backing Up a Database

Backups can be created at any time with GCP. For example, if you are about to complete a risky task, you'll want to back up your database or storage system. For these occasions, you can utilize on-demand backups, as you do not have to wait for the backup window to arrive to create a copy. Unlike automated backups, on-demand backups do not automatically get deleted. Instead, you need to delete the backups. Failing to delete them yourself results in a hefty billing charge.

On the other hand, if you decide to enable automated backups, you can specify a four-hour window during which a backup begins. The backup process begins during the lowest volume period of activity.

You can create a backup one of two ways: using Cloud Console or through the command line. To create a backup using Cloud Console, follow these steps:

1. Go to the SQL instance and click the name of the instance.

2. Select the Backup tab on the left side of the page.

3. Choose your backup options, including the time for the backup (assuming you are looking for automated backup).

4. Click Create Backup.

Once a backup is complete, it appears as part of the list of backups on the instances page.

The alternative is to use the command line. To create an asynchronous backup, use the following command:

```
gcloud sql backups create --async --instance studentroster1
```

Should you decide that an on-demand backup is more appropriate, the parameters are a bit different. For example, the query requires a start time:

```
gcloud sql instances patch studentroster1 --backup-start-time 02:30
```

In both these examples, studentroster1 is the database name and the specified instance. If you require further details, binary logging can be enabled to evaluate point-in-time recovery.

Cloud Spanner Deployment and Management

Cloud Spanner allows you to create a globally distributed enterprise-scale relational database using the Cloud Console. Unlike Cloud SQL, which leverages third-party platforms, Cloud Spanner is Google's own enterprise relational database management system (RDBMS). Depending on how many nodes and regions you decide to scale the solution by, implementing Cloud Spanner can become quite expensive relative to Cloud SQL.

EXAM TIP   For the exam, you are expected to understand how to create a Cloud Spanner database, define a schema, insert data, and query the database.

Creating a Spanner Instance

You will find the Spanner option under Storage. Once you click the button, a dashboard opens. Click the Create an Instance button on the top of the screen. As you are filling out the form, you will be able to observe the change in price based on the node and region/multiregion selected using the calculator available on the right (see Figure 7-16). It will take a few minutes for the instance to fully load. Once the load is complete, you will be able to create your schema.

Defining a Cloud Spanner Schema

You just created a Spanner instance. Now you need to create the database itself. Go to the bottom of the database creation page and click Create Database. A new form will appear asking for you to create your database and define your schema. In the example in Figure 7-17, the instance is named elearning-lms and the database is called course-schedule.

The first step is naming your table. Upon naming your table, you are asked to define the schema. To create a schema, you must add one or more columns. As seen in Figure 7-18, you must include the name of the column and the data type as well as indicate whether the value is not null. In some instances, you are given the option to limit the number of characters that can be added. After you have created one or more tables and thus completing schema creation, you can insert data into Cloud Spanner. Another option is to script

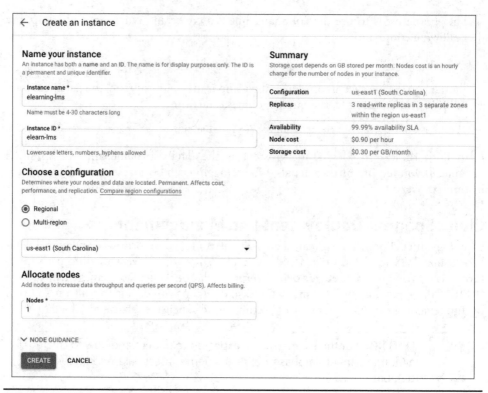

Figure 7-16 Creating the Spanner instance

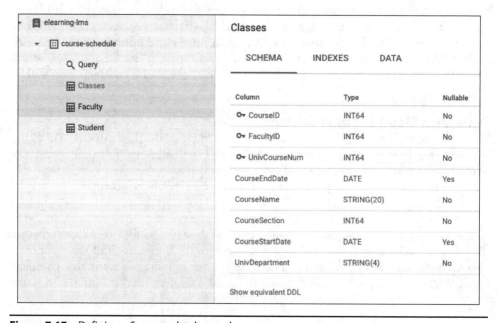

Figure 7-17 Defining a Spanner database schema

Figure 7-18
Creating a table
schema in Cloud
Spanner

the table requirements using Data Definition Language (DDL) with the table, field, and data type parameters. Using a table called Supplier, as presented in Figure 7-19, a Create TABLE DDL script is executed in Cloud Spanner.

Inserting Data into Cloud Spanner

On the left side of the database creation screen, you will find the tables you have created. In the example presented, the table created is called Faculty. Select one of the tables, click the Data tab, and then click Insert. Using the schema you've created, enter data into each of the fields to create the data entry (see Figure 7-20). Enter a few rows in one or more of the tables you have created so that you can create a simple query.

Querying Cloud Spanner

At this point, you have added data into one or more tables, and you should be able to run a basic `select` statement on one or more tables.

In Figure 7-21, the example provided illustrates all courses in which Doctor Jones (FacultyID = 500) has Michael Collins (StudentID = 51) for the upcoming semester. To create the query, go to the query tab on the left side of the page, right above the list of tables, and then enter the query in the main window and click Run. The query returns a result set of two classes.

Figure 7-19
Spanner
DDL script

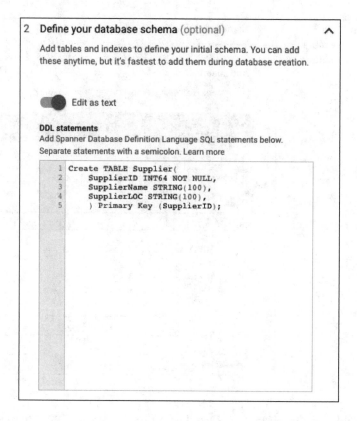

Figure 7-20
Spanner insert
data form

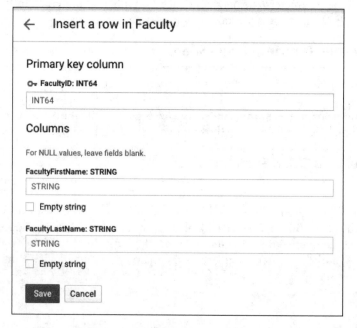

Query database: course-schedule

```
1  select * from Classes, faculty, student WHERE StudentID = 51 AND Faculty.FacultyID = 500
```

Run query ▾   Clear query   SQL query help

Suggestions: Cmd + Space Run query: Cmd + Enter

Schema   Results table   Explanation

Query complete (17.83 ms elapsed)

CourseName	CourseStartDate	CourseEndDate	CourseSection	UnivDepartment	UnivCourseNum	FacultyID	CourseID	FacultyID	FacultyFirstName	FacultyLastName	StudentID	StudentFirstName	StudentLastName
Fund. of Psych	2020-01-10	2020-05-10	2	PSYC	105	1600	5098	500	Doctor	Jones	51	Michael	Collins
Fun. of Education	2020-01-20	2020-05-10	1	EDUC	100	1500	7050	500	Doctor	Jones	51	Michael	Collins

Figure 7-21   Query output using Cloud Spanner

TIP   Only use Cloud Spanner for enterprise-scale deployments that require distributed workloads. Running a Cloud Spanner instance can cost several hundred dollars a month for a single node. Also, don't forget to delete your instance after completing any practice exercises.

BigQuery Deployment and Management

BigQuery itself is not a relational database management system. It is a managed Google database service. Google handles all maintenance and support activities. You, as a cloud engineer, are responsible for two tasks: ensuring jobs run properly and cost estimating. Understanding the various cost metrics to estimate a job and how to assign responsibility to those who need access to these estimates is an essential part of your role as an cloud engineer.

Estimating Query Cost Using BigQuery

From the Big Data menu, select BigQuery and then find a dataset from either your own data collection or an existing public data collection available in the Google Marketplace. In this example, you will use a public dataset from the Bureau of Economic Analysis:

1. Under resources, go to Add Data and select Public Datasets.

2. Locate BEA GDP and Income by Country.

3. Click View Dataset.

4. Once the dataset is loaded, click Query Table.

5. Enter one or more columns in the text box between Select and From Clause. In this case, you will enter GeoFIPS, GeoName.

6. Click Enter.

You will be presented with the result set shown in Figure 7-22. Under the query box, you should be aware of the amount of data read during the querying process.

Figure 7-22 BigQuery output results

An alternate method is to use the command-line tool to generate an estimate of the query. The structure of the command line is as follows:

```
bq --location= <LOCATION> query --use_legacy_sql=false --dry_run <SQL QUERY>
```

The location is either the regional or multiregional location you have selected for your dataset. If the dataset is coming from the public domain, this is determined by GCP. <SQL Query> is the fully qualified query you previously prepared in Figure 7-22. The estimate produced with BigQuery can be utilized with the Pricing Calculator found on the GCP website (at https://cloud.google.com/products/calculator/) to best determine the cost of your queries. A way to baseline pricing is to navigate to the On-Demand tab and enter the name of the table you are querying. Then enter the amount of storage you require (often 0) and the size of the query just executed in the Queries line within the Pricing section.

Figure 7-23
BigQuery
calculator on-
demand query
pricing output

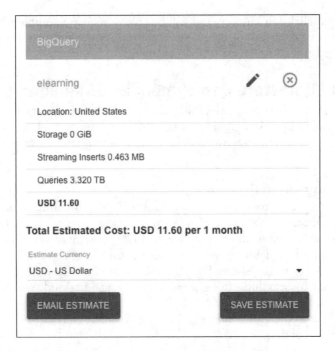

After selecting BigQuery, navigate to the On-Demand tab, enter the name of the table you are querying, set the amount of storage to 0, and enter the size of the query in the pricing section. Be sure to use the same size unit as displayed in the BigQuery console. In the example, the unit of measure is megabytes. When you click Add to Estimate, the Pricing Calculator will display the cost. In Figure 7-23, the calculator provides an estimate for the following consideration:

- Storage capacity of 0GB
- 0.463MB for streaming inserts
- 3.320TB of data per month for queries

The monthly estimate to query is $11.60.

TIP   On-demand query pricing is based on the number of bytes read. Flat pricing is based on cost predictability. With flat pricing, a customer purchases an allotment of resources for query processing; this allotment is not purchased for individual queries.

Viewing the Status of a BigQuery Job

Processing a BigQuery job may take a long time. There is a methodology to load, export, copy, and query data. Like in accounting, BigQuery processes data as it arrives in the system and exits the system. Depending on the complexity, it may process the data quickly or it may take some time. To view the status, you should go to the BigQuery navigation pane and click Job History. You will be able to review a complete history of all jobs and their status, complete or otherwise. An alternate option is to utilize the command-line editor by executing the bq show command.

Cloud Datastore Deployment and Management

Earlier in the chapter you were introduced how to create and add a fully qualified entity into a Cloud Datastore instance. Two other requirements you must know as an Associate Cloud Engineer are how to conduct basic querying and backup management activities in your role.

Querying Cloud Datastore

Unlike relational databases that utilize the SQL programming language for querying, Cloud Datastore makes use of its own querying language, called GQL(Google Query Language), which is quite similar. Cloud Datastore has its own graphical user interface (GUI) editor available to write queries against the entities that you prepare. To access the editor, go to the Query By GQL tab. Assuming you have an entity in place, query the entity by searching using a wildcard (*) against kind, which is the equivalent of a table in a datastore.

In the example shown in Figure 7-24, you find that select * from school produces a single row of data.

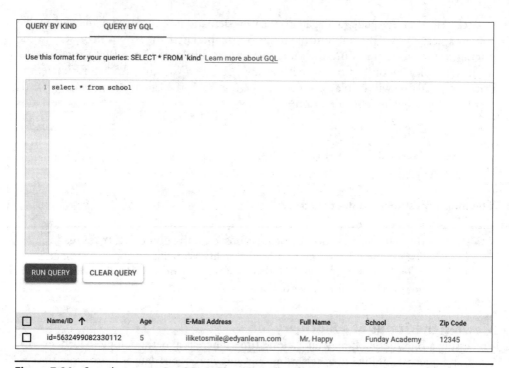

Figure 7-24   Sample query using GQL in Cloud Datastore

Backing Up Cloud Datastore

At a minimum, one Cloud Storage bucket is required to back up Cloud Datastore. To maintain the backup files, the bucket requires permissions be granted to all users who are affiliated with performing the backup. Backups are created using the `gsutil` command. To create a bucket for backup, enter the following onto the command line:

```
gsutil mb gs://<bucket_name>/
```

Permissions are required to create a backup at the database level for importing and exporting data. You will need to ensure that your system is adequately configured for `datastore.databases.export` and `datastore.databases.import`. A Datastore Import/Export Admin at a minimum will have these roles and responsibilities.

Assuming we create a bucket called school-books and we utilize the namespace students created earlier, a backup can be made using the following command line:

```
gcloud -namespace='students' gs://school-books
```

The namespace and bucket must be initialized first before you execute an `import` or `export` command. Once they are initialized, you can either import or export, like so:

To import:

```
gcloud datastore import gs://school-books//<yourfilename>.overall_export_metadata
```

To export:

```
gcloud datastore export gs://school-books//<yourfilename>.overall_export_metadata
```

Bigtable Deployment and Management

Earlier in the chapter you were taught how to configure Bigtable using the Cloud Console. While this is a convenient way to initially set up the wide-column NoSQL database, it is not the most practical long-term solution. The `cbt` command-line tool is used to support the creation, insertion, and querying of data for Bigtable. Table 7-6 provides a list of the most common commands used with `cbt`.

Because Bigtable does not support the use of SQL, the `cbt` commands and subcommands must be used to complete tasks inside of Cloud Shell for all activities ranging from the deployment to management of Bigtable. To get started with Bigtable in Cloud Shell, enter the following commands:

```
gcloud components update
gcloud components install cbt
```

Here, you are ensuring that the latest components are installed and then you are installing the Bigtable component. Once the `cbt` component is installed, you must establish the instance name so that the database can be created. To establish an instance, enter the following command into Cloud Shell:

```
echo instance = <name of instance> >> ~/.cbtrc
```

To create an instance:

```
cbt createtable <database table name>
```

Command	Definition
count	Count rows in a table
createinstance	Create an instance with an initial cluster
createcluster	Create a cluster in the configured instance
createfamily	Create a column family
createtable	Create a table
updatecluster	Update a cluster in the configured instance
deleteinstance	Delete an instance
deletecluster	Delete a cluster from the configured instance
deletecolumn	Delete all cells in a column
deletefamily	Delete a column family
deleterow	Delete a row
deleteallrows	Delete all rows
deletetable	Delete a table
doc	Print godoc-suitable documentation for cbt
help	Print help text
listinstances	List instances in a project
listclusters	List clusters in an instance
lookup	Read from a single row
ls	List tables and column families
mddoc	Print documentation for cbt in Markdown format
read	Read rows
set	Set the value of a cell (write)
setgcpolicy	Set the garbage-collection policy (age, versions) for a column family
waitforreplication	Block until all the completed writes have been replicated to all the clusters

Table 7-6 cbt Commands Provided by GCP

To read all data from a given table:

```
cbt read <database table name>
```

Using the list of commands, you can manage the Bigtable instance in a similar fashion to the command line for creating a database table.

Cloud Pub/Sub Deployment and Management

When most users store data on a cloud environment such as GCP, they like to be informed when the environment experiences a change. In this case, when the state of a Cloud Storage bucket changes, the user should be notified. Whether an item is retrieved,

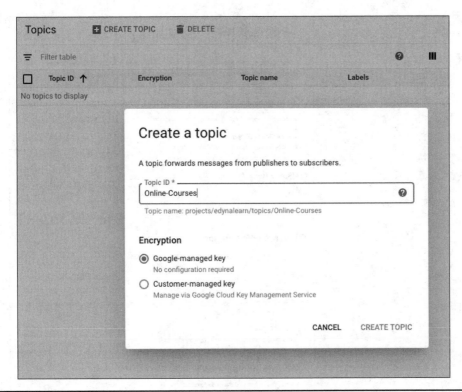

Figure 7-25 The Create a Topic interface for Cloud Pub/Sub

a file is added, the size of a folder reaches a certain threshold, or an item is deleted, all of these actions constitute a trigger in a Cloud Storage bucket. GCP has made it possible to track each of these state changes by offering a notification service called Cloud Pub/Sub. This way, you can monitor every change that occurs to your Cloud Storage objects.

You must complete two tasks to deploy a Pub/Sub message queue: create a topic and create a subscription. The *topic* is the equivalent of the application message center. The process of reading the message is called by the *subscription*, or the set of instructions.

To access Cloud Pub/Sub, navigate to the Cloud Console under Big Data and then click Pub/Sub.

You will need to first create a topic. In Figure 7-25, the Create a Topic interface asks you to enter the name of the topic and the type of encryption. You can choose a Google-managed key or you can self-manage the encryption. In the example, the name of the topic is Online-Courses.

The next step is to create the subscription, which is how one responds to the activity occurring in the Cloud Storage bucket. On the left side of the Cloud Pub/Sub main interface, select Subscriptions. Once the page opens, click the button Create Subscription to get to the Create Subscription form shown in Figure 7-26.

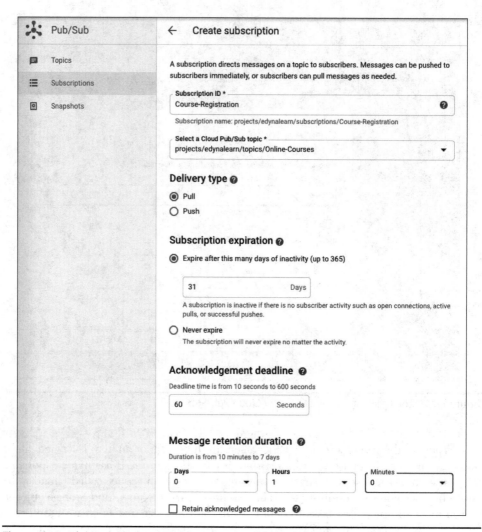

Figure 7-26 The Create Subscription interface for Cloud Pub/Sub

You will now need to fill in the following fields on the form:

- **Subscription ID:** Enter the name of the subscription.
- **Select a Cloud Pub/Sub Topic:** Select the topic you just created in the previous step.
- **Delivery Type:** Select a pull request delivery. (A push delivers a message as soon as a message is published.)
- **Subscription Expiration (Up to 365 Days or Never Expires):** How long until the message will be deleted or reactivated based on the action selected.
- **Acknowledgement Deadline:** How long should a message be held before it is sent again?

- **Message Retention Duration:** How long should the message be retained?
- **Retain Acknowledged Messages:** How long should a message be held if unacknowledged?
- **Dead Lettering:** Subscriptions are configured to support a maximum number of delivery attempts. When a message cannot be delivered, it is republished to the specific dead letter topic.

Based on the subscription type and conditions selected, either the message will be read from the topic (the pull condition) or written to a given endpoint in the Cloud Storage bucket (the push condition). For the push condition, you will need to indicate the URL for the endpoint.

Like most other storage options, there is an option to create a Pub/Sub topic and subscription using the command line. Using the Online-Courses topic we created earlier, enter the following command into Cloud Shell:

```
gcloud pubsub topics create Online-Courses
```

To create the subscription using the assigned name, Course-Registration, use the following command line:

```
gcloud pubsub subscriptions create Course-Registration --topic Online-Courses
```

TIP Make sure you understand how Pub/Sub interacts with all types of cloud storage. Equally important, make sure you review the different ways Pub/Sub is consumed in App Engine, Cloud Functions, and Cloud Run.

To test and see if the topic and subscription work, you will want to send a message. To ensure the message queue you created works properly, you can send data to the topic using a command such as this:

```
gcloud pubsub topics publish Online-Courses --message "Welcome to Online Registration"
```

To validate that the message has been received, the subscription must respond. You can send a response using a command such as the following:

```
gcloud pubsub subscriptions pull --auto-ack Course-Registration
```

Dataproc Deployment and Management

Dataproc is Google's managed Apache Spark and Hadoop service. Like BigQuery, Dataproc is designed for big data applications. You should be aware that Spark is intended for analysis and machine learning, whereas Hadoop is appropriate for batching data, with emphasis on big data applications.

EXAM TIP For the exam, you need to be familiar with creating Dataproc clusters and storage facilities as well as know how to submit jobs that run in those clusters.

To access Dataproc, go to the Cloud Console and select the Dataproc option under Big Data. To create a cluster, select Create Cluster. As shown in Figure 7-27, a Dataproc form appears asking you to provide the following information about the cluster:

- Name
- Region
- Zone
- Cluster mode
- Machine configuration (Machine family, Series, Machine type)
- CPU platform and GPU
- Machine Configuration (Series, Machine type)
- Primary disk size
- Primary disk type
- YARN cores
- YARN memory
- Autoscaling policy
- Component gateway

There are additional advanced features you can configure, such as Encryption, Preemptible VMs Networking, and Metadata properties. You choose from single node, standard node, and high availability. Single node is appropriate for development and testing, whereas high availability is often used in distributed or production environments. A high-availability cluster maintains a minimum of three nodes. Enter the values that are appropriate to your instance needs. Once this is complete, click Create. After the cluster is created, it will be listed on the Dataproc dashboard. You are now able to submit a Dataproc job.

To submit a job, click the cluster instance name. Using the example created in Figure 7-27, click edynalearn-lms and then click the Submit Job button. You will need to fill in the Submit a Job form, shown in Figure 7-28, with the details of the Dataproc job. Included in the form are the following fields:

- Job ID
- Job type (Hadoop, Spark, SparkR, PySpark, Hive, SparkSQL, and Pig)
- Main class or JAR
- JAR files
- Archive files
- Arguments
- Max restarts per hour
- Properties
- Labels

Figure 7-27
Dataproc
creation of
single-node
cluster in no
worker mode

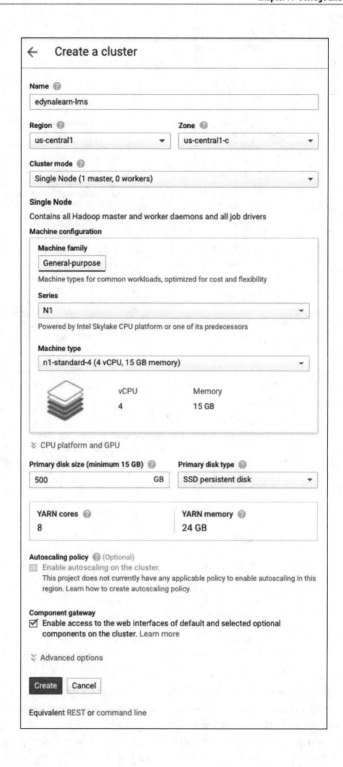

Figure 7-28
Submit a
Job form for
Dataproc

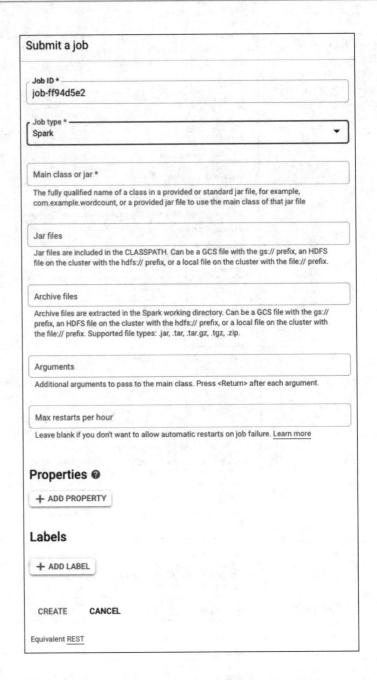

Figure 7-28 Submit a Job form for Dataproc

The difference between the JAR files option and the Main class is that JAR files are the programs that are executed, whereas the main class contains the instruction set, functions, or methods that are invoked to run the files.

Depending on the job type, optional arguments and properties are likely to be passed. The job will be listed on the Jobs dashboard once it is created (see Figure 7-29). Once a

	MONITORING	JOBS	VM INSTANCES	CONFIGURATION	WEB INTERFACES	
≡	Filter jobs					
	Job ID		Region	Type	Start time	
⊙	job-ff94d5e2		us-central1	Spark	May 21, 2020, 10:29:43 AM	

Figure 7-29   The Jobs dashboard

job is created, you can see all the executable activity by clicking the job name, which causes a log of all job activity to appear.

If you prefer to complete these activities using the command-line editor, you can use the gcloud dataproc clusters command. Here's an example of a command to pass into Cloud Shell:

```
gcloud dataproc clusters create clusterex1a2 --zone us-east1-b
```

You can pass optional parameters to refine the cluster-creation process. Submitting a job using the command line involves using the gcloud dataproc jobs command:

```
gcloud dataproc jobs submit hadoop --cluster clusterex1a2 --jar examfiles.jar
```

In this example , the examfiles.jar program submits a job to clusterex1a2.

Importing and Exporting Approaches

Each storage platform has its own methodology for importing and exporting data. Most offer a way to complete import and export tasks via a GUI using Cloud Console and through the command line using Cloud Shell or SDK, which we'll explore in this section.

EXAM TIP   For the exam, you are not expected to know how to insert or export data programmatically using SQL, GQL, or alternative methods. Instead, the goal is to learn standard command-line operators using gcloud, gsutil, kubectl, and the Cloud Console.

Importing/Exporting in Cloud SQL

To import/export from the Cloud Console, you need to locate the preferred cloud SQL instance under Cloud Storage. Once you find Cloud SQL instance, click the link. Depending on what action you want to begin with, you will either click Import or Export.

To import data, follow these steps:

1. Click the Import button. The form shown in Figure 7-30 appears.

2. Choose the file(s) you would like to import from the Cloud Storage instance.

3. Select the format (SQL or CSV) that should be imported.

4. Select the destination database for the import.

5. Click the Import button.

To export data, follow these steps:

1. Click the Export button. The form shown in Figure 7-31 appears.

2. Select the export location where you would like to store the files in Cloud Storage.

3. Select the file format (SQL or CSV) preferred for Cloud Storage.

4. Click the Export button.

TIP Consider the purpose of the dataset when selecting SQL or CSV. If your data is structured or will require extraction, choose SQL. If you know your data will follow a nonrelational pattern and has ambiguous patterns, choose CSV.

Importing and exporting data using the command line requires several steps. You cannot just select import or export and your location. Instead, you need to create your bucket, establish the instance, assign credentials, and then import or export the data. The following instructions allow you to import or export data in Cloud SQL:

1. Assuming you do not have a bucket, create a new one:

```
gsutil mb gs://<bucket name>
```

Figure 7-31
Export of Cloud
SQL data

2. You need to ensure that the service account has write access to the bucket. To identify the service account name, enter the following into Cloud Shell:

```
gcloud sql instances describe <instance name>
```

3. A listing of all credentials will appear on the command line. Once you identify the appropriate account, you can use the `gsutil acl ch` command to modify permissions on the bucket to allow write access, like so:

```
gsutil acl ch -u <service account email address>:w gs://<bucket name>
```

Here, `-u` stands for user and `w` stands for write.

4. Now that the service account has write access, you can now export and import to the bucket. Use the following import and export commands:

```
gcloud sql import sql <instance name> gs://<bucket name>/<file name>\
--database=<database name>
gcloud sql export sql <instance name> gs://<bucket name>/<file name>\
--database=<database name>
```

Importing/Exporting in Cloud Spanner

Cloud Spanner has no command-line option for importing and exporting data. Therefore, you are required to use Cloud Console. To access the import/export features in Cloud Console for Cloud Spanner, go to Storage and select the Cloud Spanner option.

To import data into your database of choice, click the following link on the Import/Export page: *To import data from Cloud Storage into a new Cloud Spanner database.* You need to select the source bucket/folder for content to reside in. Then, enter the

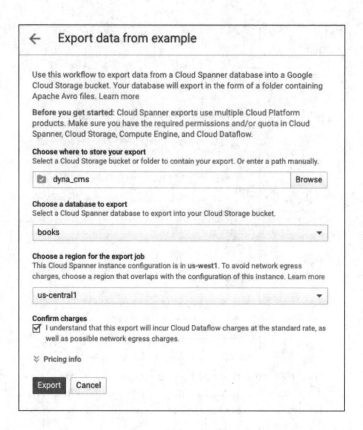

Figure 7-32
Cloud Spanner
export data
interface

name of a new database, not the existing one that will store the data being imported. After that, pick the region in which you prefer the import to be housed. You will need to approve of these changes by acknowledging that there are charges associated with Cloud Spanner and import/export activity. For you to proceed, check the Confirm Charges box and click Import. Upon completion of these steps, the changes are reflected in the Import/Export log in the Cloud Spanner dashboard.

Exporting data follows a similar process; the only difference is you click a button and not a link. Select the database and then click the Export button. You will need to choose where you want to store the data (bucket/folder). Next, select the database you intend to export. Pick the region in which you prefer the data to be stored. Finally, you will need to acknowledge that there are charges associated with these changes. Check the Confirm Charges box (see Figure 7-32). Once you approve the statement, click Export. It will take a few minutes for the data to export. The results of the export are listed on the Database dashboard under Import/Export activity.

Importing/Exporting in BigQuery

BigQuery allows a cloud engineer to import/export using both Cloud Console and the command line. To access import/export capabilities using Cloud Console, go to Big Data and click the BigQuery button.

Creating a BigQuery import is similar to creating a database table. Under Resources, select the database table you would like to import. Then, on the right side, click the Create Table button. In the form that appears, shown in Figure 7-33, you need to select the source where your import will come from. Your choices include Empty table, Google Cloud Storage, Upload, Drive, and Google Bigtable. Either the data exists already on a Google Cloud Platform system or is local to the user desktop. You have the option to select where the data is coming from. Selecting the location also dictates the file format.

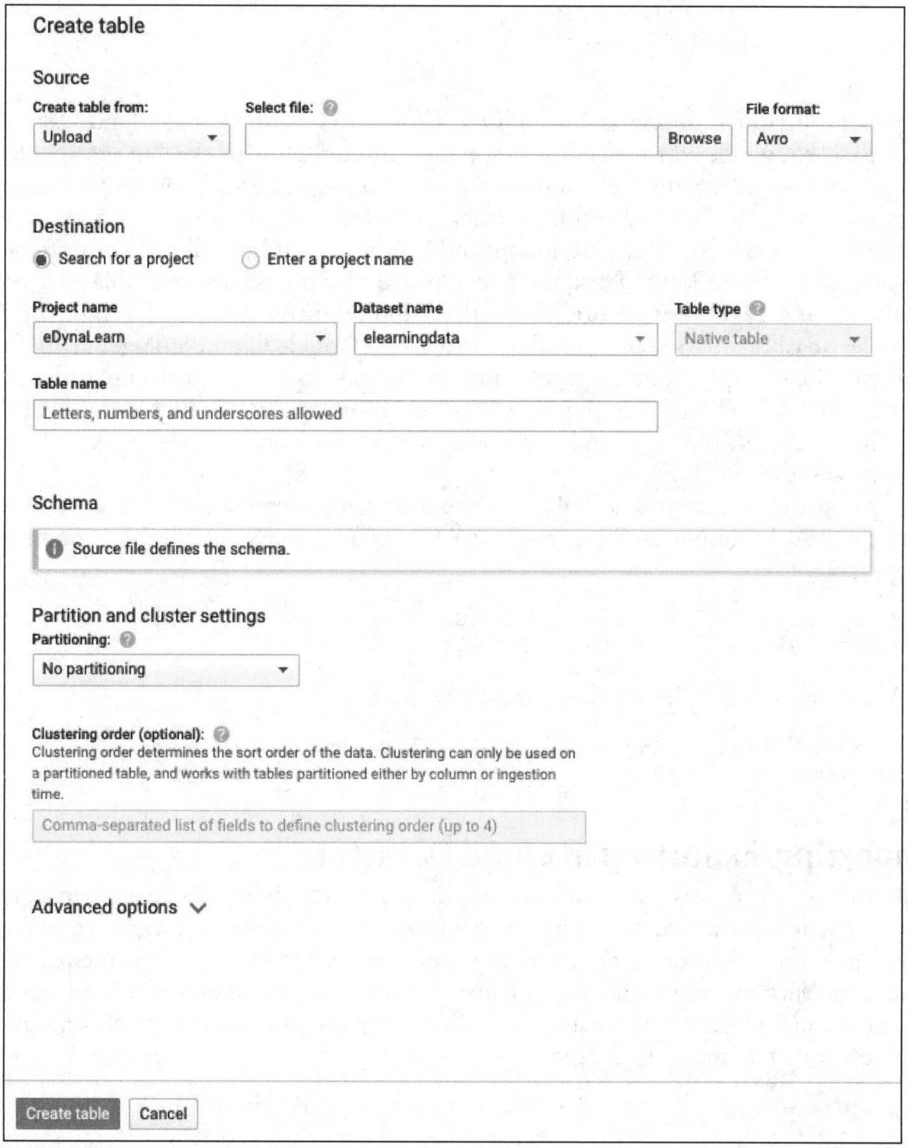

Figure 7-33   Import into BigQuery

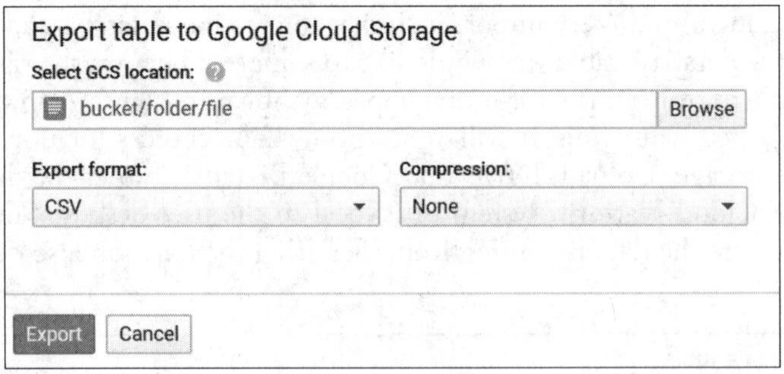

Figure 7-34
BigQuery export

At present, BigQuery supports Avro, JSON, CSV, ORC, Parquet, and Cloud Datastore Backup. Next, you need to select the destination. Either select an existing project, dataset, and table type. Alternatively, you can start a fresh project. Other conditions you may want to consider configuring include schema, partition and cluster settings, and encryption. All of these settings can be found under Advanced. Once all choices have been selected, click Create Table. The data is now loaded into the destination table selected.

To create a BigQuery export, locate the Export button on the very right of the BigQuery dashboard. Select either Export to GCS (Google Cloud Storage) or Explore Data Studio. Google Cloud Storage is used for data storage, whereas Data Studio is an analysis tool. There are three requirements for exporting data in BigQuery: identifying GCS location, file type, and compression type (see Figure 7-34). Select all three options and then click Export.

If you prefer to complete a BigQuery import/export using command line, you must use bq load for import and bq extract for export. Here's example of a command-line import:

```
bq load --autodetect --source_format=CSV authors.books gs://schooldata
/cardcatalog.csv
```

And here's an example of a command-line export:

```
bq extract --destination_format CSV --compression GZIP 'authors.books'
gs://elearn-lms/library.zip
```

Importing/Exporting in Cloud Datastore

Datastore only supports command-line import/export capability. Because a datastore is based on a document structure, very few parameters are needed to create the command-line request for import or export. As an engineer, you need to identify the namespace that groups the entities and provide the intended bucket name for an export. For an import, two additional pieces of information are required: path and filename. Here's a sample structure for a command-line import:

```
gcloud datastore import gs://<bucket> /<path>/<file>.overall_export_metadata
```

And here's a sample structure for a command-line export:

```
gcloud datastore export --namespaces= <name> gs://<bucket>
```

Importing/Exporting in Bigtable

Bigtable does not have one set method for import/export. You can export Avro, Parquet, and SequenceFile files directly from the table pages of Bigtable using Cloud Console. Similarly, Cloud SDK only supports data importing of CSV files. However, if your intention is to migrate data from another database, Bigtable requires the use of HBase. For this example, you only need to be familiar with the HBase method of migrating data to and from another data source.

The first step in importing or exporting a Bigtable table is to download the JAR file:

```
curl -f -O https://search.maven.org/remotecontent?filepath=com/google/cloud/
bigtable/bigtable-beam-import/1.14.1/bigtable-beam-import-1.14.1.jar
```

Using the JAR file you just downloaded, gather the project name, table name, bucket name, number of maximum workers for the project, and the zone that will run the dataflow. These are all prerequisites for creating import and export commands.
Here's an example of an import:

```
java -jar bigtable-beam-import-1.6.0-shaded.jar import \
    --runner=dataflow \
    --project=school-project\
    --bigtableInstanceId=book-instance \
    --bigtableTableId=book-table1 \
    --sourcePattern='gs://library-bucket/book-table1/part-*' \
    --tempLocation=gs://book-bucket1/jar-temp \
    --maxNumWorkers=20 \
    --zone=us-central1-a
```

Exporting into Bigtable requires a few parameter modifications from an import. The majority of those changes are in the filename structure.

```
java -jar bigtable-beam-import-1.14.1.jar export \
    --runner=dataflow \
    --project=school-project \
  --bigtableInstanceId=book-instance \
    --bigtableTableId=books-table1 \
    --destinationPath=gs://books-bucket1/books-table1 \
    --tempLocation=gs://library-bucket/jar-temp \
    --maxNumWorkers=60 \
    --zone=us-central1-a
```

Importing/Exporting in Cloud Dataproc

Cloud Dataproc is not a database platform; it is intended for analysis, manipulation, machine learning, and complex data operations. You would use Dataproc for purposes that do not require persistency. Dataproc has an import and export capability to save cluster configuration data. You can only execute such commands using the command-line tools.

To create an import or export, you need to identify the cluster name, region, and destination. Here's an example of an import:

```
gcloud beta dataproc clusters import sys_cluster \
    --region=us-central1 --source=output.yaml
```

Here's an example of an export:

```
gcloud beta dataproc clusters export sys_cluster \
    --region=us-central1 --destination= output.yaml
```

Chapter Review

GCP offers several storage options. Memorystore, a cache service, persistent disks, and network disks are available for consumption by Compute Engine or Kubernetes Engine. When you are looking for virtually unlimited, expandable capacity, Cloud Storage is a better option. Cloud Storage is GCP's object storage solution. For those who are looking for database-driven models, GCP offers relational and NoSQL alternatives.

Cloud SQL and Cloud Spanner are two relational database options. Whereas Cloud SQL can utilize MySQL, PostgreSQL, or SQL Server, Cloud Spanner is Google's globally distributed database system. Both systems are ideal for transaction-oriented activities. Scaling even a single database node, especially Cloud Spanner into specific multiregions, can be extremely costly. Be sure to evaluate pricing as you configure instances. While Big-Query is not a relational database, it is a platform that analyzes relational models found in data warehouses. It can evaluate very large datasets. NoSQL options include Datastore and Firebase, both of which are document databases, whereas Bigtable is a wide-column table database.

For each of the databases, you became familiar with basic configuration and management tasks using the Cloud Console and/or command line. While more of the services use `gcloud`, a few utilize command-line utilities such as `gsutil`. You were provided examples of how to import, export, move, query, and rename objects across the various databases.

The end of the chapter presented you with how to load data into Cloud Storage, relational and NoSQL databases, Dataproc, and Cloud Pub/Sub. The use of the `gsutil` command and Cloud Console allows you to upload and move data between buckets.

Cloud Pub/Sub is useful in improving application resiliency and load management. One last notable activity is that you learned how to create a topic and subscription. Upon creating the topic and subscription, the data in the queue becomes readable by subscribers.

Questions

1. Your team recently implemented a new electronic health records system at City Hospital. The government mandates that all patient records be retained for seven years regardless of whether the patient actively sees a physician at the hospital regularly. What kind of storage would you recommend the hospital implement for patient health records that are not accessed after 90 days?

   A. Standard

   B. Coldline

    C. Nearline

    D. Archive

2. The researcher team at City Hospital is investigating data from one of its clinical trials held in 2019. The dataset has 2 million records across 150 columns of data. The clinical team is looking for a relational database platform that can easily ingest and evaluate this dataset. What tool would you recommend?

    A. Cloud SQL

    B. Cloud Spanner

    C. BigQuery

    D. Cloud Firestore

3. A team of scientists is preparing a statement of work that requires them to evaluate data patterns captured from different smart device sensors. The data has little structure, given that the scientists intend to use over 200 different smart devices in their experiment. What type of storage should the team indicate it intends to use in the statement of work?

    A. Cloud Firestore *for: mobile, web, IoT*

    B. Cloud Spanner

    C. Cloud Datastore

    D. Bigtable

4. Of all the NoSQL databases, which of the following has many relational database characteristics?

    A. Bigtable

    B. Cloud Datastore

    C. Cloud Firestore

    D. Cloud Spanner

5. Your organization, an accounting firm, is looking to configure an archive for data it no longer actively accesses but is required to keep for recordation purposes. The leadership team is looking for an affordable solution. The team has decided that any record where there are multiple copies should be archived after 90 days. Previous records must be accessed quarterly for bookkeeping. What would you recommend?

    A. Create a bucket lifecycle rule that archives data with a new version after 90 days to nearline storage.

    B. Create a bucket lifecycle rule that archives data with a new version after 90 days to coldline storage.

    C. Create a bucket lifecycle rule that deletes all versions of the data except the most recent at 90 days.

    D. Create a bucket lifecycle rule that archives all regional storage every 90 days and copies it to coldline storage.

6. An automatic daily backup of the edynalearn Cloud SQL instance occurs at 2:30 A.M. each day. Which command would you use?

A. `gcloud sql instances patch edynalearn --backup-start-time 02:30`

B. `gcloud sql backups create –async --instance edynalearn`

C. `gcloud sql database create –async --instance edynalearn`

D. `gcloud sql backup patch edynalearn --backup-start-time 02:30`

7. GCP oversees all aspects of database management for Cloud Spanner and Cloud SQL, except for which of the following?

A. Tuning the operating system

B. Applying appropriate database and system patches

C. Scheduling system backups

D. Creating databases and tables

8. What is a prerequisite for creating a database in Cloud Spanner?

A. SQL Data Definition Language (DDL)

B. Encryption

C. Tables

D. Indexes

9. Your team is looking to estimate how much it will cost to run a query with 2,000,000 records using BigQuery. You expect that this volume of records will increase by 10 percent monthly over the next 12 months. You want to estimate how much it will cost to run the query three months from now. You are using on-demand pricing. What should you do?

A. Use the command line to dry run a query to estimate the number of bytes read. Then convert that bytes estimate to dollars using the Pricing Calculator. Multiply by 1.3.

B. Use the command line to dry run a query to estimate the number of bytes returned. Then convert that bytes estimate to dollars using the Pricing Calculator. Multiply by 1.3.

C. Use the command line to dry run a query to estimate the number of bytes read. Then convert that bytes estimate to dollars using the Pricing Calculator. Multiply by 0.3.

D. Use the command line to dry run a query to estimate the number of bytes returned. Then convert that bytes estimate to dollars using the Pricing Calculator. Multiply by 0.3.

10. Cloud Memorystore allows for region configurable memory up to what size?

A. 100GB

B. 50GB

C. 1TB

D. 300GB *Cloud Memory store Max*

11. Loading and moving data can be done on the command line using which of the following commands?

A. `gcloud`

B. `gsutil` *load/move date*

C. `mb`

D. `bq extract`

12. What is the best-suited file format to handle compression and large datasets using BigQuery?

A. CSV

B. JSON

C. Avro *(Binary form)*

D. ZIP

13. Which of the following requires the use of an external solution for importing/exporting data?

A. Cloud Spanner *Cloud Console*

B. Cloud SQL *Command-line utility*

C. Cloud Dataproc

D. Bigtable *HBase→ JAR*

14. Your team recently rebuilt a set of servers. The team leadership is looking for the most efficient way to restore the configuration of their cluster instances. What method would you recommend for achieving the configuration restoration?

A. Export the configuration from old_server using Cloud Dataproc. Import the configuration to new_server using Cloud Dataproc.

B. Export the configuration from old_server using Bigtable. Import the configuration to new_server using Bigtable.

C. Export the configuration from old_server using BigQuery. Import the configuration to new_server using BigQuery.

D. There is no way to rebuild a server using an existing configuration file from an old cluster instance.

15. An organization runs 10 million queries a month. It has seen an average increase in its spend month over month of around 4 percent annually. The CIO has asked the cloud administrators to try and figure out a way to reduce the cloud budget spend. What methods would you suggest the team look into? (Choose two.)

   A. Consider using Google Search Appliance.

   B. Add budget alerts to better forecast querying costs in the future.

   C. Limit the number of queries a user can submit per hour.

   D. Switch from on-demand pricing to fixed pricing.

Answers

1. **B.** The threshold of 90 days is most appropriate for coldline storage. Standard storage is for frequently accessed data. Nearline is intended for those who seek access to records every 30 days or so. Archive is for storing records not accessible for more than 365 days.

2. **C.** BigQuery can be used to easily ingest and evaluate this dataset. CloudSQL and Cloud Spanner are relational databases but are not intended to do analysis to this degree, especially with the number of columns being analyzed. Cloud Firestore is a NoSQL database.

3. **A.** The team should indicate it intends to use Cloud Firestore in the statement of work. Near-real-time data collection is necessary using a NoSQL data solution. While Bigtable and Cloud Datastore are both NoSQL solutions, Cloud Firestore is specifically designed for mobile, web, and IoT distribute data capture. Cloud Spanner is a relational database.

4. **B.** Cloud Datastore requires data to be structured in a document format. Examples of how data is stored include user profiling, catalogs, and gaming profiles. Cloud Spanner is a relational solution. Cloud Firestore and Bigtable are both NoSQL database solutions. Interestingly, of all the NoSQL databases, Cloud Datastore shares the most commonalities with a relational database solution.

5. **B.** At the end of each quarter, a new copy of the data should replace the existing set of data in coldline storage, hence 90 days. Nearline storage is for 30 days. Nothing in the object lifecycle ruleset says to archive or delete the data, only provide a new version; therefore, answers C and D are incorrect.

6. **A.** Only the command in answer A is correct. Although answers B and C include on-demand queries using the `--async` parameter, they do not include automatic backup requirements. Only answers A and D include automatic backup configurations; however, the command shown in answer D is incorrect.

7. **D.** An administrator is still responsible for creating the database and configuring the tables for their database. All other activities are completed by GCP.

8. **A.** You must use the SQL Data Definition Language (DDL) to create tables and indexes in Cloud Spanner. Encryption is irrelevant.

9. **A.** Volume will increase by 30 percent over three months. Therefore, the first thing to consider is to multiply by 1.3, not 0.3. The second thing to evaluate is the difference between the words *read* and *returned*. For on-demand pricing, you need to measure how much is read, not returned, to calculate a price. Therefore, the correct answer is A.

10. **D.** The maximum capacity is 300GB. All other answers are incorrect.

11. **B.** `gsutil` is the utility to loading or move data. `mb` allows you to make buckets. `gcloud` is not intended for loading or moving data. `bq extract` is for analyzing and extracting data in BigQuery.

12. **C.** Avro is best suited for large file data compression. CSV and JSON are not intended for large datasets. ZIP is not applicable.

13. **D.** Bigtable requires the use of HBase and JAR files to migrate data. The other solutions all make use of either Cloud Console or a command-line utility.

14. **A.** Dataproc allows for an administrator to create a cluster configuration file. BigQuery may be an analysis tool, but it does not create a configuration file. Bigtable is a NoSQL database that does not yield a configuration file. Answer D is irrelevant.

15. **B** and **D.** The team should integrate budget alerts to better understand spend patterns so it can report back to the CIO exactly what projects are resulting in high consumption costs. A second option is to switch from an on-demand to fixed consumption model. With an on-demand model, your consumption is measured as you query in real time. With fixed, you are paying a fixed rate for a given number of queries. The more an organization purchases, the lower the cost is for the organization. The Google Search Appliance is not utilized for cloud consumption purposes. As for answer C, the administrator can limit the number of queries all they want; however, the query load determines the cost. A complex, large query may still yield a significant cost burden on an organization. This will likely not solve any problems.

Networking

In this chapter you will learn to

- Plan, configure, deploy, and manage Virtual Private Cloud (VPC) resources using Cloud Console and Cloud SDK
- Understand how to implement various load-balancing techniques available in Google Cloud Platform (GCP)
- Create and manage ingress and egress firewall rules
- Configure Cloud DNS

Network solutions necessary to run many of the GCP features such as Compute Engine are discussed in this chapter. Accessing resources requires connectivity between a host system and the user. The use of a Virtual Private Cloud (VPC) is central to the Google Cloud strategy. Ensuring stability and preventing unauthorized traffic inside a VPC require the use of a load balancer and firewalls. There are several types of load balancers, so in this chapter you will learn the difference between them and how to create and configure various load-balancing options. Implementation practices regarding firewall rules, as a way to prevent malicious traffic from accessing your GCP instances, are also addressed at length.

Users must connect to the GCP instances but often do not have access to them; therefore, a method to connect the users to the network is required. You learn how to create a virtual private network that enables the connection between the users and GCP instances. Finally, this chapter also covers how to manage IP addresses under various conditions and how to utilize Cloud DNS, Google's domain name service.

IP Address Management

Exam objectives identify several IP address–related topics to be familiar with as part of your networking skills in preparation for the exam. First, you need to understand the difference between ephemeral and static IP addresses. Second, you need to know how to expand Classless Inter-Domain Routing (CIDR) blocks. Finally, make sure you understand how to reserve an IP address.

Static and Ephemeral IP Addresses

A static IP address is a fixed IP address. The address maintains an association with a project unless the administrator releases it. An organization uses a static address to apply consistency for services such as a web application or website. Many virtual machines utilize a different type of address where as long as the resource uses the IP address and remains active, there is no change. This IP address type is known as an ephemeral IP address. A virtual machine running an application often maintains the same IP address until the instance is stopped or deleted. Once either of those two states is reached, the IP address is released.

When a user connects to a network, an IP address is assigned to the networking equipment. There may be times when the equipment that is assigned is associated with a private network. In some cases, the network can utilize a single public IP address. RFC 1918 standardizes the private assignment of IP addresses to a single IP address. There are three IP ranges that are dedicated to private assignment:

IP Address Range	Prefix
10.0.0.0–10.255.255.255	10/8
172.16.0.0–172.31.255.255	172.16/12
192.168.0.0–192.168.255.255	192.168/16

If you are inside a private network, you can assign a unique address on the network, but not outside it. A private IP address cannot communicate directly with external computers because they are not globally unique and hence addressable from the public Internet.

Expanding the CIDR Block Range

Classless Inter-Domain Routing, also known as a CIDR block, is a bitwise, prefix-based standard for presenting IP addresses and routing properties. By using a CIDR block, routing facilitation occurs with blocks of addresses, whereby addresses are grouped into single routing table entries. CIDR blocks replace the old Class A, B, C system by extending the IPv4 address range. To extend the primary IP range of an existing subnet, you need to modify the subnet mask.

Setting the mask prefix length to a smaller number makes more addresses available on a given subnet mask. Using an auto mode network, the largest subnet mask that can be used is /16. Using a broader range conflicts with the creation of the primary IP ranges of other subnets. Similarly, the same rule applies to a custom network in auto mode. Once it is in place, you cannot expand or contract the primary IP range of a subnet. If you realize later on that you need more addresses, you can extend the range at that time; therefore, your initial IP address expansion should only account for what you absolutely need.

EXAM TIP A CIDR address is made up of two values: a network address to establish the subnet, and the host identifier. CIDR notation spells out the numbers using a network address and mask. With CIDR notation, a slash added at the end of the address expresses how many bits of an IP address are allocated to a network mask. Note that you can create a larger IP allocation with a smaller number such as /10, which offers 4,194,304 available addresses, versus /14, which offers 262,144 available addresses. Therefore, a small number after an IP address yields a large pool of available addresses. You should be aware that managing IP ranges within subnets can get rather complex within larger environments. If you intend to manage a range of IP addresses, make sure that they do not conflict with one another.

To make CIDR block range modifications, go to the VPC Networks page under Networking. You should see all available networks and subnets in your assigned project, as shown in Figure 8-1.

Now click a network that requires expansion. Once you do, a more detailed state of the VPC appears. At the top of the page, click Edit. On the next page, select the subnet under the Subnets tab and then click Edit again.

For example, to broaden your CIDR block range, go to the IP Address Range field and change /12 to /10. With this use case, you are making more addresses available for devices in this subnet. After you change the range, click Save to apply your changes and make them active. Should you decide that you want to reduce the CIDR block range, you need to re-create the subnet.

To modify the CIDR block range using `gcloud`, use the following command:

```
gcloud compute networks subnets expand-ip-range dynlearn-network
--prefix-length 10
```

This command changes the CIDR block range to /10 from the previously set range of /12.

Name ∨	Region	Subnets	Mode	IP address ranges	Gateways	Firewall Rules	Global dynamic routing	Flow logs
dynalearn-network		1	Custom			0	Off	
	us-central1	dynlearningus		10.0.0.0/8	10.0.0.1			Off
default		24	Auto ▾			7	Off	
	us-central1	default		10.128.0.0/20	10.128.0.1			Off
	europe-west1	default		10.132.0.0/20	10.132.0.1			Off
	us-west1	default		10.138.0.0/20	10.138.0.1			Off
	asia-east1	default		10.140.0.0/20	10.140.0.1			Off

VPC networks   ➕ CREATE VPC NETWORK   ↻ REFRESH

Figure 8-1 View of all networks and subnets in a project

Reserving an IP Address

There are times when you may want to reserve an external IP address. A reservation can be made using Cloud Console or the command line. To reserve a static IP address using Cloud Console, go to the Networking option in the navigation area and then select External IP Address under Virtual Private Cloud (VPC).

On the next screen, you will see a list of all IP addresses currently reserved. To add a new reservation, click the Reserve Static Address button. As shown in Figure 8-2, a form appears asking for the following information:

- IP address name
- Description
- Network service tier (Premium or Standard)
- IP version (IPv4 or IPv6)

Figure 8-2
Reserving
an IP address

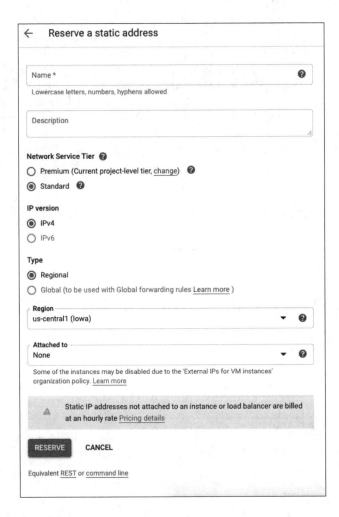

- Type (Regional or Global)
- What instance the IP address is attached to

If you choose the Premium network service tier, all traffic is routed across the Google Global Network, whereas the Standard tier transfers just some data. If you decide to reserve an IP address, you also need to attach it to an instance. Should you simply want to reserve the IP address without instance association, GCP charges you per hour for usage of an IP reservation.

Using the command line requires the same parameters be passed as described in Cloud Console. To create a static IP address in us-central1 using the Standard tier, enter the following command:

```
gcloud beta compute addresses create dynalearn-network --region=us-central1
--network-tier=STANDARD
```

Virtual Private Cloud Management

A Virtual Private Cloud (VPC) is like a hardware-based network infrastructure, except it is software-defined. In the case of Google Cloud Platform, a VPC provides the networking functionality to virtual machines running on Compute Engine, Google Kubernetes Engine (GKE) clusters, and App Engine flexible environments. Because a VPC is a cloud-based resource on Google Cloud Platform, services can be made global, scale, and offer flexibility.

VPC networks are global resources that maintain regional virtual subnetworks across all of Google's data centers. The VPCs are connected by a global wide area network while being isolated from one another. Resources communicate with each other on a VPC such as two Compute Engine virtual machines transmitting data between one another, assuming a firewall rule does not block traffic.

VPCs consist of *subnets,* a type of regional resource associated with an IP address range. The IP addresses associated with subnets are private so that resources, including APIs and third-party services, can communicate with one another. VPCs do not have to be standalone; they are sharable inside an organization utilizing a project. Assuming users across an organization have the appropriate permissions, it is possible to create resources in a shared environment.

Creating Virtual Private Clouds

You can create a Virtual Private Cloud using Cloud Console or the gcloud command-line interface. To create a VPC using Cloud Console, go to the Networking section in the navigation area and select the option VPC Networks from the VPC Network submenu. The page that loads shows a list of all existing VPC network connections. To create your VPC, click the Create VPC Network button. As shown in Figure 8-3, a form appears that allows you to configure a new VPC network. You have several options to consider when you choose Automatic for the Subnet Creation mode:

- **Name**   The name of the VPC. You are unable to modify this once it is in place.
- **Description**   Indicate the purpose of the VPC.

Figure 8-3
Automatic VPC
configuration

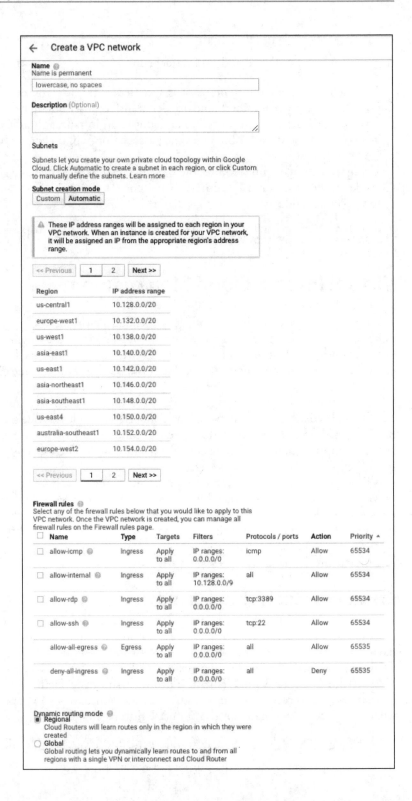

Automatic Subnet Creation Mode

- **Subnets**   Custom, or select an automatic configuration. If you choose Automatic, you are selecting predefined IP address ranges. An assignment is per region in the configured VPC network.

- **Firewall rules**   You have four choices: ICMP, Internal, RDP, and SSH tied to *egress* (outgoing), and *ingress* (incoming) traffic management. An explanation for each rule type can be found in the "Firewall Rules" section, later in this chapter. Select one or more of these options to secure the environment.

- **Dynamic routing mode**   Select either Regional (single route based on selected region) or Global (location-agnostic, as there is international coverage).

- **Server policy**   Select either None required or Create a custom policy. This setting allows for the domain name service (DNS) to identify specific requirements for a given project.

Custom Mode

Should you decide to configure the VPC using the Custom mode, you are limited to knowing the name, description, subnet name, region, and IP address range as well as determining whether you would like private Google access or flow logs, as shown in Figure 8-4. Private Google access allows a virtual machine instance that only has internal private IP address access to reach the public IP addresses of a Google API and its services. Furthermore, private Google access allows access to certain Google Cloud services that are restricted to internal IP addresses. Flow logs are utilized to document traffic samples based on network flows sent from and received by virtual machine instances, Compute Engine, and Kubernetes Engine nodes. Logs can capture data that is useful for network monitoring, forensics, real-time security analysis, and expense optimization. The collection of log data can become expensive to store and manage, but it's useful should a diagnostics event require such details. In identifying the IP address range, be sure to understand CIDR notation, discussed in the "IP Address Management" section earlier in this chapter.

Upon configuring the necessary parameters in either scenario, click Create to create the VPC. The newly configured VPC appears in the list of available VPC options along with the associated subnets.

If you prefer, you can also create the VPC with the `gcloud` command. You use the `gcloud compute networks create` command. Here's an example of how to create an automatic VPC using default configurations:

```
gcloud compute networks create dynalearn-networks --subnet-mode=auto
```

Should you prefer to create a custom VPC, the only difference from the initial command line is modifying the `--subnet-mode` parameter to equal `custom`, not `auto`. However, there are additional flags to qualify the command-line statement fully. Mandatory requirements include the VPC name, IP range, and region. Optional configuration flags include the flow logs and private IP Google access. Here's an example of a fully qualified custom VPC configuration:

```
gcloud beta compute networks subnets create dynalearning-ntwk-subnet1
--network=dynalearn-networks --region=us-central1-a --range=10.10.0.0/16
```

Figure 8-4
Custom VPC
configuration

Creating a Shared Virtual Private Cloud

Shared VPC, also known as XPN in the API and command-line interface, enables an engineer to export subnets from an existing VPC network to a host project or other service project inside the same organization. Instances inside a service project may have network connections to shared subnets within a host project. This section describes how to create and configure a shared VPC using the `gcloud` command. While Cloud Console does support the ability to create a shared VPC configuration, the exam focus is on the command-line interface. You need to use the appropriate administrative roles at the organization or folder level before creating the shared VPC connection. Here is the default command:

```
gcloud compute shared-vpc enable <host project ID>
```

You would need to identify the host project name, assuming the goal is to support the project at the organizational level. On the other hand, if the Shared VPC Admin role is at the folder level, you would construct a command line that would differ slightly:

```
gcloud beta compute shared-vpc enable <host project ID>
```

Once you have created the shared VPC connection, it is necessary to associate projects with the `associated-projects` command line. Depending on if your VPC is at the organizational or folder level, the command line differs slightly.

Here's the command at the organizational level:

```
gcloud compute shared-vpc associated-projects add <service Project ID> \
--host-project <host Project ID>
```

And here's the command at the folder level:

```
gcloud beta compute shared-vpc associated-projects add <service Project ID> \
--host-project <host Project ID>
```

When organizations do not exist, but traffic still flows between two or more projects, an administrator should consider VPC Peering. A VPC Peering connection is a type of network connection between two VPCs that enables an administrator to route traffic between each connection using either a private IPv4 or IPv6 connection. Traffic stays inside the Google network with a shared VPC.

 TIP VPC networks only support IPv4 unicast traffic. GCP networks do not support broadcast, multicast, or IPv6 traffic within the network; VMs in the VPC network can only send to IPv4 destinations and only receive traffic from IPv4 sources. As a cloud engineer, you are able to create an IPv6 address for a global load balancer.

VPC Network Peering allows the administrator to establish services across the VPC network by using internal IP addresses. If services are offered to other organizations, the use of an internal IP address allows the organizations to connect. Using shared VPC services is especially useful when third-party enterprises may want to leverage an internal service but you want to own control beyond the single organization. VPC Network Peering can only be configured using the command line at this time using the `gcloud compute networks peerings create` command.

Here's an example of how to create a peer relationship between two VPCs:

```
gcloud compute networks peerings create <peer host name> \
    --network <host name a>\
    --peer-project <peer project a>\
    --peer-network <peer project b>\
    --auto-create-routes
```

On the other system, you need to create a peering connection using the conditions of `--network <host name b>`, `--peer-project <peer project b>`, and `--peer-network <peer project a>`. Executing both `gcloud` command lines yields a connection between two private networks.

Compute Engine and VPC

You can configure Compute Engine resources within a VPC using either Cloud Console or the `gcloud` commands. In Chapter 3, you learned how to create a virtual machine instance. In Figure 8-5, you are introduced once again to the Virtual Machine instance creation interface. You already know how to configure basic parameters, but advanced features such as firewall management and setting up a network connection were not addressed at that time. This section covers these advanced features that are accessed by clicking the form link "Management, security, disks, networking, sole tenancy," which opens up an extended interface with separate tabs (see Figure 8-6) to configure each feature.

Upon opening the Networking tab, you are able to configure network settings. First, click Network Interface so that you can identify the VPC created earlier and establish the subnet. You have the choice of creating a custom network or using automatic features. For the example in Figure 8-7, Automatic is chosen.

The VPC and subnetwork used earlier in the chapter are shown as well. You also need to decide about the type of internal and external IP address. The example applies a custom ephemeral IP address, although you can apply a static IP address too. Whether you are creating a new instance or modifying an existing instance, the configuration of a VPC in a VM instance can easily be managed using the instance's interface.

Figure 8-5
Creating a
virtual machine
instance form

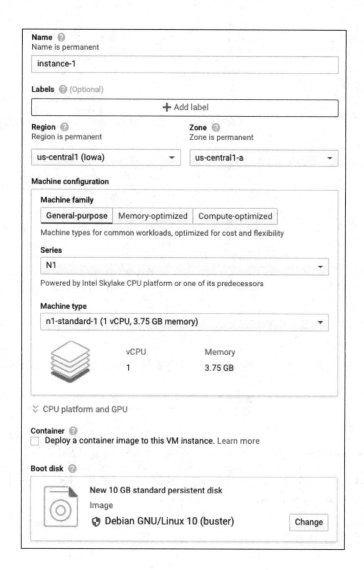

Figure 8-6
Configuring
networking
for Compute
Engine instances

An alternative to configuring the network settings for the VM instance using Cloud Console is using the `gcloud compute instances` command. At a minimum, you need to identify the instance name, subnet name, and zone name. Here's a typical example that includes all parameters and flags:

```
gcloud compute instances create <instance name> --subnet <subnet name>
--zone <zone name>
```

Figure 8-7
Configuring
an automatic
network
connection

Firewall Rules

Google Cloud firewalls are software-defined, not hardware-based. Firewall rules allow or deny traffic from the VM instance you configure. Once enabled, firewall rules are always enforced, protecting an instance regardless of system configuration. Firewall rules are defined by the network, whereas connections are managed at the instance level.

When creating a GCP firewall rule, you are asked to identify the VPC network and related components applicable to the rule. Components include the type of traffic based on protocol, ports, sources, and destinations. Managing firewall rules is possible using Cloud Console, the `gcloud` command-line interface, or a REST API, although for the exam, you only need to understand using Cloud Console and `gcloud`. Here are some firewall rule considerations to keep in mind:

- Firewall rules, whether during creation or modification, can be associated with an instance using targeted components.
- Firewall rules allow for incoming (ingress) or outgoing (egress) traffic, not both simultaneously.
- Firewall rules support IPv4 traffic exclusively using CIDR notation.
- Firewall rules support either one of two core actions: allow or deny.
- Firewall rules must be associated with a VPC network and enforceable.
- Firewall rules are stateful; they do not reassemble fragmented TCP packets.
- Firewall connections are limited by the number of stateful connections supported by the given machine type.

The four types of firewall rules to be aware of are found in Table 8-1.
Traffic is blocked under three conditions:

- If the traffic is GRE
- If the traffic is using protocols other than TCP, UDP, ICMP, AH, ESP, or SCTP to external IP addresses
- If egress traffic is processed to TCP destination port 25 (SMTP)

Firewall rules consist of several components:

- Direction (ingress versus egress)
- Priority
- Action (allow or deny)
- Target

Rule	Description
`default-allow-internal`	Allows ingress connection for all protocols and ports using instances in the network. Has the second lowest priority at 65534. Permits incoming connections to instances from others in the same network.
`default-allow-ssh`	Allows ingress connection on TCP port 22 using any source available to an instance in the network. Priority is 65534.
`default-allow-rdp`	Allows ingress connection on TCP port 3389 using any source available to an instance in the network. Enables connections to RDP clients including Microsoft Remote Desktop Protocol. Priority is 65534.
`default-allow-icmp`	Allows ingress ICMP traffic to any source across any instance available on a network. Supports the use of tools such as ping. Priority is 65534.

Table 8-1 Types of Firewall Rules

- Source/destination
- Protocol/port
- Status

[handwritten: Traffic priority - ensures application/subnet has a certain uplink bandwidth at all time]

By default, two firewall rules are automatically created, an ingress rule and an egress rule, directing allowable or deniable traffic to IP address 0.0.0.0/0. The priority is 65535.

Creating Firewall Rules Using Cloud Console

Creating firewalls rules can be accomplished by going to the Cloud Console navigation. Under Networking and the subsection VPC Network, select Firewall Rules. Upon clicking the option, all predefined rules and any firewall rules established previously are listed (see Figure 8-8). To create a new firewall rule, click Create Firewall Rule.

A form appears asking for various parameters to create the new firewall rule, as seen in Figure 8-9. Unless the field says optional in the label, all fields are required.

- Name
- Description
- Logs
- Network
- Priority
- Direction of traffic
- Action on match
- Targets
- Source filter
- Source IP ranges
- Protocols and ports

Once all the required fields are filled in and you are ready to proceed, click Create. New rules are visible within the list of existing rules on the listing page.

	Name	Type	Targets	Filters	Protocols / ports	Action	Priority	Network ↑	Logs	Hit count	Last hit
☐	edynaleam-site-tcp-443	Ingress	edynaleam-site-deployment	IP ranges: 0.0.0.0/0	tcp:443	Allow	1000	default	Off	—	—
☐	edynaleam-site-tcp-80	Ingress	edynaleam-site-deployment	IP ranges: 0.0.0.0/0	tcp:80	Allow	1000	default	Off	—	—
☐	default-allow-icmp	Ingress	Apply to all	IP ranges: 0.0.0.0/0	icmp	Allow	65534	default	Off	—	—
☐	default-allow-internal	Ingress	Apply to all	IP ranges: 10.128.0.0/9	tcp:0-65535 udp:0-65535 icmp	Allow	65534	default	Off	—	—
☐	default-allow-rdp	Ingress	Apply to all	IP ranges: 0.0.0.0/0	tcp:3389	Allow	65534	default	Off	—	—
☐	default-allow-ssh	Ingress	Apply to all	IP ranges: 0.0.0.0/0	tcp:22	Allow	65534	default	Off	—	—

Figure 8-8 Listing of firewall rules

Figure 8-9
Firewall
Rules form

Creating Firewall Rules Using gcloud

You can use the command-line interface to manage the full life cycle of firewall rules. The default command is

```
gcloud compute firewall-rules create
```

Numerous flags, such as `--action`, `--allow`, `--direction`, `--network`, `--priority`, and `--source-ranges`, can be used to qualify the firewall rules. Four components must be included in a firewall rule: action, type of protocol, source/destination, and ports. Here is an example of a firewall rule using `gcloud`:

```
gcloud compute firewall-rules-create http-allow-rule --direction=INGRESS
--allow=TCP:80 --target-tags=red-tags
```

Virtual Private Networks

A virtual private network (VPN) allows a user to securely connect a peer network to a Virtual Private Cloud (VPC) network using an IPsec-based VPN connection. Traffic that travels between two networks is encrypted by a VPN gateway. The connection is then decrypted by the other VPN gateway. Connections are protected as the data travels over the Internet. Alternatively, you can create a connection between two VPN instances. With GCP, you can create a VPN using Cloud Console or `gcloud`.

Configuring a VPN Using Cloud Console

To create a VPN using Cloud Console, locate Hybrid Connectivity under Networking and open the VPN submenu. If you have never created a VPN before, you are asked to initiate the service. Otherwise, a page appears giving you two options: the ability to create a high availability VPN or a classic VPN. Select classic VPN unless you need 99.9 percent service level agreement (SLA) guarantees.

The next page provides requirements to configure the VPN to Google Compute Engine gateway, as seen in Figure 8-10. You will also need to establish the appropriate VPN tunnels, as presented in Figure 8-11.

The first part of the form (shown in Figure 8-10) asks you to identify a VPN name, description, network, region, and IP address. If a static IP address is not already reserved, you can configure the IP address from the form directly.

The Tunnels section of the form (shown in Figure 8-11) requires you to establish network endpoints for your newly created VPN. The first thing you need to do is determine the name, description, and remote peer IP address. Next, you need to establish the Internet Key Exchange (IKE) protocol type that best fits the project. Part of creating an IKE is configuring a shared secret and string of characters to help authenticate a user. You can auto-generate a shared secret string, which is mandatory for setting the VPN endpoint.

The three types of routing (dynamic, route-based, and policy-based) are described in Table 8-2.

Figure 8-10
Compute
Engine VPN
configuration

Dynamic routing requires the creation of a new cloud router, which is configurable from this interface. The dynamic routing option allows for the Border Gateway Protocol (BGP), a field that must also be filled out under the dynamic option, to learn the best traffic path possible.

Routing Type	Definition
Dynamic	Using the Border Gateway Protocol (BGP), dynamic routing makes use of the Cloud Router to automatically manage the exchange of routes to support traffic management. The mode of the VPC network controls the behavior of the Cloud Router to determine how peer networks respond to GCP resources in a given region or across multiple GCP regions.
Route-based	Creating a route-based VPN means specifying a list of defined IP addresses in a given range. Those addresses are prescribed as the only ones to be used to support routes in the VPC networks and peer resources.
Policy-based	Decisions are made by the network administrator, using configurations that are prescribed using specific IP ranges and subnetworks.

Table 8-2 Types of Router Definitions

Figure 8-11
VPN tunnel
configuration
form

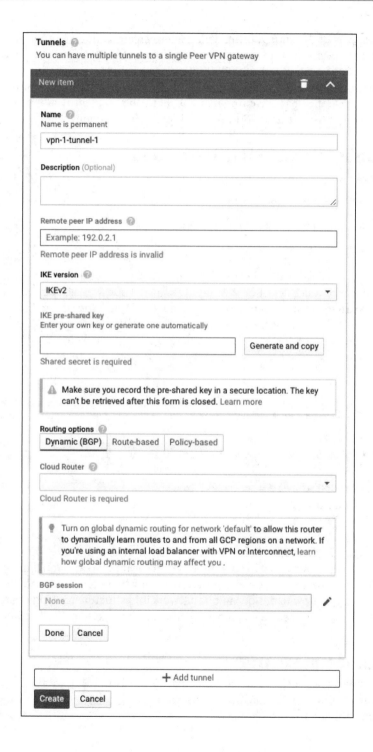

As part of dynamic routing, you need to create a Cloud Router. In this form, you will need to specify an autonomous system number (ASN) that is used by BGP. The range is either 64512–65534 or 4000000000–4294967294.

Choose route-based management if you require a minimum of one remote network IP range. Policy-based routing requires that you also identify at least one remote network IP range, a local subnetwork, and maintain a local IP range.

Configuring a VPN Using gcloud

The following three commands are often used to create and configure a VPN:

```
gcloud compute target-vpn-gateways

gcloud compute forwarding-rule

gcloud compute vpn-tunnels
```

Each one has a specific purpose. The purpose of the `target-vpn-gateways` command is to create a classic VPN gateway. Using `gcloud compute forwarding-rules` allows traffic to be directed to a load balancer. When you use `gcloud compute vpn-tunnels`, the purpose is to create a classic VPN tunnel between a target VPN gateway and a peer address. Such a configuration is available for classic and high-availability options. The structure for each of these commands is as follows.

- `target-vpn-gateways`:

  ```
  gcloud compute vpn-tunnels create <name> --peer-address=<peer address>
  --shared-secret=<shared secret> --target-vpn-gateways=<target VPN gateway>
  ```

- `forwarding-rules`:

  ```
  gcloud compute forwarding-rules create <name> --TARGET_SPECIFICATION=<vpn
  gateway name>
  ```

- `vpn-tunnels`:

  ```
  gcloud compute vpn-tunnels create <name>--peer-address=<peer address>
  --shared-secret=<shared secret> --target-vpn-gateways=<target VPN gateway>
  ```

 EXAM TIP For the Associate Cloud Engineer exam, you are only expected to know how to configure the VPN using `gcloud`. You are not expected to go into great detail about network infrastructure. Knowing the terminology and how to design various network infrastructure topologies are not required unless you intend to become a Google Certified Professional Cloud Architect.

Load Balancing

A load balancer helps manage user capacity by distributing traffic across several instances of an application. Through load distribution, load balancing mitigates the risk that an application performs inefficiently.

Internal or External IP Address	Regional or Global	Supported Network Tier	Proxy or Passthrough	Traffic Type	Load Balancer Type
Internal	Regional	Premium	Passthrough	TCP/UDP	Internal TCP/UDP
Internal	Regional	Premium	Proxy	HTTP/HTTPS	Internal HTTP(S)
External	Regional	Premium Standard	Passthrough	TCP UDP	External TCP/UDP network
External	Global (Premium tier)	Premium Standard	Proxy	TCP	TCP proxy
External	Regional (Standard tier)	Premium Standard	Proxy	SSL	SSL proxy
External	Regional (Standard tier)	Premium Standard	Proxy	HTTP HTTPS	External HTTP(S)

Table 8-3   Cloud Load Balancing Configurations

With Google Cloud Platform, load balancers are available to manage traffic across a single region or several regions. Load balancing in GCP is measured using several metrics:

- Internal or external
- Regional or global
- Supported network type
- Proxy or passthrough
- Traffic type
- Load balancer type

Table 8-3 summarizes each Google Cloud Platform load balancing option, including support for internal or external IP address, load balancer position is regional or global, supported network tier, and traffic types.

Proxy vs. Passthrough

A *proxy* acts as a middleman between a client and the servers fulfilling the requests. Two transmission sessions are created: one between the client and the proxy and another from the proxy to the server. A *passthrough* only establishes a single transmission session from the client to the servers. Why is this difference important? The simplest answer is that it is far easier to manage SSL/TLS CA certificates on a single load balancer, acting as a proxy, than having to manage them on each individual server. In typical proxy deployments, the transmission sessions from the client to the load balancer are encrypted using TLS to port 443. However, in a session from the load balancer to the servers, this is not the case. Yet, a secure communication solution is provided. For passthrough deployments, the load balancer does not interfere with the transmission sessions and simply lets the server do all the work, whether the transmission sessions are encrypted (port 443) or not (port 80).

Deciding when to use these configurations may seem a bit confusing. You have two decision points to consider: global versus regional load balancing and external versus internal load balancing. Once those two determinations are made, you are best able to determine the type of load balancer appropriate for the organization.

You should consider using a global load balancer when the backend is distributed across regions. However, users may need access to content or an application, and capacity might not be ideal when a single IP address is offered. If IPv6 management is required, global load balancing is the appropriate fit. Whereas global load balancing focuses on distribution management, regional load balancing requires a single location, or the intended system requires IPv4 termination exclusively.

Where the load is distributed also influences the selection of the most appropriate load balancer. Should traffic distribution come from the Internet to a Google VPC network instance, external load balancing is ideal. However, global load balancing requires the use of Premium tier services exclusively, whereas regional load balancing supports Standard tier hosting. Internal load balancing is suitable for applications that run inside of GCP only.

GCP offers six load balancer types, as described in Table 8-4.

In summary, external load balancers are intended for Internet traffic distribution, whereas internal load balancers originate within GCP only. There is only one internal load balancer offering: internal TCP/UDP. Otherwise, all the load balancers are external.

Load Balancer Type	Description
Internal HTTP(S)	A managed service offering, the internal HTTP(S) load balancer provides load balancing support for Layer 7 application data. Traffic is routed using URL maps. The load balancer uses an internal IP address that acts as a frontend to a backend system.
External HTTP(S)	Google Front Ends (GFEs) are external-facing HTTPS load balancers supporting global distribution on Google's worldwide network. For Premium tier services, GFE provides cross-regional load balancing. The load balancer manages traffic to the closest healthy backend where capacity exists. Traffic is terminated as close as possible to a given user.
Internal TCP/UDP	An organization is able to load-balance internal TCP/UDP traffic behind an internal IP address. The IP address is load-balanced and accessible to a virtual machine (VM) instance. The internal IP address uses the internal TCP/UDP configuration to support the frontend of an internal backend instance. Regional load-balanced instance groups enable autoscaling across regions.
External TCP/UDP	Using incoming IP protocol data such as address, port, and protocol type, an organization can load-balance traffic on its own system. The solution is a regional, non-proxied load-balancing option. Typical use cases include using this load balancer for UDP traffic or for TCP and SSL traffic on portals not supported with an SSL or TCP proxy load balancer. Network load balancing is considered "passthrough" since the connections are not proxied from clients.

Table 8-4 Load Balancer Types

Load Balancer Type	Description
SSL proxy	SSL proxy load balancing can be implemented on Google Front Ends. They are distributable globally. Assuming the organization selects Premium tier network services, an SSL proxy is global. Multiple backends can be deployed across multiple regions. Load balancers automatically direct user traffic to the closest regional data center offering available capacity. Standard network tier only allows single region support.
TCP proxy	TCP proxies are implemented on Google Front Ends globally. Premium tier support offers TCP proxy support globally, including backends across multiple regions. Load balancers automatically direct user traffic to the closest regional data center with available capacity. Standard tier only offers direct traffic management to backends in a single region.

Table 8-4 Load Balancer Types

Configuring a Load Balancer Using Cloud Console

To create a load balancer, go to the Cloud Console navigation area under Networking and select Load Balancing under Network Services. You will need to create a new load-balancing instance by clicking the Create Load Balancer button at the top of the screen. From there, you have three options to pick from, as seen in Figure 8-12: HTTP(S) Load Balancing, TCP Load Balancing, and UDP Load Balancing. Depending on the load-balancing class desired, click the appropriate Start Configuration button.

You need to decide the presentation of the load balancer. You have two choices: "From the Internet to my VM" and "Only between VMs." Select "From the Internet to my VM" and then click Continue.

Now, you have four areas to configure:

- Load balancer name
- Backend configuration
- Host and path rules
- Frontend configuration

First, you need to configure the backend. Either you will map to a backend service (see Figure 8-13) or backend bucket (see Figure 8-14).

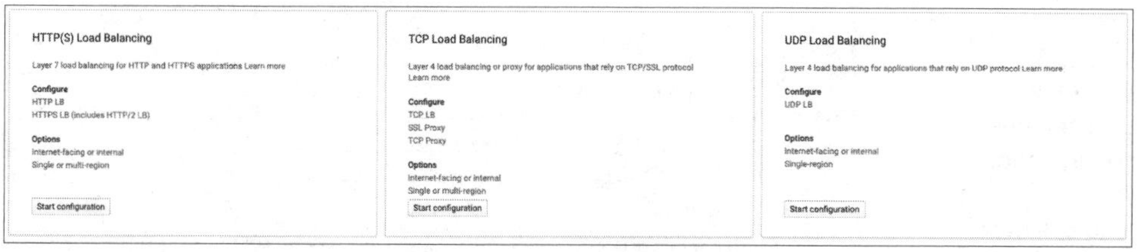

Figure 8-12 Choice of load balancers

Figure 8-13
Backend service
configuration
for HTTP/HTTPS
load balancer

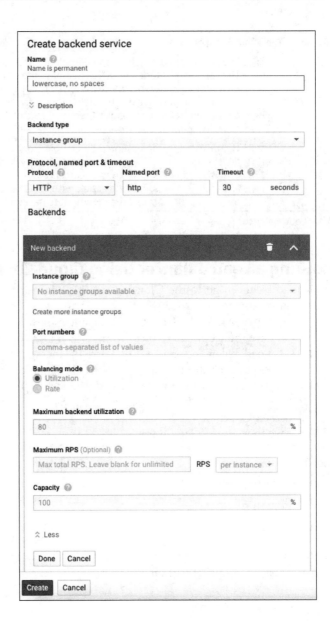

Create backend service

Name ⓘ
Name is permanent

lowercase, no spaces

⌄ Description

Backend type

Instance group ▾

Protocol, named port & timeout
Protocol ⓘ   Named port ⓘ   Timeout ⓘ

HTTP ▾   http   30   seconds

Backends

New backend   🗑 ⌃

Instance group ⓘ

No instance groups available ▾

Create more instance groups

Port numbers ⓘ

comma-separated list of values

Balancing mode ⓘ
● Utilization
○ Rate

Maximum backend utilization ⓘ

80   %

Maximum RPS (Optional) ⓘ

Max total RPS. Leave blank for unlimited   RPS   per instance ▾

Capacity ⓘ

100   %

⌃ Less

Done   Cancel

Create   Cancel

Figure 8-14
Backend bucket
configuration
for HTTP/HTTPS
load balancer

Create backend bucket

Name ⓘ
Name is permanent

lowercase, no spaces

⌄ Description

Cloud Storage bucket

🪣 bucket   Browse

Cloud CDN ⓘ
☐ Enable Cloud CDN

Figure 8-15
Load balancer
Cloud Storage
bucket
configuration

In Figure 8-15, an association configuration to the dyna_cms Cloud Storage bucket is made. Enabling Cloud CDN is optional.

By default, the host and path rules, as well as the frontend configuration, are configured on your behalf. Should you want to create a name for the frontend IP and port, you can do so under Frontend Configuration, as seen in Figure 8-16.

Figure 8-16
Frontend
configuration
for HTTP/HTTPS
load balancer

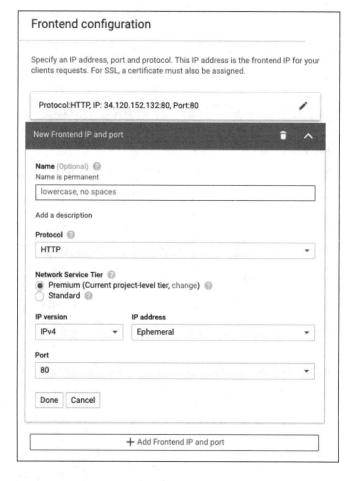

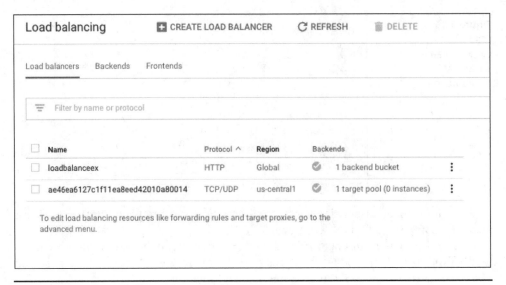

Figure 8-17   Listing of all provisioned load balancers

Once all sections are complete, you are asked to confirm the configuration. If you are satisfied with the selections, click Create.

Once provisioned, the load balancer appears in the main console list in Figure 8-17.

Configuring a Load Balancer Using gcloud

If you prefer to configure a load balancer using `gcloud`, use a command with the following structure:

```
gcloud compute <group> <command> <--flags selected>
```

Beyond the HTTPS load balancer mentioned in the previous section, there are many other alternatives to create a network load balancer. Key commands that should be applied in creating a load balancer command line are presented in Table 8-5.

Mimicking the creation of the HTTP load balancer created in the Cloud Console, the following command lines are used.

To create a health check:

```
gcloud compute health-checks create http http-basic-check \ --port 80
```

To create a backend service:

```
gcloud compute backend-services create web-backend-service \ --protocol HTTP \
--health-checks http-basic-check \ --global
```

To add an instance group as the backend to the backend services:

```
gcloud compute backend-services add-backend web-backend-service \
--instance-group=dynalearn-ex \ --instance-group-zone=us-central1-a \ --global
```

Command	Description
backend-buckets	Read and manipulate backend buckets.
backend-services	List, create, and delete backend services.
forwarding-rules	Read and manipulate forwarding rules to network load balancers.
health-checks	Read and manipulate health checks for load-balanced instances.
http-health-checks	Read and manipulate HTTP health checks for load-balanced instances.
https-health-checks	Read and manipulate HTTPS health checks for load-balanced instances.
security-policies	Read and manipulate Cloud Armor security policies.
ssl-certificates	List, create, and delete Compute Engine SSL certificates.
ssl-policies	List, create, delete, and update Compute Engine SSL policies.
target-pools	Control Compute Engine target pools for network load balancing.
url-maps	Map HTTPS and HTTPS URLs to backend services and backend buckets.

Table 8-5   Commands for Load Balancing When Using `gcloud compute`

To create a URL map to route the incoming requests to the default backend service:

```
gcloud compute url-maps create web-map-https \ --default-service web-backend-service
```

Cloud DNS

Cloud DNS is GCP's domain name resolution service. Every time you go to a website (for example, www.google.com), the website maps to an IP address. An IP address and other resources map to a domain name service (DNS), which is a distributed database. The Cloud DNS database maps the IP address (a series of numbers) to publishable zones and records it without requiring an administrator to handle the technical details. The two zone types are public and private. A *public zone* is visible to anyone with an Internet connection. A *private zone* is available to only those who have access to the VPC network. When you're creating a Cloud DNS entry, there is an assumption that you have already purchased a domain name from a domain registrar. If you have not already done so, you can buy a domain name from Google Domains at https://domains.google/.

When creating a DNS record in Cloud DNS, you need to be familiar with specific terminology to populate the appropriate form fields. Table 8-6 presents those terms.

EXAM TIP   For the exam, Google expects you to understand how to create the services for Cloud DNS, which includes configuring zones and setting up a record set.

Term	Description
Public zone	Public zones allow access to your web-based platform to be visible to all Internet users.
Private zone	Private zones allow access to your web-based platform to be visible to only those users who are granted Virtual Private Cloud access.
Zone name	A DNS zone is a portion of a namespace that is managed by a specific part of an organization.
DNS name	The specific domain and extension that is translatable from a record to an IP address.
DNSSEC	DNS security extensions, also known as DNSSEC, provide a way to authenticate DNS response data. DNSSEC adds cryptographic signatures to existing DNS records.
Resource record type	The resource record type allows for different kinds of DNS resolution to occur.
TTL	Time to live (TTL) is the limit allowed (or lifetime) for data to stay active in a computer or network.
IPv4 address	IPv4 address is a 32-bit number that uniquely identifies a network interface on a computer system accessible publicly or privately.
IPv6 address	IPv6 addresses are represented as eight groups of four hexadecimal digits, each group representing 16 bits.
A	An A record is used to find the IP address of a network-connected device connected to the Internet from a domain name.
AAAA	Similar to an A record, but it allows you to specify the IPv6 address of the server, rather than the IPv4 address.
CNAME	A canonical name (CNAME) is a type of DNS record that maps an alias name to a true domain name (for example, www.dynalearning.com to dynalearning.com).
NS	NS stands for nameserver. The NS record points to which DNS server is authoritative for a given domain name.
SOA	SOA (start of authority) resource record identifies for the DNS server what the best source of information is for the specified domain name.

Table 8-6   Key Cloud DNS Terminology

Understanding Zone Types

GCP Cloud DNS supports three different zone types—managed, public, and private. Most often, cloud engineers work with managed zones because they are associated with a project. A managed zone holds all of the DNS records for DNS name suffixes (www .dynalearning.com). A project may have several managed zones, and each zone must have a unique name. With Cloud DNS, a managed zone is the resource type that supports an entire DNS zone. That means all records on the same Google Server will map to the same nameservers. A nameserver responds to a DNS query against a managed zone based on your zone configuration. A project can support many managed zones, but you are charged daily for each managed zone that exists.

A public zone is Internet-facing. Cloud DNS provides public authoritative nameservers, allowing you to respond to queries regardless of location. DNS records in public zones are specific to publishing services to the Internet. Whereas public zones are Internet-facing, private zones allow an organization to manage custom domain names against Compute Engine resources, load balancers, and other GCP resources without needing to provide the underlying DNS infrastructure or use the public Internet. A private zone is a container of DNS records that allows a user to connect with one or more Virtual Private Cloud (VPC) networks, assuming they are authorized. The zone must be located in the same project where Cloud DNS defines it.

Furthermore, you must also authorize the project to be in the same private zone. To query records hosted in a managed private zone, use DNS peering. A DNS peering zone is a type of Cloud DNS–managed private zone that enables name resolution order of other VPC networks. Peering zones can also resolve the names that are defined in other VPC networks. It is important to remember that only authorized networks can query a private zone. If you do not provide proper authorization to the networks, it will be impossible to query the zone. Finally, private zones do not support DNSSEC or custom domain name set types, known as nameservers (NS).

Managed Zone Creation Using Cloud Console

To create a Cloud DNS service, go to the Cloud Console navigation area and Locate Networking. Under Networking Services, you will find Cloud DNS. If this is the first time you have ever created a zone, click the button Create Zone. Otherwise, a form similar to the one in Figure 8-18 is presented.

On the form, select whether the zone should be public or private. Public zones are Internet-facing, whereas private zones point to GCP resources that require authorization. For private zone resources, the resource being queried for the zone and project are often the same.

The zone name is descriptive within the organization, whereas the DNS name is the actual domain name registered with a domain registrar (for example, dynalearning.com).

DNSSEC provides an extra layer of security for public-facing (public zone) sites only. This involves a type of cryptography that prevents various kinds of Internet attacks from occurring to public-facing websites. If you chose private zone, this option will not be available. Should you choose a private zone, an option to select which network to connect to appears. A list of all available networks is populated in the drop-down box. If no networks are available, select Default.

One additional drop-down, called Options, appears if you select a private zone. Four options appear beside the default private network:

- **Forward queries to another server**   Forwarding allows you to configure target nameservers for specific private zones.

- **DNS peering**   DNS peering enables you to request a record from one zone namespace to another VPC network.

Figure 8-18
Creating a new
managed zone

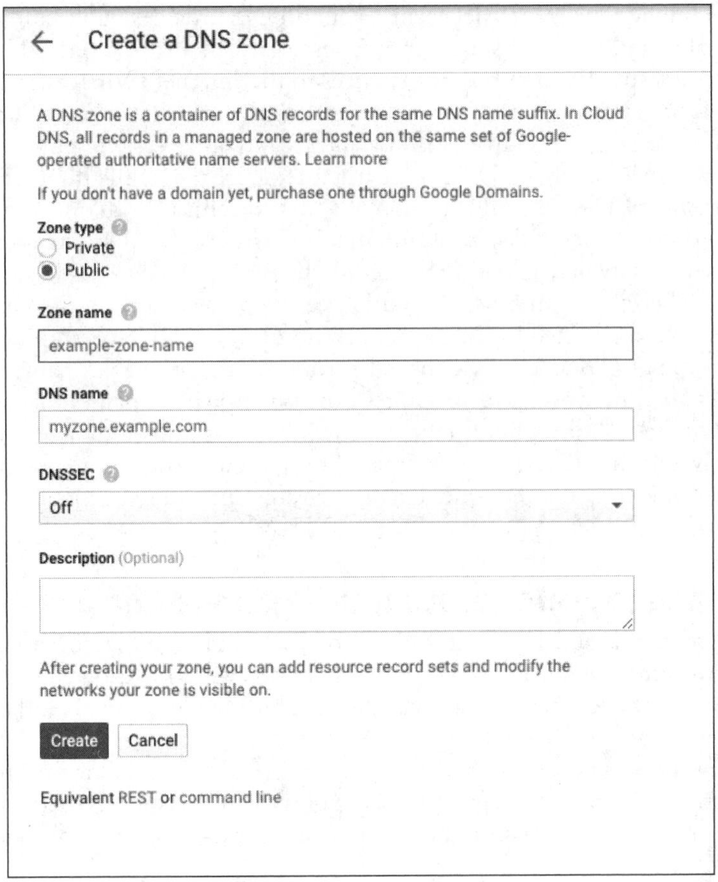

← Create a DNS zone

A DNS zone is a container of DNS records for the same DNS name suffix. In Cloud DNS, all records in a managed zone are hosted on the same set of Google-operated authoritative name servers. Learn more

If you don't have a domain yet, purchase one through Google Domains.

Zone type ⑦
○ Private
● Public

Zone name ⑦

example-zone-name

DNS name ⑦

myzone.example.com

DNSSEC ⑦

Off   ▼

Description (Optional)

After creating your zone, you can add resource record sets and modify the networks your zone is visible on.

Create   Cancel

Equivalent REST or command line

- **Manage reversed lookup**   A private zone with appropriate attribution that requires Cloud DNS to perform a PTR (pointer) lookup against Compute Engine DNS data.

- **Use a Service Directory namespace**   A type of Cloud DNS private zone that allows for the complete authority of service information within a Service Directory namespace.

Once all fields have been filled out for the DNS zone creation, click the Create button. You are then brought to a page that provides a list of all zone details (see Figure 8-19). You will find that SOA (start of authority) and NS (nameserver) records have been provisioned. The parameters associated with the TTL (time to live) records are also made available. You can edit the records by clicking the pencil icon should you need to make any modifications.

You will likely need to add A, CNAME, TXT, and MX records for a public-facing website. If you decide to add these other records, click the Add Record Set button.

Figure 8-19   List of all Cloud DNS records

A new form will appear to create a new record set (see Figure 8-20). You will need to enter parameters such as DNS name, resource record type, TTL, TTL unit, and the IPv4 address.

You have a variety of resource record type configurations to select from that yield slightly different form fields (see Figure 8-21). For the most part, though, each recordset varies ever so slightly in the data requirements.

Figure 8-20
Creating a new
record set

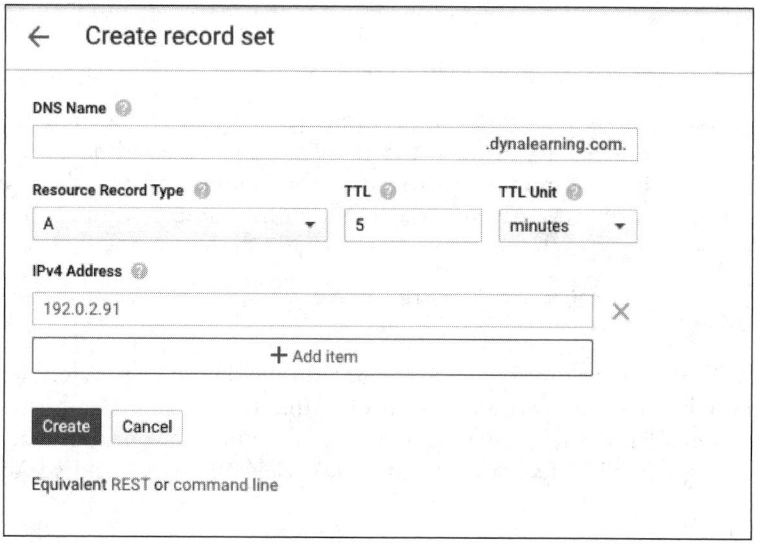

Figure 8-21
List of resource
record types

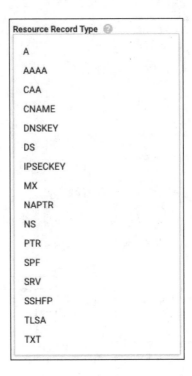

Resource Record Type
A
AAAA
CAA
CNAME
DNSKEY
DS
IPSECKEY
MX
NAPTR
NS
PTR
SPF
SRV
SSHFP
TLSA
TXT

Managed Zone Creation Using gcloud

There are two command types you need to be familiar with when using `gcloud` to create DNS zones:

```
gcloud beta dns managed-zones
```

```
gcloud dns record-sets transaction
```

Assuming you are creating a public-facing web application using a public zone, you would need to identify the managed public zone name and the DNS suffix name. Using the example provided in the Cloud Console, the managed public zone is `dynalearning-ex` and the DNS suffix name is `dynalearning.com`. Using `--description` is an optional parameter. On the command line, enter the following:

```
gcloud beta dns managed-zones create dynalearning-ex --description=
--dns-name=dynalearning.com
```

There may be times when the managed zone should be private. The difference between a public zone and a private zone involves the zone's visibility and network type. You must indicate that the visibility is set to private for a private zone, but that is not necessary for managed public zones. Selecting the type of network is also required. You have five options.

The most likely option is the default, which is for a standard private network. If you want to set up a managed private zone, enter the following:

```
gcloud beta dns managed-zones create dynalearning-ex --description=
--dns-name=dynalearning.com. --visibility=private --networks=default
```

The structure of the command line requires a known transaction to create a new record with different resource types. You must also specify the resource type. For each record set, you need to initiate, set, and execute the transaction.

Here's how to create an A record:

```
gcloud dns record-sets transaction start --zone=dynalearning-ex

gcloud dns record-sets transaction add 127.0.0.1 --name=dynalearning.com.
--ttl=3600 --type=A --zone=dynalearning-ex

gcloud dns record-sets transaction execute --zone=dynlearning-ex
```

And here's how to create a CNAME record:

```
gcloud dns record-sets transaction start --zone=dynalearning-ex

gcloud dns record-sets transaction add training.dynalearning.com
--name=www.dynalearning.com. --ttl=300 --type=CNAME --zone=dynalearning-ex

gcloud dns record-sets transaction execute --zone= dynalearning-ex
```

Finally, here's how to create a TXT record:

```
gcloud dns record-sets transaction start --zone=dynalearning-ex

gcloud dns record-sets transaction add "Hello World"
--name=www2.dynalearning.com. --ttl=300 --type=TXT --zone=dynalearning-ex

gcloud dns record-sets transaction execute --zone= dynalearning-ex
```

Chapter Review

This chapter covered the networking concepts you may be tested on for the Associate Cloud Engineer exam. The first part of the chapter reviewed creating various types of VPCs using Cloud Console and `gcloud`, including a standalone VPC, shared VPC, peering VPC, and subnets. You learned how to configure Compute Engine resources, including virtual machine instances, with VPC. Once you became familiar with all facets of VPCs, you were then introduced to firewall rule configuration and creating a VPN.

Additional topics that Google might test you on include load balancing, IP address management, and Cloud DNS. It is essential to know the six types of load balancers, some of which are external facing while others are internal traffic sources. Load balancers are either available on a global or regional basis. IP management, which includes knowing the difference between static and ephemeral addresses, expanding the CIDR block range, and reserving an IP address are other areas to review. Pay special attention to CIDR notation and IP address availability rules. The last topic covered in this chapter was Cloud DNS, Google's authoritative naming service for mapping domain names to IP addresses. A DNS zone can be either public or private with Cloud DNS.

Questions

1. VPC networks are what type of resource, even though they maintain regional virtual subnetworks across all of Google's data centers?

   A. Multiregional

   B. Zonal

   C. Global

   D. Persistent

2. There are four primary firewall rule types. Which of the following is not one of the four?

   A. TCP

   B. ICMP

   C. RDP

   D. SSH

3. Which of the following flags is optional in creating a managed VPC based on the following command line?

   ```
   gcloud beta dns managed-zones create dynalearning-ex --description=
   --dns-name=dynalearning.com. --visibility=private --networks=default
   ```

   A. --dns-name

   B. --description

   C. --visibility

   D. --networks

4. Which of the following CIDR blocks offers the largest range of IP addresses?

   A. 10.0.0.0/20

   B. 10.0.0.0/16

   C. 10.0.0/10

   D. 10.0.0.0/8

5. Which types of firewall rules determine incoming and outgoing traffic flow? (Choose two.)

   A. Ingress

   B. Egress

   C. Direction

   D. Flows

6. The cloud administrator at DynaLearning needs to configure a new managed zone using `gcloud`. The administrator is looking to enable a user to request records from one zone namespace to another VPC network. Which of the options best fits the description?

   A. Forward queries to another server

   B. DNS peering

   C. Managed reverse lookup

   D. Use a Service Directory namespace

7. Joe needs to create a new record set in Cloud DNS. He wants to configure an alias for an IPv4 record. Which of the following record set types will Joe use?

   A. A

   B. AAAA

   C. NS

   D. CNAME

8. You recently purchased a new domain from Google Domains. You want to configure the new domain using Cloud DNS. When you create the managed DNS zone, which records are automatically created? (Choose two.)

   A. NS ~ *nameserver - name of authoritative nameserver w/in domain DNS*

   B. TXT

   C. CNAME

   D. SOA *Start of Authority information about domain*

9. There have been numerous malware attack attempts at DynaLearning recently. The CIO is concerned that the public website and newly launched learning management system (LMS) may be vulnerable. What would you recommend the technical team do to prevent a DNS attack? (Choose two.)

   A. Add IAM policies to the service account.

   B. Include DNSSEC in the DNS record.

   C. Include AAAA in the DNS record.

   D. Implement firewall rules to filter incoming and outgoing traffic.

10. You just built a new Linux VM for your single-instance WordPress website. You need to modify some of the administrative features per the instructions available on the Google Marketplace. The machine seldom shuts down, yet it requires optimal performance. What type of IP address would you suggest be attached to the VM?

    A. Static

    B. Ephemeral

    C. Persistent

    D. Dynamic

11. A cloud administrator has recently reserved a single IP address for a new web application being built. The application still remains on a staging server, which has not been associated to the IP address. The administrator is trying to understand why the most recent invoice is so expensive. What could be a reason why?

   A. The cloud administrator selected the wrong hosting region for the IP address.

   B. The cloud administrator is paying per hour for the reservation, as there is no application tied to the IP.

   C. The cloud administrator selected the Premium tier instead of the Standard tier for the IP address.

   D. The cloud administrator purchased multiple ephemeral IP addresses.

12. Which of the following load balancers is only available as an external, globally distributed Premium offering?

   A. Internal or external HTTP/HTTPS

   B. Internal or external TCP/UDP

   C. SSL proxy

   D. TCP proxy

Answers

1. **C.** VPC networks are global resources. Although it is possible for a VPC to be supported in more than one region, multiregional is an invalid response. Zonal and persistent are location types for disks.

2. **A.** TCP is a protocol, not a type of firewall rule. Internal, ICMP, RDP, and SSH are firewall rule types.

3. **B.** All of the flags are required to create a managed VPC exception for `--description`.

4. **D.** The smaller the number at the end of the slash (/), the bigger the range is for available IP addresses. In this case, /8 is the smallest number listed, so 10.0.0.0/8 offers the largest range of IP addresses.

5. **A** and **B.** Ingress (incoming) and egress (outgoing) are the two types of firewall rules that govern traffic management. Direction and flow do not match what's being asked for in the question.

6. **B.** DNS peering best fits the description. Managed reverse lookups require Cloud DNS to perform a PTR lookup against Compute Engine DNS data. Using a Service Directory namespace allows for the complete authority of service information within a Service Directory namespace. Forwarding queries to another server allows you to configure target nameservers for specific private zones.

7. **A.** The A record set type is the one Joe will use. Although AAAA is an alias record type, it is intended for IPv6 only. CNAME is a type of DNS record that maps an alias name to a true domain name. The NS record points to which DNS server is authoritative for a given domain name.

8. **A** and **D.** When you create a managed DNS zone, the NS and SOA records are automatically created for you. You will need to add the CNAME and TXT records after the managed DNS zone is created.

9. **B** and **D.** DNSSEC provides an extra layer of security to IPv4-based public-facing websites and applications. Also, adding specific rules to the firewall to filter suspicious traffic will also mitigate some risks. On the other hand, adding IAM policies to a service account will have no effect whatsoever on protecting the environments. Also, an AAAA record is an alias for an IPv6 address.

10. **A.** To keep a consistent URL and maintain optimal performance, using a static IP address is the best solution. Given this is a public website, changing an IP address each time an instance is restarted is not ideal; hence, ephemeral is not the best choice. Permanent and dynamic are not IP types.

11. **B.** If you do not attach an instance to a reserved IP address, GCP charges you by the hour to maintain the reserved IP address, which is why the most recent invoice is so expensive in the given scenario. The hosting region may be applicable when it comes to other GCP resources, but not IP reservations. Also, there is no such thing as a Standard tier versus a Premium IP tier reservation. Similarly, although purchasing multiple IP addresses will most certainly cost the organization more money, this reason is not applicable given that the administrator confirmed the procurement of a single IP address.

12. **D.** Only TCP proxy requires global/Premium-level services exclusively. All the other load balancer types offer both Standard and Premium services.

Deployment Management

In this chapter you will learn to
- Deploy a solution using Cloud Marketplace
- Deploy an application infrastructure using Deployment Manager

If you have come this far in the book, you have deployed Compute Engine, Kubernetes Engine, App Engine, storage, and network resources as some of the capabilities available in the Google Cloud Platform (GCP). As part of the Associate Cloud Engineer exam, Google expects you to understand how to deploy applications. To do so, you should know how to use Cloud Marketplace and Deployment Manager. Google Cloud Marketplace offers preconfigured applications that users can deploy within the Google Cloud infrastructure.

Your organization may decide it wants to build its applications too. Deploying applications and distributing them in Cloud Marketplace requires the creation of deployment templates. In this chapter, you learn about Deployment Manager, which lets you deploy applications into Cloud Marketplace without having to to configure the application yourself.

Deploying Solutions Using Cloud Marketplace

You need to understand two functional areas of Cloud Marketplace for the exam: browsing and deploying. First, you need to know how to browse Cloud Marketplace to find preconfigured templates that have already been created. You should not have to reinvent work previously created by others. Second, if you are looking to deploy applications or compute, storage, or network resources that are unavailable using Cloud Marketplace preconfigured templates, you can use Deployment Manager to easily configure these resources without much effort.

Browsing the Cloud Marketplace Catalog

When you are looking to deploy commercial off-the-shelf products, virtual machines with open source applications, or readily available productivity for user consumption, GCP offers predefined templates for solutions with Deployment Manager. You can find these templates in Cloud Marketplace, accessible from the Google Cloud Console.

Why would you want to use Cloud Marketplace? Instead of having to build your instances completely from scratch, most of the configuration work is already done for you. You can simply execute the solution by clicking a button versus having to build a solution that takes some time to create and requires customization. However, if you desire precise control over operating system or application configurations and customizations, it might be best to create your own solution. To locate Cloud Marketplace, go to the Cloud Console navigation area under Products and select Marketplace (see Figure 9-1).

Upon clicking the Marketplace option, you are presented with Cloud Marketplace featured solution templates. Categories include datasets, virtual machines, GCP-ready solutions, APIs and services, operating systems, developer stack, databases, blog and CMS, healthcare, security, and financial security. You have the option to browse or search the Cloud Marketplace directory. Also, you can use one of the categories found on the left-hand column to locate a product. The page along with the categories is shown in Figure 9-2.

You can drill down within a given page by clicking any of the categories, as this acts as a filtering mechanism. For example, selecting the Database link filters the list to just the databases available in GCP. What you see represented are specific templates created that support a given database platform. When you get to the specific section, you can even filter based on license type (paid, free, or bring your own license). The filtering option is consistent across Cloud Marketplace, whether it is for operating systems or security applications.

When it comes to billing, if you select a paid Cloud Marketplace option, you are charged based on consumption and number of units. These charges are present on your monthly GCP invoice. If you elect to pay using your license, to run your instance, you will need to provide GCP with a valid license.

Figure 9-1
The Marketplace option in Google Cloud Console

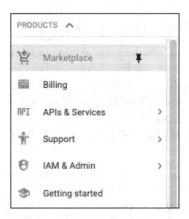

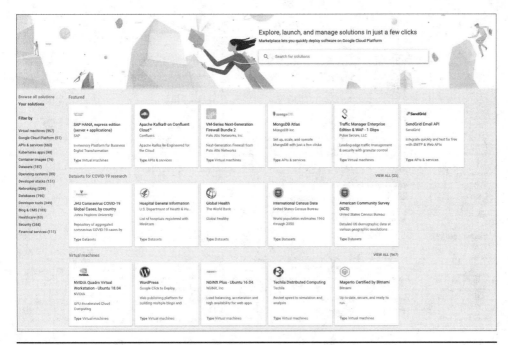

Figure 9-2   Example of a featured page in Cloud Marketplace

TIP   There are times when you will find the same application on Cloud Marketplace available from different vendors or service providers. Before deploying a template, make sure to look at the configuration and cost for deployment. Deployments can differ significantly depending on price, storage requirements, memory utilization, CPU utilization, and, of course, version.

Deploying a Cloud Marketplace Solution

Once you have searched Cloud Marketplace and located the template that meets your organizational needs, the next step is to launch the template directly from Cloud Marketplace. Figure 9-3 shows an example of the typical information provided for a solution in Cloud Marketplace (in this case, a solution called Drupal). The type of information disclosed might include the GCP environment, infrastructure requirements, last updated date, category, price, version, operating system, template contents, and a detailed description.

On the right side of the page are estimated prices to run the template. When you click the Launch button at the top of the page shown in Figure 9-3, you will be asked to update the configuration to meet your business needs.

Figure 9-3 Drupal solution overview page

You will need to select your project and then click Open. For this example, we selected eDynaLearn. You can configure the instance using the following fields:

- Deployment name
- Zone
- Machine type
- Boot disk type
- Boot disk size in GB
- Networking
- Firewall
- Stackdriver (now called Google Operations Suite)

As you are making your modifications, notice the price change for your instance in the right-hand column. In Figure 9-4, the solution increased from $24.75 a month to $50.54 a month as we increased the number of vCPUs to 2, increased the boot disk size to 20GB, and changed the boot disk type from Persistent to SSD. Also, we modified the zone from a default option to us-central1-a.

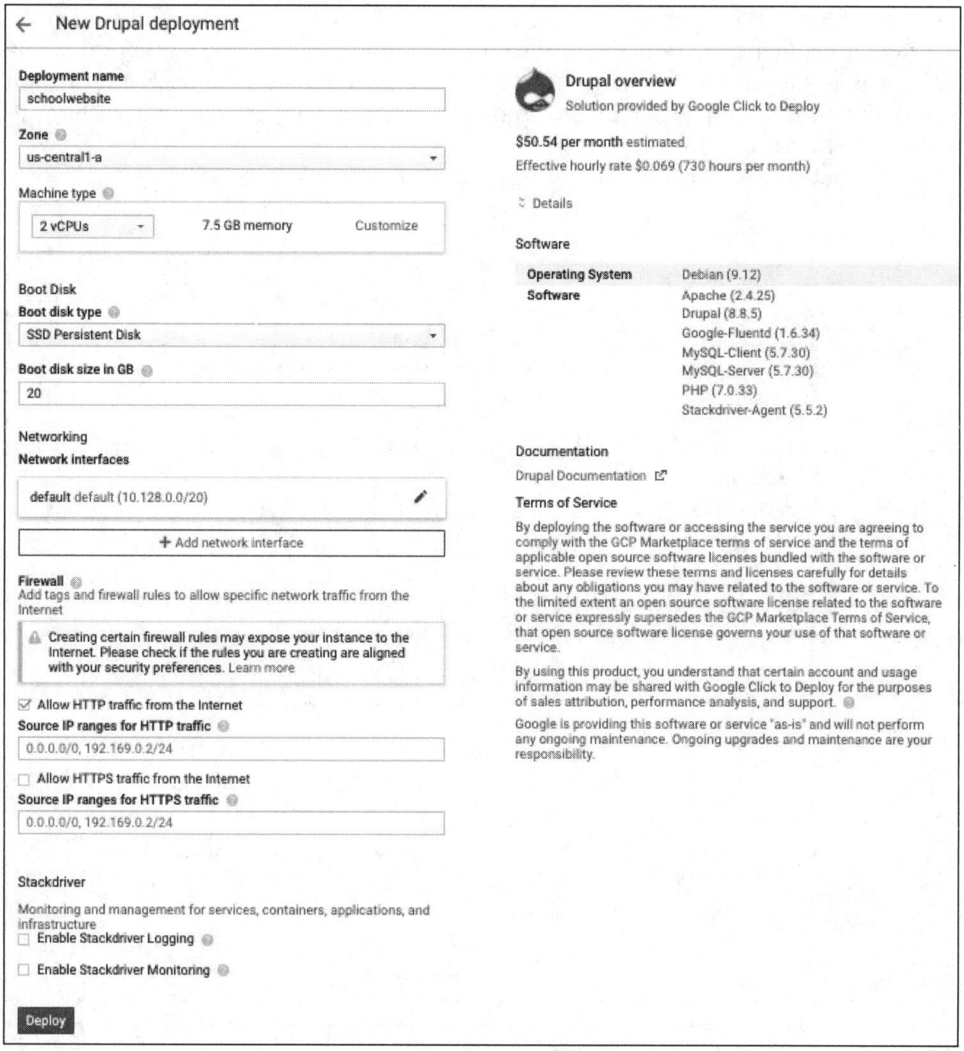

Figure 9-4   Configuring a template from Cloud Marketplace

If you select any of the Stackdriver check boxes at the bottom of Figure 9-4, you may not necessarily see a change in the deployment price. However, utilizing monitoring does increase the rate slightly.

Once you are satisfied with your configuration, click Deploy. You will be able to monitor the current status of the deployment in real time as the files are unpacked. As seen in Figure 9-5, the Deployment Manager provides summary data about the current state of the deployment as well as how to access administrative control points once the process is complete.

After the deployment, the login information for the administrative panel appears along with helpful hints on how to manage the application (see Figure 9-6). Such information includes the system-provided address, username, and password for the administrator to begin using the application.

You are now ready to begin configuring your system (see Figure 9-7).

Figure 9-5 Current Cloud Marketplace deployment state

Figure 9-6
Information
on how to
administer
Drupal

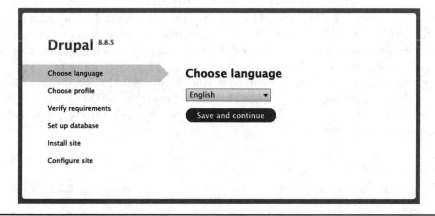

Figure 9-7   Drupal configuration screen

Deploying Applications Using the Deployment Manager

Enterprises often have unique technical requirements. They may find that the templates available in Cloud Marketplace fill a majority of their needs, but some unique configurations must be applied that are not offered. Sometimes, it is not easy to configure and distribute the configurations. That is when you would consider deploying an application using the GCP Deployment Manager to preconfigure your solutions.

Developing Deployment Manager Templates

Deployment Manager configurations are written using the YAML syntax. You must adhere to a specific file structure in order to configure the Deployment Manager templates properly. The structure starts with resources and entities, for which you need to provide their name, type, and properties. Names help identify the resources explicitly, types help qualify the resources (for example, an instance type), and properties provide specific configurations.

Here is a sample definition of a virtual machine called `dynalearn-deployment-vm`:

```
resources:
type: compute.v1.instance
name: dynalearn-deployment-vm
properties:
machineType: https://www.googleapis.com/compute/v1/projects/dynalearn-
deployment-vm/zones/us-central1-f/machineTypes/f1-micro
diskType:
Devicename: Boot
Type: SSD
boot: true
autodelete: false
[KEY]:[VALUE]
[KEY]:[VALUE]
```

As you can see in the example, the project name is fully qualified, as is the information regarding `machineType` and `diskType`. All of these items vary depending on your specific configuration file syntax and business parameters. Figure 9-8 shows an example of a fully qualified YAML file, provided by Google, that you might find on GitHub or on GCP at https://cloud.google.com/deployment-manager/docs/configuration/templates/create-basic-template.

If you have successfully created a template, you likely want to import the template and use it. To import your template, you need to add an `imports` section to your configuration file. You will need to add a relative or absolute path from the directory as well. Some examples include the following:

```
imports:
  - path: path/to/an_example_vm.jinja
  - path: basic_vm.py
  - path: template_vm.jinja
```

You would put the `imports` path before the `resources` section of the YAML file.

```
# Copyright 2016 Google Inc. All rights reserved.
#
# Licensed under the Apache License, Version 2.0 (the "License");
# you may not use this file except in compliance with the License.
# You may obtain a copy of the License at
#
#     http://www.apache.org/licenses/LICENSE-2.0
#
# Unless required by applicable law or agreed to in writing, software
# distributed under the License is distributed on an "AS IS" BASIS,
# WITHOUT WARRANTIES OR CONDITIONS OF ANY KIND, either express or implied.
# See the License for the specific language governing permissions and
# limitations under the License.

resources:
- name: vm-created-by-deployment-manager
  type: compute.v1.instance
  properties:
    zone: us-central1-a
    machineType: zones/us-central1-a/machineTypes/n1-standard-1
    disks:
    - deviceName: boot
      type: PERSISTENT
      boot: true
      autoDelete: true
      initializeParams:
        sourceImage: projects/debian-cloud/global/images/family/debian-9
    networkInterfaces:
    - network: global/networks/default
```

Figure 9-8   Sample YAML file from Google

Using and Launching Deployment Manager Template Files

Managing configuration templates can be a cumbersome process. Templates are a type of text file that allows you to define resources and import them into the configuration easily and in a standalone fashion. The reason you would use a Deployment Manager template file is simple: reusability. You have two options in writing these files: Python and Jinja2.

 EXAM TIP   Unless the template is simple to create, use Python, as this is highly recommended by Google. The exam is likely to use Python only, given its popularity and widespread implementation within GCP. If you want to learn more about Jinja templating, go to https://palletsprojects.com/p/jinja/.

Launching a deployment template file requires the use of the `gcloud deployment-manager deployments` command. As with other command-line operations, you can execute this command using Cloud Shell or Cloud SDK.

If you want to deploy a template with a deployment name of example-deployment, you would use the following:

```
gcloud deployment-manager deployments create example-deployment --config vm.yaml
```

If you need to know the current state of your deployment, you would use the `describe` command, as follows:

```
gcloud deployment-manager deployments describe example-deployment
```

Chapter Review

In this chapter, you were introduced to Cloud Marketplace and Cloud Deployment Manager. These two utilities help cloud engineers deploy compute resources easier, faster, and more efficiently in GCP. Cloud Marketplace allows vendors from around the globe to provide templated resources using industry-standard commercial off-the-shelf proprietary and open source applications. These resources are organized into categories based on using criteria such as license type and product type. Up until this point, you have had to learn how to heavily configure resources in order to support deployments in your organization with Cloud Marketplace, which involves searching or filtering for a prebuilt configuration and properly sizing the resources to meet the organization's capacity needs. There may be times, though, that a prebuilt resource will not be sufficient for organizational requirements. In these cases, you can configure deployment templates using Deployment Manager. As a cloud engineer, you will create a YAML file, which is a type of configuration file to describe the resources that must be deployed. Once everything is configured, you can use `gcloud` commands to deploy the resources.

Questions

1. What are the options for finding templates in Cloud Marketplace? (Choose two.)

   A. Search

   B. Filter

   C. Console

   D. Pages

2. How does Google handle products that require a paid license?

   A. They will not allow you to use GCP until you pay for the service.

   B. They will charge you based on consumption and units consumed.

   C. They only support open source products.

   D. They invoice you for storage. The product vendor invoices you for incurred services.

3. What type of file is used to deploy a Deployment Manager template?

    A. XML

    B. JSON

    C. YAML

    D. TXT

4. A GCP engineer wants to evaluate the state of a recent deployment named compute-dep-vm. What command would the engineer enter into Cloud Shell?

    A. `gcloud deployment-manager deployments create compute-dep-vm`

    B. `gcloud deployment-manager deployments describe compute-dep-vm`

    C. `gcloud deployment-manager deployments search compute-dep-vm`

    D. `gcloud deployment-manager deployments list compute-dep-vm`

5. What is the preferred language for creating Deployment Manager templates?

    A. Go

    B. C#

    C. Python

    D. PHP

6. What section of the Cloud Console do you navigate to in order to find the Marketplace option?

    A. Compute

    B. Networking

    C. Storage

    D. Products

7. Which of the following is not one of the parameters in the YAML file to create a Deployment Manager template?

    A. Name

    B. Location

    C. Type

    D. Properties

8. To save the template using your YAML file, what section would you add before `resources` to call out the file path?

   A. `destination`

   B. `save`

   C. `imports`

   D. `directory`

9. Which of the following parameters does not influence a visible change in price when configuring a Cloud Marketplace template?

   A. Stackdriver

   B. Machine type

   C. Disk type

   D. Region/zone

10. Which button would you click to initiate a new template in Cloud Marketplace?

    A. Create

    B. Start

    C. Launch

    D. Execute

Answers

1. **A** and **B.** Search and Filter are the two options available in Cloud Marketplace for a user to actively launch an existing template. You would access Cloud Marketplace from the Cloud Console. You would view the Search and Filter options on a page. Console and Pages are both incorrect answers.

2. **B.** Google has an arrangement with the vendors who post their templates on Cloud Marketplace. Google charges you, the customer, a fee based on consumption and the number of units against your project. All of the other answers are incorrect.

3. **C.** YAML files are a type of configuration file used to deploy a Deployment Manager template. XML, JSON, and TXT files are not used in GCP by Deployment Manager.

4. **B.** The command `describe` allows an administrator to evaluate the current state of a deployment. The commands `create` and `list` do not allow the administrator to see the current state of a deployment, and `search` is not a qualified command.

5. **C.** Python and Jinja2 are the only two template languages Google supports to create Deployment Manager templates. However, only Python is listed as a possible answer. The other languages, Go and PHP, are used elsewhere in GCP, but not to create Deployment Manager templates.

6. D. Marketplace is the very first option in the Cloud Console. You can find it under Products. All of the other options do not have Marketplace listed under them, although there are resources in Cloud Marketplace available.

7. B. Location is not one of the parameters that qualifies a resource or entity. Only name, type, and properties are included in a YAML file.

8. C. The term `imports` can be found right above the `resources` section in the YAML file. The other options—`destination`, `save`, and `directory`—are not terms you would find in a YAML file for saving the path of the file.

9. A. Selecting Stackdriver does not influence a change in the calculated price. All of the other features listed—machine type, disk type, and region/zone—heavily influence the price of a deployment.

10. C. On each information page, you can find details about a product. At the top of each page is the Launch button, which you click to initiate a new template. All of the other terms—Create, Start, and Execute—are irrelevant.

## CHAPTER 10

Access and Security

In this chapter you will learn to
- Manage identity and access management features in Google Cloud Platform (GCP)
- View, assign, and define identity and access management (IAM) roles
- Understand how to support service accounts under various states
- View auditing logs for projects and managed services

In Chapters 1 and 2, you were introduced to fundamental concepts on identity and access management (IAM) to build your organization and project hierarchy structure. Concepts included knowing the difference between primitive, predefined, and custom roles. Also, you were introduced to both Google-managed and user-managed service accounts. You also began to explore the nuances between the different user role types, including creator, administrator, user, and viewer. In this chapter, we explore IAM in greater depth.

IAM questions often play a large part in Google Cloud exams. Make sure to read this chapter a few times to acclimate yourself with the different concepts covered. You should know that GCP prefers using Cloud IAM; however, since Cloud IAM was not available until a few years ago, the mode of assigning permissions has changed. Before having an identity and access management platform, Google gave users access to primitive roles as a broad means of role management. Organizations using primitive assignment often gave too much control to their users. With any platform, you want to provide a user with the least privileges possible needed to do their job effectively and efficiently. You will learn how to apply various role types, including predefined and custom roles, using IAM to control access.

Managing Identity and Access Management

Part of your daily responsibilities in managing a Google Cloud infrastructure is to understand access and security controls. Common activities you are responsible for and will be tested on for the Associate Cloud Engineer exam include the following:

- Viewing IAM account assignments
- Assigning IAM roles
- Defining custom roles

In this section, you learn how to complete all of these tasks using the IAM tools available using the Cloud Console.

Cloud Identity Access Management Basics

Google Cloud Platform has its own identity and access management platform called Cloud IAM. With Cloud IAM, a user can manage the access to and control of an identity based on the role or resource. For example, a virtual machine, GKE cluster, and Cloud Storage bucket are all GCP resources. These resources are often tied to the organizations, folders, and projects you use to organize those resources. There is a strong likelihood of a role-based relationship between one or more of these resources.

Cloud IAM does not directly grant permissions to an end user. Permissions are grouped into roles, which are granted to members of an authenticated group. Cloud IAM policies dictate and apply what roles are granted to which group members. Authenticated members are validated each time they try to access a resource to determine whether the action is permissible.

You must understand three fundamental concepts during a discussion of Cloud IAM. You need to know the dynamic between members, roles, and policies. A *member* is representative of the type of user—be it a Google account (end user), service account (apps and virtual machines that are not humanly accessible), Google group, G Suite group, or Cloud Identity domain, which has access to one or more resources. Identities are defined by the user e-mail address, a service or Google account, or the organizational domain name tied to the G Suite or Cloud identity domain account. *Roles* group permissions together, and permissions help determine which operations can support resources. Granting a role to a member means granting the permissions given a role association. *Policies* in Cloud IAM associate members to a given role. When a member is supposed to have access to a type of role or resource, you associate that policy with that member and apply it to the resource.

Now that you are familiar with the principal design of Cloud IAM, you are ready to begin implementing role assignments.

Viewing Identity and Access Management Role Assignments

To locate the IAM functionality, go to Cloud Console and find the option IAM & Admin and then select the IAM submenu, as seen in Figure 10-1.

Once you select IAM, a page similar to the one presented in Figure 10-2 appears. On the page, you will find all the member accounts associated with the project (in this case, eDynaLearn). The member accounts for the eDynaLearn project include a mix of Google accounts (end user) and several service accounts (apps and virtual machines that are not human accessible). Other member accounts can be added at a later time. In the particular example in Figure 10-2, member jack@dynlearning.com is a Compute Admin, Owner, Organization Administrator, Storage Admin, Storage Object Viewer,

Figure 10-1
The IAM & Admin
option in the
Cloud Console
navigation area

App Engine Admin, and Kubernetes Engine Admin. That means for any of these resource types where that level of permissions is needed, the dynalearning.com account is granted permission.

Before Cloud IAM, GCP supported primitive roles. A member either was given Owner, Editor, or Viewer permissions. Owners could manage a role or entity, and they inherited the permission of Editor. Editors could modify any system entity as well as systemwide view capabilities. Viewers could only complete read-only tasks. A distinction for Owners is they also could configure project billing.

Figure 10-2   Viewing IAM by members

When Google introduced Cloud IAM, setting permissions became more fine-grained. Identities can now be tailored to just those permissions that are necessary to complete a task, and nothing more. In Figure 10-3, you can see a list of predefined roles for the project eDynaLearn and the applicable permissions. For example, only two users have role of Compute Admin assigned whereas five users have Editor access.

Since Cloud IAM combines both primitive, predefined, and custom roles, you will often find a mixture of more than just primitive roles in this display view. To view each role, click the arrow on the left next to the role text to expand the view.

For those users who prefer to see all users and roles assigned to a project using a command-line editor such as Cloud Shell, the following command is used:

```
gcloud projects get-iam-policy <project id>
```

Using the example in this section, the command would be as follows:

```
gcloud projects get-iam-policy edynalearn
```

Figure 10-3
Viewing IAM
members by role

Permissions for project "eDynaLearn"

These permissions affect this project and all of its resources. Learn more

View By: MEMBERS   ROLES

≡ Filter tree

☐	Role / Member ↑	Name	Inheritance
☐	▶ App Engine Admin (1)		
☐	▶ App Engine Deployer (1)		
☐	▶ Cloud Build Service Account (1)		
☐	▶ Cloud Build Service Agent (1)		
☐	▶ Cloud Dataflow Service Agent (1)		
☐	▶ Cloud Functions Service Agent (1)		
☐	▶ Cloud Memorystore Redis Service Agent (1)		
☐	▶ Cloud Run Service Agent (1)		
☐	▶ Cloud Source Repositories Service Agent (1)		
☐	▶ Compute Admin (2)		
☐	▶ Compute Engine Service Agent (1)		
☐	▶ Compute Viewer (4)		
☐	▶ Container Analysis Service Agent (1)		
☐	▶ Container Scanner Service Agent (1)		
☐	▶ Dataproc Service Agent (1)		
☐	▶ Editor (5)		
☐	▶ Firebase Rules System (1)		
☐	▶ Kubernetes Engine Admin (1)		
☐	▶ Kubernetes Engine Service Agent (1)		
☐	▶ Monitoring Admin (1)		
☐	▶ Monitoring Editor (1)		
☐	▶ Organization Administrator (2)		
☐	▶ Owner (1)		
☐	▶ Service Account User (1)		
☐	▶ Storage Admin (1)		
☐	▶ Storage Object Viewer (3)		

Predefined Roles

Predefined roles are intended to provide fine-grained access to specific GCP services. You would use predefined roles for common use cases that do not require particular access control requirements. There are many predefined roles, unlike primitive roles. Throughout the book, you have been introduced to several, including Compute Engine, App Engine, Kubernetes Engine, Billing, and BigQuery, to name a few. Two predefined roles that are quite pervasive throughout the Google Cloud Platform are the Kubernetes Engine and Billing roles. Tables 10-1 and 10-2 provide all the fine-grained roles, titles, and descriptions for each predefined role for these two resource types.

 EXAM TIP Unlike primitive roles, there are many predefined roles in Cloud IAM. While you do not need to know all of them, you should become familiar with those mentioned throughout the book. Also, consider reviewing resource-specific IAM roles, as there is always the possibility the exam will ask questions about these roles. To review a list of all the predefined roles, go to https://cloud.google.com/iam/docs/understanding-roles.

Role	Title	Description
roles/container .admin	Kubernetes Engine Admin	Provides full management access to clusters and their Kubernetes API objects. To use this role, you must set a service account on nodes. You also need to grant the Service Account User role (roles/iam .serviceAccountUser).
roles/container .clusterAdmin	Kubernetes Engine Cluster Admin	Provides management access to clusters. To set a service account on nodes, you need to grant the Service Account User role (roles/iam .serviceAccountUser).
roles/container .clusterViewer	Kubernetes Engine Cluster Viewer	Provides read-only access to Kubernetes clusters.
roles/container .developer	Kubernetes Engine Developer	Provides access to Kubernetes API objects inside clusters.
roles/container .hostServiceAgentUser	Kubernetes Engine Host Service Agent User	Allows the Kubernetes Engine service account to host projects and configure shared network resources for cluster management. Also provides access to evaluate firewall rules in the host project.
roles/container .viewer	Kubernetes Engine Viewer	Provides read-only access to GKE resources.

Table 10-1 Kubernetes Engine Predefined Roles

Role	Title	Description
roles/billing .admin	Billing Account Administrator	Provides access to see and manage all facets of a billing account
roles/billing .creator	Billing Account Creator	Provides access to create a billing account
roles/billing .projectManager	Project Billing Manager	Provides access to assign a project billing account or disable the billing account
roles/billing .user	Billing Account User	Provides access to associate a project with a billing account
roles/billing .viewer	Billing Account Viewer	Can view billing account cost transactions

Table 10-2 Billing Predefined Roles

Assigning IAM Roles

You now understand the difference between primitive and predefined roles. In the previous section, you learned how to view the organizational users, called members, who have been assigned roles to the project. Now, you can add IAM roles to accounts and groups within a project.

To add IAM roles, go to the Cloud Console, locate the IAM & Admin section of the console, and select the IAM submenu option. A new page opens, displaying all of the existing members and role assignments. On the top of the page, click the Add link to open up a form similar to Figure 10-4.

You need to identify an existing account in the domain, or you can identify a Google account. In the example, you see that bobbys@dynalearning.com is added. He has been assigned two roles so far. Each time a new role is added, you can select the appropriate role and permission using the drop-down menu, as shown in Figure 10-4. Once role assignment is complete, click Save. The new member and granted roles appear on the IAM page.

Validating and Reviewing Added Roles

To confirm your users are properly assigned the appropriate roles and permissions, you may want to double-check IAM from time to time. Assuming you assigned fine-grained permissions when granting a role, you have the ability to review a list using Cloud Console. You also have the ability to see role-based permission assignment using a command-line utility.

To review role-based permissions, use the command line in Cloud Shell:

```
gcloud iam roles describe <role>
```

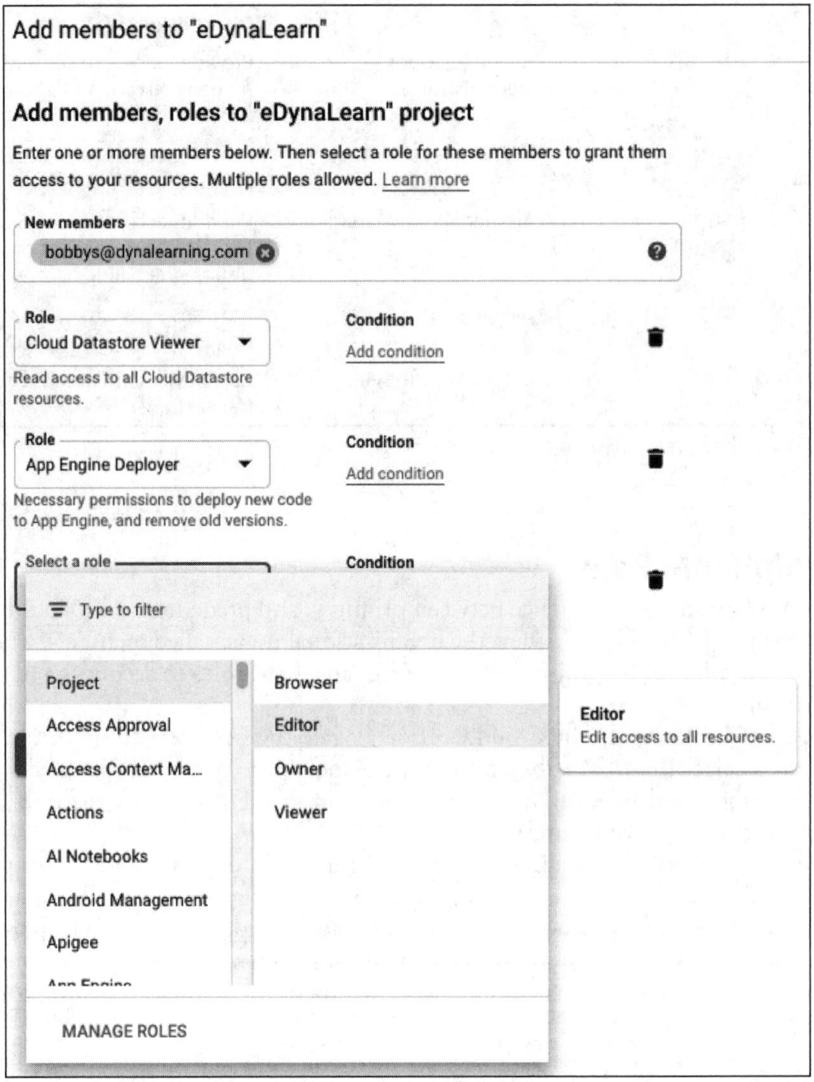

Add members to "eDynaLearn"

Add members, roles to "eDynaLearn" project

Enter one or more members below. Then select a role for these members to grant them access to your resources. Multiple roles allowed. Learn more

New members

bobbys@dynalearning.com ⊗   ❓

Role
Cloud Datastore Viewer ▼   Condition   🗑
                                    Add condition

Read access to all Cloud Datastore
resources.

Role
App Engine Deployer ▼   Condition   🗑
                                    Add condition

Necessary permissions to deploy new code
to App Engine, and remove old versions.

Select a role   Condition   🗑

≡ Type to filter

| Project | Browser |
| Access Approval | Editor | Editor
| Access Context Ma... | Owner | Edit access to all resources.
Actions	Viewer
AI Notebooks	
Android Management	
Apigee	
App Engine	

MANAGE ROLES

Figure 10-4   The form for adding IAM role

An example of the command-line output for all resources associated with the Admin role can be found in Figure 10-5.

There may also be times you need to view all the permissions associated with a role. As you know, there are only three primitive roles: Owner, Editors, and Viewer. For predefined roles, there are many more options. If you go to the Cloud Console, choose IAM & Admin and go to the Roles option, a new page will appear that shows all the predefined roles established by Google. There are over 500 predefined roles. As shown in

```
jack@cloudshell:~ (edynalearn)$ gcloud iam roles describe roles/admin
description: Full access to all resources.
etag: AA==
includedPermissions:
- accessapproval.requests.approve
- accessapproval.requests.dismiss
- accessapproval.requests.get
- accessapproval.requests.list
- accessapproval.settings.delete
- accessapproval.settings.get
- accessapproval.settings.update
- accesscontextmanager.accessLevels.create
- accesscontextmanager.accessLevels.delete
- accesscontextmanager.accessLevels.get
- accesscontextmanager.accessLevels.list
- accesscontextmanager.accessLevels.replaceAll
- accesscontextmanager.accessLevels.update
- accesscontextmanager.accessPolicies.create
- accesscontextmanager.accessPolicies.delete
- accesscontextmanager.accessPolicies.get
- accesscontextmanager.accessPolicies.getIamPolicy
- accesscontextmanager.accessPolicies.list
- accesscontextmanager.accessPolicies.setIamPolicy
- accesscontextmanager.accessPolicies.update
- accesscontextmanager.accessZones.create
- accesscontextmanager.accessZones.delete
- accesscontextmanager.accessZones.get
- accesscontextmanager.accessZones.list
- accesscontextmanager.accessZones.update
- accesscontextmanager.policies.create
- accesscontextmanager.policies.delete
- accesscontextmanager.policies.get
- accesscontextmanager.policies.getIamPolicy
- accesscontextmanager.policies.list
- accesscontextmanager.policies.setIamPolicy
- accesscontextmanager.policies.update
- accesscontextmanager.servicePerimeters.commit
- accesscontextmanager.servicePerimeters.create
- accesscontextmanager.servicePerimeters.delete
- accesscontextmanager.servicePerimeters.get
- accesscontextmanager.servicePerimeters.list
- accesscontextmanager.servicePerimeters.replaceAll
- accesscontextmanager.servicePerimeters.update
- actions.agent.claimContentProvider
```

Figure 10-5   Output from command line for verifying role-based Admin permissions

Figure 10-6, the BigQuery User role is associated with 24 known permissions. This is just one example of a predefined role. Should an administrator require a custom role, there is the possibility of defining custom IAM roles, which will be discussed in the next section.

Taking what you've learned, you can apply the information to a specific user and role-based permission using the following command:

```
gcloud projects add-iam-policy-binding <resource> --member user:<user email>
--role <role id>
```

Figure 10-6 BigQuery User role as seen in the Roles page found in Cloud IAM

Here's an example using bobbys@dynalearning.com with a resource name of elearning-tools and a role of compute.admin:

```
gcloud projects add-iam-policy-binding elearning-tools --member user:bobbys@
dynalearning.com --role roles/compute.admin
```

EXAM TIP On the exam, you may be asked to assign a user the most appropriate role. Security best practices recommend assigning users least privileges and employing separation of duties. What does this mean? You only assign a user what they absolutely require and nothing more. As to separation of duties, if doing two tasks by the same person presents a risk, the user should be prohibited from completing both tasks to avoid any malicious or unintentional harm.

Defining Custom IAM Roles

There may be instances when the predefined roles may offer too few or too many permissions. Perhaps the permissions require some modification in order to meet the role of least privilege for your organizational need. For these cases, you will want to create a custom IAM role. To define a custom IAM role, go to the Cloud Console and locate the Roles option under the IAM & Admin section. Once the page loads, click the Create Role link. You will find a page similar to Figure 10-7.

On that page, you are able to enter the title of the custom role, add a description, set the ID of the custom role, define what stage the custom role is currently at (alpha, beta, or general availability), and select the appropriate permissions that are supported. In the example shown in Figure 10-7, four permissions were added before the Create button was clicked.

Figure 10-7
Form for creating
a custom role

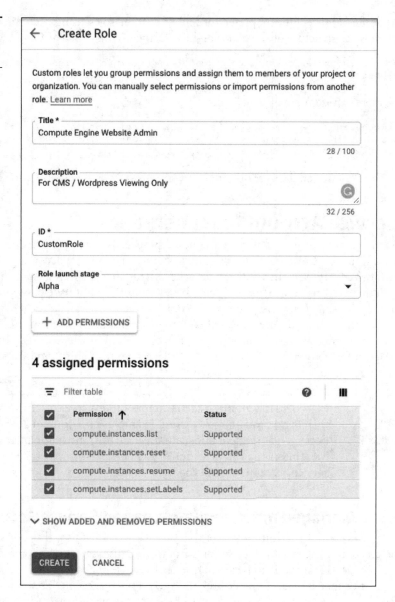

TIP   If a permission is not available when you're trying to create a custom role, it will indicate the status as Not Supported. Otherwise, you will be able to add the permission to the list as needed based on availability by checking the box and clicking Add.

Some cloud engineers prefer to deploy custom roles using a command-line editor. Here is the structure of the command line using a utility such as Cloud Shell:

```
gcloud iam roles create <role id> --project <project id> --title <title> \
--description <description> --permissions <permission> --stage <stage>
```

Here's an example of the output:

```
gcloud iam roles create ComputeEngVMEX --project=eDynaLearn --title='VM
for New Website Permissions' \ --description='Custom Rules' --permissions=
compute.instances.list --stage=alpha
```

In the example, all flags are optional, but you must state the role ID, project ID, and title.

Service Account Management

Service accounts are a different account type because they are used by applications or virtual machine instances, not by human beings. The service accounts are used to make authorized API calls. In GCP, service accounts are identified by e-mail addresses that are unique to the accounts. Interestingly, these accounts do not have passwords, so they cannot log in using browsers or maintain cookies.

For the exam, you are expected to know three skills. First, you must know how to manage service accounts with limited privileges, also known as *scopes*. Second, you must assign a virtual machine instance to a service account. Third, you must know how to grant access to a service account in another project.

 EXAM TIP   It is important to remember that a service account is GCP's way of managing programmable users. Examples of programmable users include bots such as prebuilt applications, cron jobs, and automations. If a human must intervene with a resource, you need to select a user account type; service accounts are not the right choice.

User-Managed and Google-Managed Service Accounts

Instances are only permitted to have one service account. Also, the service account must be created in the same project as an instance. As discussed in Chapter 2, there are two types of service accounts: User-managed and Google-managed.

A user-managed account creates the new service accounts as well as the Compute Engine default service account. An advantage to a user-managed account is that you can create and manage your service accounts using Cloud IAM. Once created, you grant the account IAM roles and set the instance to run as the service account. Apps that run on instances enable the service account credential to have the opportunity to request additional Google APIs. Furthermore, the user-managed service accounts come with a Compute Engine default service account. New Projects are associated with a default service account. They are always identifiable with a standard naming nomenclature:

[PROJECT_NUMBER]-compute@developer.gserviceaccount.com

While Google creates the Compute Engine default service account for you during project creation, the cloud engineer has full control over it. As a cloud engineer, you are granted the Project Editor role. You can limit the service account roles to prevent Google APIs that a service account may access.

Google-managed service accounts are service accounts created and managed by Google. These service accounts are assigned to a project automatically. A Google-managed service account represents different Google services, each of which has some access to a Google Cloud project. By default, all projects enable Compute Engine to have a Google API service account that uses an e-mail account with a standard nomenclature:

[PROJECT_NUMBER]@cloudservices.gserviceaccount.com

The account is intended to run internal Google processes exclusively. That means the account is meant to run internal Google processes not listed in a service account of Cloud Console. The account is automatically granted the Project Editor role on the project. It is also listed as part of the IAM section within Cloud Console. The service can only be deleted when the project is deleted. However, a cloud engineer can modify the roles granted at any time, including revoking access to a project if desired. It is strongly encouraged that limited changes be made to a Google-managed services account.

Managing Service Accounts with Limited Privileges

Service accounts are associated with virtual machines instances. A service account is used to complete this action when you are trying to grant an instance to operate automatically without human intervention. There are two ways in which service accounts with limited permissions can be managed. One is using Cloud IAM. The other is using *scopes*, a legacy form of permission assignment.

In GCP, scopes are a type of permission granted to the virtual machine instance that is associated with API authorization. Each service account has specific roles assigned to a virtual machine, not unlike a human. To configure your VM, the cloud engineer must configure both Cloud IAM roles and scopes. You already know how to configure IAM roles; now you need to configure scopes for the service accounts.

While still used, an access scope is a legacy method of specifying permissions for your instance. Using access scopes is not a secure method. It is a way to define the default OAuth scope used in requests from the client libraries or when using the `gcloud` tool. When you create a new virtual machine instance, you configure an access scope to limit the privileges of a service account. At any time you may modify service account privileges as well by shutting down the instance and modifying the access scopes as necessary. Since access scopes are applicable on a per-instance basis, you set the access when you create the instance. The permission maintains itself only for as long as the instance exists; otherwise, the permission remains in place. Best practices recommend that a cloud engineer set the full cloud-platform access scope on an instance. Once it is set, the cloud engineer should securely limit the service account's API access with the appropriate Cloud IAM roles.

 TIP If you have not enabled the API on a project that the service account belongs to, nothing will happen. For example, you may want to grant an access scope to the Cloud Storage on a virtual machine instance to call the Cloud Storage API—that is, only if the actual API is enabled in the project.

Sample access scopes can be accessed on the following pages:

- **Full control access to Compute Engine methods:**
  https://www.googleapis.com/auth/compute
- **Read-only access to Compute Engine methods:**
  https://www.googleapis.com/auth/compute.readonly
- **Read-only access to Cloud Storage:**
  https://www.googleapis.com/auth/devstorage.read_only

To configure a scope, go to Cloud Console and locate Compute Engine. Next, find VM Instances and select the instance you would like to modify. Stop the instance. It will take a few minutes. Once the instance has stopped, click the name of the instance and then click the Edit link. Scroll to the bottom of the Edit page, where you will find a section labeled Access Scopes. The section allows you to select from three options:

- Allow default access
- Allow full access to all Cloud APIs
- Set access for each API

Most cloud engineers select Allow default access for service account creation. There are times, however, when that is not sufficient. If you want to provide more control, grant full access but enable IAM roles to tighten access for specific users. Should you wish to set individual roles for users, select the Set access for each API option. Figure 10-8 presents an example of assigning access scopes for each API to the VM instance, elearning-tools.

Instead of configuring access scope using Cloud Console, you can configure scopes using Cloud Shell:

```
gcloud compute instances set-service-account <instance name>\
     --service-account <service account name  --scopes <scope>
```

Using this convention, the output would look like this:

```
gcloud compute instances set-service-account elearning-tools\
23574600376-compute@developer.gserviceaccount.com  --scopes compute-
rw,storage-rw
```

Figure 10-8
Assigning the
scope "Set access
for each API"

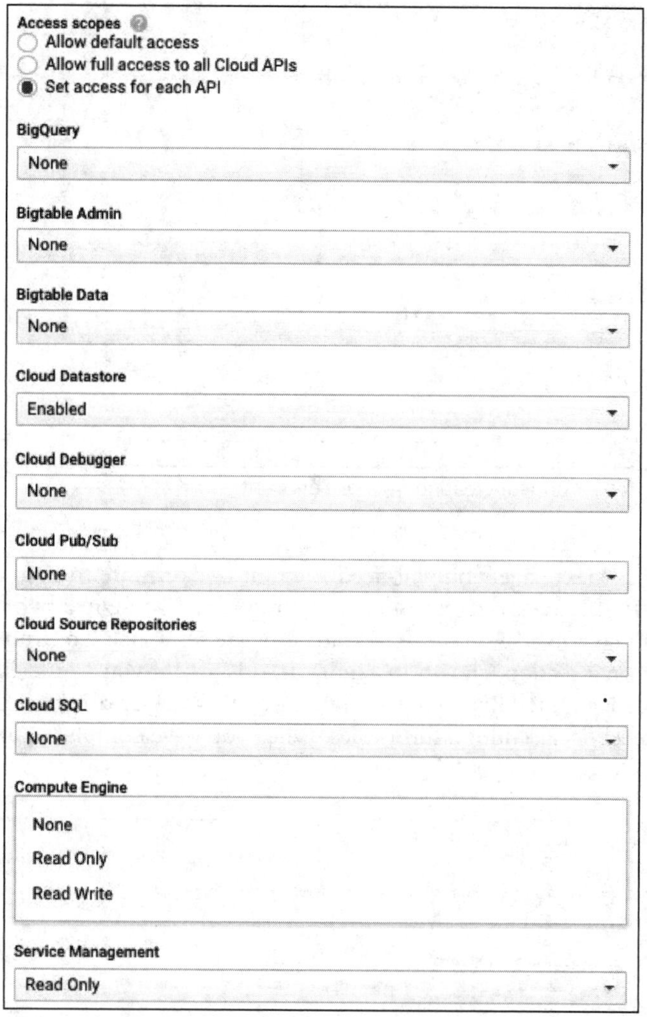

Assigning Service Accounts to VM Instances

At times, you may be responsible for having to create a service account for a VM instance (hence, user-managed account creation). To assign a service account to a VM instance, go to the Cloud Console and locate IAM & Admin. Next, select the Service Accounts option. Once the page opens, click the Create Service Account link on the top of the page. A form such as the one shown in Figure 10-9 appears and requires you to provide the service account's name, ID, and description. By default, the service account's name and ID are the same. The description is optional, although it's strongly recommended that you fill in the field. Once you complete all the requirements, click Create.

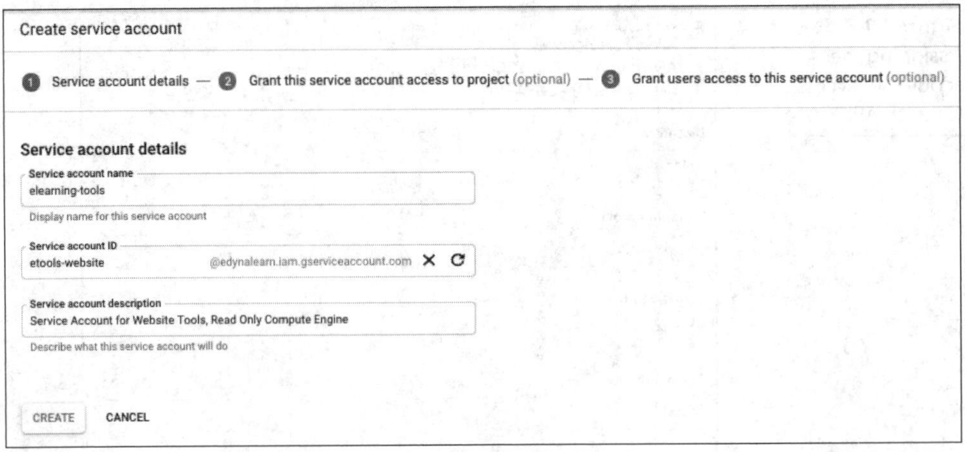

Create service account

① Service account details — ② Grant this service account access to project (optional) — ③ Grant users access to this service account (optional)

Service account details

Service account name
elearning-tools

Display name for this service account

Service account ID
etools-website   @edynalearn.iam.gserviceaccount.com ✕ ⟳

Service account description
Service Account for Website Tools, Read Only Compute Engine

Describe what this service account will do

CREATE   CANCEL

Figure 10-9   Form for creating a service account

On the next page, you will need to grant one or more roles to the service account. In Figure 10-10, the service account, elearning-tools, is assigned two roles: Compute Viewer and Storage Object Viewer. No conditions are set. Click Continue once you are ready.

The final section, shown in Figure 10-11, asks if you would like grant user access to a service account. This is completely optional. You can either assign service account user roles or service account admin roles. Once you have completed this task, click Done.

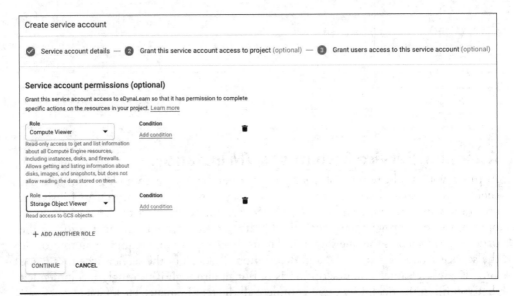

Figure 10-10   Assigning roles to service account

Figure 10-11   Granting user access to a service account

Now that the custom service account is created, go to the virtual machine instance that requires the service account. To locate the virtual machine, go to Cloud Console, locate Compute Engine, and then select the VM Instances menu option.

It helps if you stop the VM you intend to add the service account to on this page. Once you have done this, click the name of the instance, click Edit, and then scroll to the bottom of the page. Under the option Service Accounts, select the drop-down menu and you will find the service account that was just created. In this case, the service account, elearning-tools, appears in the drop-down menu, as seen in Figure 10-12. Select this option and click Save.

Once you have made all your changes to the service account, restart your virtual machine instance.

As you are planning your access control and security strategy, remember that giving a user access to a service account is not a best practice. Service accounts are intended for specific discrete activities using a strictly programmatic approach. With a user account, a user is unable to deny completing activities. If a user can complete activities behind an ambiguous user name, be it another human user or a programmatic user, you are unable to track who has committed specific actions when you monitor and log them. If something goes wrong, you will be unable to determine the identity of the bad actor interrupting operational continuity. You need to ensure you follow the rules regarding

Figure 10-12
Drop-down menu of service accounts in the VM Instances page

the principle of least privilege because you do not want a user to have more access to a system that they should be allowed. Users should not be able to access an OS for a VM granted high privileges with service account roles and make changes to an environment where access should be limited.

Assuming all of the steps to create a VM instance are complete, you can use the following `gcloud` command to assign a service account to an instance:

```
gcloud compute instances create <instance name> --service-account=<service
account email address>
```

Here is the output for the example created earlier in this chapter:

```
gcloud compute instances create elearning-tools --service-account=elearning-
tools@edynalearn.iam.gserviceaccount.com
```

NOTE If you are looking to grant access to a service account for a project, always go to the IAM & Admin | IAM page of the Cloud Console and add a new member to the desired project. You use the service account e-mail address when adding a new member entity.

Viewing Audit Logs for Projects and Managed Services

Audit logs play a vital role in understanding your security posture and behavior, and you will learn more about auditing in the next chapter. To access and view logs, navigate to Operations in the Cloud Console and then locate Logging and select the Logs Viewer submenu. A page similar to Figure 10-13 appears. In the example, a log of all Compute Engine activities appears. Note that you have a navigational drop-down with audit logging options to select from. Via this menu, you are able to conduct an audit for a project or managed service.

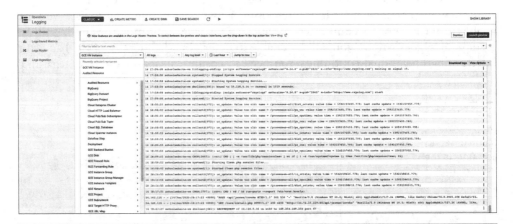

Figure 10-13 Sample log file from Google Operations Suite

Chapter Review

At the beginning of the chapter, we reviewed some concepts you were introduced to earlier in the book—that is, primitive, predefined, and custom roles. While primitive roles are limited to just three options (Owner, Editor, and Viewer), Cloud IAM offers resources fine-grained access control. Following the notion of least privilege, the use of predefined roles allows a user only the minimum set of permissions required to complete an activity or task. A cloud engineer can create a custom role if a user is unable to complete an action or task using a predefined role.

We also covered three exam objectives you should master: managing identity and access management tasks, managing service accounts, and viewing audit logs for projects and managed services. You were taught how to use Cloud Console and a command-line utility to assign IAM roles, define custom IAM roles, manage service accounts, assign service accounts to a VM instance, and grant access to service accounts in another project.

The difference between a cloud engineer and service account assigning permissions is that the service account is not human. A service account is intended for managing Google API-based operations with defined permissions. Although you learned how to configure service accounts, keep in mind that you can always utilize the Google-managed service accounts.

Questions

1. You recently stood up a development Compute Engine VM instance with the appropriate IAM roles. You need to replicate the development instance and create a production project by having the same IAM roles in the new project. Using Google best practices, what would you do?

   A. Use `gcloud iam roles copy` and specify the organization in which the project is located.

   B. Go to the Cloud Console Platform and create a new role from an existing role's functionality.

   C. Go to the Cloud Console Platform, create a new service account, and assign the necessary roles.

   D. Use `gcloud compute instances create` and apply the same roles that were applicable to the development environment.

2. DynaLearning was recently notified by the government that its financial records are not accurate. The organization is due for an external financial audit by two government accountants. In order to protect sensitive employee data, what can the cloud engineers do so that only the financial records are made available?

   A. Add an auditor group to the existing predefined IAM roles.

   B. Create Billing Creator and Admin Groups that are part of a new Custom IAM group.

   C. Add two auditor user accounts, each containing the appropriate predefined roles.

   D. Create user accounts for each auditor with admin privileges.

3. You are looking to verify all IAM users and roles assigned to the newly created project `etools-webinars`. How would you go about validating this?

   A. Run `gcloud iam roles describe <project>` and then review the output.

   B. Go to the specific project and locate the Roles section within IAM; then, review the roles and their status.

   C. Go to the specific project, locate IAM, and review by filtering by Members.

   D. Run `gcloud projects get-iam-policy <project>` and review the output.

4. Smart Student, Inc., recently deployed G Suite for Education as their preferred business productivity solution. Every user in the organization has been provisioned a G Suite account. Some of these users are responsible for maintaining enterprise applications recently migrated to and hosted on Google Cloud Platform. How would you grant those G Suite users access to GCP?

   A. Given that each user has an e-mail address, grant the user the required IAM roles with their G Suite e-mail account.

   B. Add each user as a new member in IAM by manually entering in each identity.

   C. Go to the domain and add each user first. Then allow Cloud Identity to recognize each user based on the domain.

   D. G Suite for Education Users and Google Cloud Platform user accounts cannot be integrated seamlessly.

5. All of the following are primitive roles except for which one?

   A. Editor

   B. Owner

   C. Viewer

   D. Developer

6. What is the most efficient way to audit all access and security activity over a month-long period of time for a virtual machine instance?

   A. Use Google Operations Suite (formerly Stackdriver) audit logs.

   B. Run `gcloud projects get-iam-policy <project id>`.

   C. Run `gcloud iam roles list <project>` and review the output.

   D. Run `gcloud iam roles describe <project>` and review the output.

7. When granting access to a service account in another project, what do you need to configure?

   A. Go to IAM and enter the member user name only.

   B. Go to IAM and enter the service account e-mail address.

C. Go to IAM and enter the member e-mail address.

D. Go to IAM and enter the service account name only.

8. When you're assigning users roles and permissions for assigned resources, what are two Google best practices with Cloud IAM?

    A. Separation of duties

    B. Authorization management

    C. Least privilege

    D. Resource allocation

9. Once a service account is fully configured, which of the following `gcloud` commands could you run to assign the service account when creating a virtual machine instance?

    A. `gcloud compute instances create <instance name> --service-account=<project id>`

    B. `gcloud compute instances create <instance name> --service-account=<service account email>`

    C. `gcloud compute instances create --service-account <instance name>=<service email>`

    D. `gcloud compute instances create instances --service-accounts=<service account email> --project id=<project id>`

10. William is trying to explain to Theodore the purpose of access scopes. William states that scopes are a type of permission granted to a type of resource exclusively. Which of these best fits the description?

    A. Virtual machine

    B. Persistent disk

    C. Object storage

    D. Block storage

11. Custom roles allow for four stages of deployment. Select the one stage that is not recognized under this categorization.

    A. General availability

    B. Alpha/beta

    C. Disabled

    D. Functional

12. What is the key difference between user-managed and Google-managed Cloud IAM service accounts?

   A. Google-managed service accounts are service accounts created and managed by humans whereas user-managed accounts create default Compute Engine service accounts that are managed by Google.

   B. Google-managed service accounts create default Compute Engine service accounts that can be managed by humans. User-managed accounts create service accounts that are automated and managed by Google exclusively.

   C. Google-managed service accounts are service accounts created and managed by Google whereas user-managed accounts create default Compute Engine service accounts that can be managed by humans.

   D. Google- and user-managed service accounts are capable of being managed by humans; however, Google accounts offer extra automation.

Answers

1. **A.** Google best practices recommend the quickest way to migrate an instance from development to production is to copy the instance. This assumes that the system has one or more custom roles defined. That said, part of the responsibility of a cloud engineer is to also properly maintain custom roles between environments. Google does occasionally make modifications to predefined roles, which could potentially include one of the custom roles you've created. Answer B would not have any logical impact in IAM. Answer C is not appropriate, as the question makes no mention of service accounts. Answer D involves creating a new instance, but creating a copy is a more efficient method to handle this activity.

2. **C.** Following the concept of least privilege, adding the two users to an appropriate group and not provisioning them for more access than they require is the best approach. Creating additional IAM groups is unnecessary, which is what is mentioned in answer A. For answers B and D, too much authority is being given to the external auditors for a highly secure environment.

3. **B.** If you want to review all possible predefined roles against a project, you would go to the Roles menu option under IAM. Both command-line options (answers A and D) would not provide adequate information. Finally, answer C only provides member-specific data against projects and roles. It does not offer a holistic view of all roles.

4. **A.** Because G Suite for Education is part of the school's infrastructure, you can integrate G Suite e-mail addresses inside GCP directly, as Google recognizes G Suite identities for Cloud IAM. All other options are incorrect because the product stack is highly integrated with Google Cloud Platform.

5. **D.** Developer is not a primitive role. Editor, Owner, and Viewer are primitive roles.

6. **A.** Only Google Operations Suite provides auditing capabilities. All of the `gcloud` command-line operations will provide output, but they will not offer extensive auditing output with granular, sortable data output.

7. **B.** You need to enter the service account e-mail address into the other project to assign the necessary permissions. All of the other answers are incorrect.

8. **A** and **C.** Least privilege and separation of duties are the two best practices associated with predefined roles and Cloud IAM. Authorization management and resource allocation are bogus concepts.

9. **B.** The construction of this command is accurate and reflects all the proper requirements for assigning a service account to a virtual machine. All of the other commands either have wrong variables or wrong placement of variables.

10. **A.** Access scopes are associated with virtual machine instances as a resource. All of the other items listed are types of resources but not associated with scopes.

11. **D.** Functional is the only choice listed that is not a category associated with a custom role. All of the other categories are applicable.

12. **C.** Google-managed accounts are machine-managed service accounts that are fully controlled by Google. User-managed accounts are created for a VM instance but are fully managed by a human being. Except for answer C, none of the answers reflect these options entirely because of the conditions described.

## CHAPTER 11

Operations and Pricing

In this chapter you will learn to
- Provision an Operations Suite Workspace
- Understand how to install the Stackdriver API agent for monitoring and logging
- Create Google Operations Suite alerts based on resource and custom metrics
- Configure log sinks for external systems and to export logs
- View and filter the various log output types available in Google Operations Suite
- Plan and create price estimates using the Google Cloud Platform (GCP) Pricing Calculator

This last chapter of the book is about operations management for the Google Cloud Platform. Throughout the book, you have learned about Operations Suite, formerly known as Stackdriver, on a use-case-specific basis. Here, we will address the primary business concepts and technical capabilities you need to familiarize yourself with as a cloud engineer.

In this chapter, you will continue to see references to Stackdriver despite the product name change by Google Cloud Platform in March 2020. Google has rebranded all of its Stackdriver products to Google Operations Suite. Within the Google Operations Suite, products include Cloud Monitoring, Cloud Debugger, Cloud Error Reporting, Cloud Logging, Cloud Profiler, and Cloud Trace. However, Google has kept the core API name for the Operations Suite, the Stackdriver API series, throughout Google Cloud (see Figure 11-1). GCP has also added a new API to Operations Suite: the Dashboard API.

The last section of this chapter addresses the Pricing Calculator. You will learn how to utilize the Pricing Calculator for virtually all of the products and services offered by Google Cloud Platform.

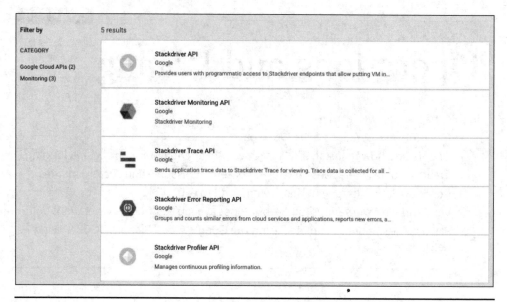

Figure 11-1   List of Stackdriver APIs available in Google Operations Suite

Overview of Google Operations Suite

Google Operations Suite is a collection of cloud tools available in the Google Cloud Platform to help monitor, troubleshoot, and improve application performance. Application performance monitoring requires real-time, responsive analytics. Google Operations Suite, assuming the Stackdriver API is enabled for a project, collects metrics, logs, and traces across GCP and applications. A cloud engineer can create one or more dashboards to meet the organization's needs to determine system performance, including alerts, notifications, and performance indicators.

To better understand the full Google Operations Suite set of offerings, Table 11-1 lists each service and provides a description of it.

Google Operations Suite	Description
Cloud Monitoring	Cloud Monitoring provides alerting policies, metrics, health check results, and uptime check results based on criteria set by a cloud engineer. You can integrate Cloud Monitoring with various third-party integration and notification solutions. In addition, Cloud Monitoring dashboards, which leverage the Dashboard API, are standard and customizable dashboards. Integrated into GCP are visualization tools to meet project needs for managing alerts, notifications, logs, and monitoring data.

Table 11-1   Google Operations Suite Features

Google Operations Suite	Description
Cloud Debugger	Cloud Debugger is a testing tool that enables a cloud engineer to inspect the state of an application, without reducing the application or having to stop it. With Cloud Debugger, the output does not produce logging statement entries, making it easier to diagnose issues.
Cloud Error Reporting	Cloud Error Reporting analyzes and aggregates all errors in one or more cloud applications. When errors are detected, notifications are sent out based on set conditions.
Cloud Logging	Cloud Logging is a comprehensive analysis tool that allows a cloud engineer to store, search, analyze, monitor, and establish alerts for logging data and events from Google Cloud. Other cloud platform integrations are also supported. Included is access to the BindPlane service, a common application component that allows a cloud engineer to collect log data from over 150 on-premises or hybrid cloud systems.
Cloud Profiler	Should your applications experience performance degradation, Cloud Profiler provides real-time profiling of resources in production with the goal of identifying and eliminating issues.
Cloud Trace	Specific to App Engine, Cloud Trace provides latency samples and reporting. Sample output includes per-URL statistics and latency distribution.

Table 11-1   Google Operations Suite Features

Workspaces

Cloud Monitoring requires an organizational tool to monitor and collect information. In GCP, that tool is called a Workspace. The Workspace brings together Cloud Monitoring resources from one or more GCP projects. It can even bring in third-party account data from other cloud providers, including Amazon Web Services. The Workspace collects metric data from one or more monitored projects; however, the data remains project bound. The data is pulled into the Workspace and then displayed.

Provisioning a Workspace

A Workspace can manage and monitor data for one or more GCP projects. A project, however, can only be associated with a single Workspace. A Workspace requires that your project be provisioned with the following user roles in IAM:

- Monitoring Editor
- Monitoring Admin
- Project Owner

Before you create a new Workspace, you need to identify who in the organization has roles in a given project. To do so, go to Cloud Console and select IAM & Admin. Each user role is listed beside the member name (see Figure 11-2). You should filter your user list to only actual users in order to remove service accounts.

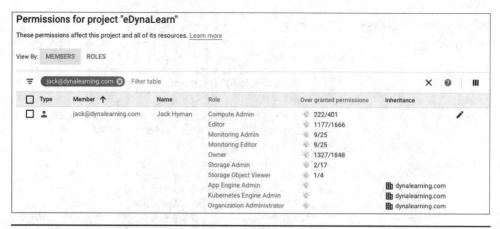

Figure 11-2 User role identification in IAM & Admin

If you need to add the three roles, you should do so at this time if the appropriate user roles have not been granted permission. Once this is done, close IAM & Admin. You can now create a new Workspace.

Creating a Workspace

A Workspace can only be created using the Cloud Console. To create a Workspace for an existing GCP Project, follow these steps:

1. To create a single Workspace, go to the toolbar and select the intended project for the Workspace.

2. Ensure you have the project permissions to create the Workspace for the intended project. If you do not, apply the necessary authorizations, as discussed in the previous section.

3. Once you have appropriately identified the necessary permissions, go to the Cloud Console navigation area and select Monitoring.

4. If you already have a Workspace associated with the project, you will see a window that presents Monitoring Overview. Otherwise, a Workspace is generated.

At this point, one of two options will appear:

- Assuming you have never created a multiproject Workspace before, a first Workspace is created. This Workspace is called the host project. The Workspace and project will have the same name under these conditions.

- If you have created a multiproject Workspace in the past, you have a few options to consider. You can either create a new Workspace or add the project to an existing Workspace. Google describes these as the Add Workspace Approach and Merge Workspace Approach, respectively.

Add Workspace Approach

When two new Google Cloud Projects exist and you intend to create a multiproject Workspace, but no host project is associated with a single Workspace, you need to follow these steps:

1. Create your initial Workspace.

2. Go to the Monitoring navigation pane and select Settings.

3. In the Settings window, select Add GCP Projects.

4. In the dialog window, select the second project and click Add Projects.

5. Now that the operation is complete, the Settings window indicates that both Google Cloud projects are available in the Workspace. The first project is the host project in this case.

Merge Workspace Approach

The assumption for a "merge" approach is that both projects already have Workspaces and both are host projects. In this case, you need to merge the Workspaces to create a single Workspace. To do this, follow these steps:

1. Select the first project. You are going to keep this project as the default.

2. In the Monitoring navigation pane, select Settings.

3. In the Settings window, choose Merge.

4. Select the second project that will be part of the Workspace.

5. To save the change, click Merge.

6. After a few minutes, the merge operation will be complete. In the Settings window, both projects will be members of the Workspace, but the first project is listed as the host project.

Enabling Stackdriver APIs for Monitoring and Logging

For the exam, you only need to know how to enable, disable, and install the Stackdriver API for Cloud Monitoring and Cloud Logging. Although you can collect third-party analytics data, that is not in scope for the exam. To quickly install, enable, or disable the Stackdriver APIs, follow these steps:

1. Go to the Cloud Console navigation area.

2. Locate APIs and Services.

3. Click Library.

4. The page shown in Figure 11-3 opens. Enter **Stackdriver** in the search box.

5. Press ENTER.

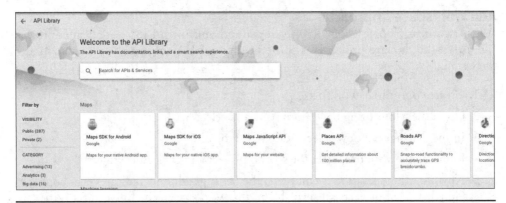

Figure 11-3 The API Library page and search box

6. The results for all Stackdriver APIs appear. You will select each of the APIs needed to evaluate your environment (Stackdriver API, Stackdriver Monitoring API, and so on).

7. For each API not enabled, click the button Enable.

Monitoring with Operations Suite

Operations Suite offers a variety of services that collect predefined and custom metrics, logs, and events data for resources within a project. Measures can be collected across all GCP projects, be it Compute Engine, Kubernetes Engine, App Engine, or Cloud Functions, or directly from storage and database instances. Metrics may include utilization, read and seek time, execution time, load, and count measures. Operations Suite also offers you the ability to evaluate the health of various services and resources at a fairly granular level. The most important thing to keep in mind is that Operations Suite capabilities are not limited to just GCP alone; other cloud platforms such as Amazon Web Services and on-premises architectures can utilize Operations Suite to evaluate performance.

Configuring Stackdriver for Metrics and Logging

Operations Suite supports the alerts creation based on predefined metrics. A metric is a defined measurement using a resource based on a regular period of time. Metrics leverage mathematical calculations to measure outcomes. Examples of metrics available using Operations Suite, and specifically the Stackdriver API, include maximum, minimum, average, and mean. Each of these mathematical calculations might evaluate CPU utilization, memory usage, and network activity.

To create an alert for a resource, a few prerequisites must be in place. First, you need to assume that you have a working virtual machine with an approved configuration to install the Stackdriver agent for monitoring. This instance should also be able to install the logging agent too. You can install the agents on a variety of operating system environments, including Linux AMI, CentOS, Red Hat Enterprise Linux (RHEL), Windows, SUSE Linux Enterprise Server (SLES), SUSE, Debian, and Ubuntu.

 TIP The AWS Linux AMI is not an image offered on GCP. It is, however, supported with Google Operations Suite because of its integration with the Stackdriver Monitoring API agent. The other images listed are all GCP-supported images.

To install the agent on the VM instance running Linux AMI, CentOS, or RHEL, follow the command prompts:

1. Open the command-line connection in your VM using the SSH. Access requires `sudo` command-line control.

2. Modify the directory path to have write access to the appropriate directory path. An example is the home directory.

3. Add the agents package repository in the command-line tool:

```
curl -sSO https://dl.google.com/cloudagents/add-logging-agent-repo.sh
sudo bash add-logging-agent-repo.sh

curl -sSO https://dl.google.com/cloudagents/add-monitoring-agent-repo.sh
sudo bash add-monitoring-agent-repo.sh
```

The next step in the process is to establish the Workspaces. You can either create a single Workspace or multiple Workspaces, as described in "Creating a Workspace," earlier in the chapter.

 TIP You can monitor third-party resources, including Amazon Web Services, in a Workspace. When you are configuring the Workspace, you need to establish the resource and source parameters for the integration at the time of setup.

Once you have created the desired Workspace configuration, you must install and validate the agents that exist. To install each agent service, enter the following into the SSH shell:

Monitoring:

```
curl -sSO https://dl.google.com/cloudagents/install-monitoring-agent.sh
sudo bash install-monitoring-agent.sh
```

Logging:

```
curl -sSO https://dl.google.com/cloudagents/install-logging- agent.sh
sudo bash install-logging-agent.sh
```

To verify that each of the services are active, enter the following:

```
sudo service stackdriver-agent status
```

Configuring Monitoring for Metrics

With the consolidation of products under Google Operations Suite, many metrics-related features were redesigned and consolidated under each of the respective operations tabs. For Monitoring, that is especially true. You are no longer prompted after the installation of Stackdriver to create basic outputs, including reports by e-mail, to establish basic alerting policies, or to create and establish uptime checks. Each of these activities has its own functional area under the Monitoring navigation menu within the Cloud Console. To access each area, locate Monitoring under the Cloud Console (see Figure 11-4).

You can select any of the areas under the submenu to access specific features, including Metrics Explorer, Alerting, or Uptime Checks. However, to get a holistic picture of all monitoring capabilities enabled, select the Overview option, which results in the page shown in Figure 11-5.

You'll want to be familiar with a few important tasks, including getting reports sent to you by e-mail, establishing alerting policies based on a defined parameter, and creating a health check for your project.

Figure 11-4
Monitoring
navigation menu

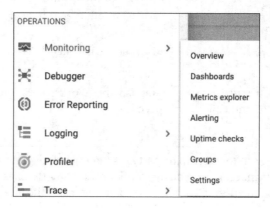

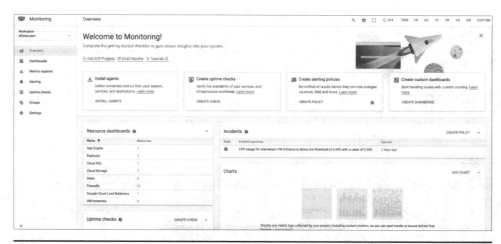

Figure 11-5   Monitoring Overview page

Creating E-mail Reports

At the top of the Overview page, right below the Welcome to Monitoring section, you will find the Email Reports link. Click the link so that you can establish your reporting parameters and the associated frequency (see Figure 11-6). You can produce Alert Policy Incidents and Utilization Groups reports. The frequency of distribution is either daily or weekly.

You can also access the Email Reports settings when you click the Settings menu option under Monitoring (see Figure 11-7).

Figure 11-6
Email Reports
settings,
accessed from
the Monitoring
Overview page

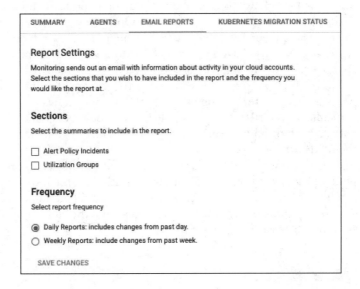

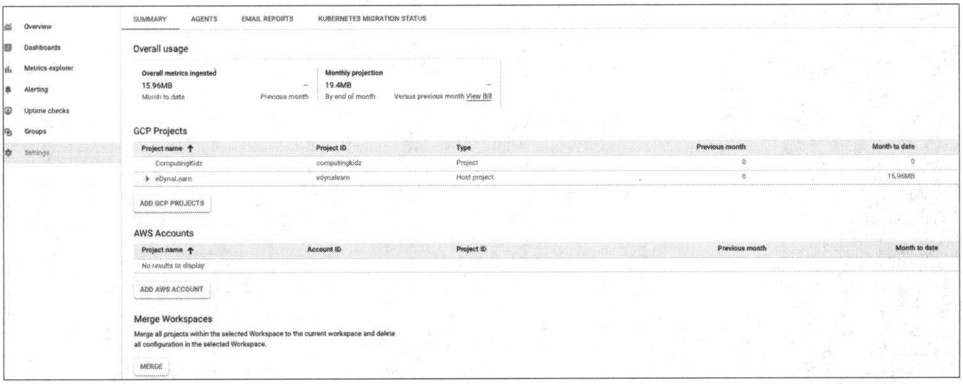

Figure 11-7 Monitoring features under the Settings menu, including Email Reports

Creating Alerting Policies

To create an alert, go to the Alerting option under Monitoring. On the Alerts overview page, you are able to view the summary of all alerts currently operating. An alert is intended to trigger a notification when an incident occurs. Policies are intended for alerts that describe a set of conditions that require monitoring. These conditions may be associated with an unhealthy system or resource consumption. An example of a policy might be to measure CPU utilization, disk read bytes, and disk write bytes. In the example presented in Figure 11-8, a policy for a VM Instance resource with CPU Usage metrics is presented. You may also want to more granullary group data; for example, by project_id, using the Group By option. Should you want to create advanced aggregator options, click the arrow next to Show Advanced Options. By expanding the menu, you are able to create an aligner parameter, define an alignment period, and also create a secondary aggregator. You also have the option of adding a legend template. Key definitions associated with alerting policies are found in Table 11-2.

Under the Configuration section, the triggers are identified. In the case of the example, whenever there is a time series violation that indicates the condition is above the threshold 5 ms for 10 minutes, a policy alert should be set off. Whenever you are satisfied with the condition of creating the policy, click Add. The new policy appears as part of the Alerts overview.

Creating policy conditions does not fulfill all the requirements for creating a new policy. You may optionally select the notification channel, which is the method by which a policy violation alert is sent to a user. Also, you can add documentation to an alert as a way to help the cloud engineer better understand the context of the policy alert. Once all conditions are satisfied, click Save.

Figure 11-8 Policy creation interface

Term	Definition
Aligner	Allows for the data points within an individual time series to be brought together under an equal period of time. When aligned for each time series, data points are aggregated into a single point. The value of the single point is determined by the aligner option used.
Alignment period	The period determining the time interval in which aggregation takes place.
Aggregator	Describes the way to aggregate data points across a times series. By default, an aggregation results in a single line so that the values are the result of applying the aggregators across a time series.
Legend template	A type of template used for a charted time series. Intended to replace an auto-generated description on a chart.

Table 11-2 Monitoring and Alerting Policy Definitions

Creating Metrics for Resources Using Metrics Explorer

You have already created a policy that includes the integration of metrics. There are times, however, you may not want threshold-based policies that produce alerts. Instead, you are looking to better understand the data collected visually for your project by building charts. With Metrics Explorer, the goal is not to produce alerts and notifications. Instead, it is merely to create graphical representation of specific resources based on one or more conditions. Based on the created metric query, you can distribute the output via a dashboard, a URL, or in JSON format. You also have the option to use Metrics Explorer for observation and monitoring. To utilize Metrics Explorer as a way to evaluate resources, follow these steps:

1. Go to the Monitoring section of Cloud Console and select the Metrics Explorer option.

2. The Metrics Explorer window appears (see Figure 11-9). You can either build a metric using a query builder or select an option using the drill-down interface.

Figure 11-9 Metrics Explorer overview page

Figure 11-10
Saving resource
metrics as a
dashboard, URL,
or JSON file

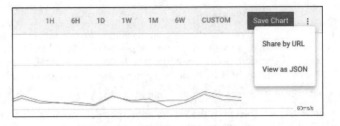

3. Find the resource type and metric desired for the specific evaluation.

4. Enter any filters, group by, and aggregator parameters.

5. Click Add Metric to add the query created using the drop-down options on the page.

6. If you would like to make a modification to the view, including the way the metrics are presented graphically, go to the View Options tab on the Metrics Explorer overview page. That is where you can modify the presentation as well as update the parameters for Threshold, Compare to Past, and Log Scale on Y-axis.

7. Once all resource metrics are captured, go to the right side of the page, where you can either save the query or create a new dashboard. Alternatively, you have the ability to save the metrics as a URL or JSON file by clicking the three dots next to the Save Chart button (see Figure 11-10). Follow the prompts to save each output type, as instructed.

EXAM TIP   For the exam, creating a metric is limited to the drill-down option because querying is a new feature with the release of the Google Operations Suite.

Creating Stackdriver Custom Metrics

The difference between prebuilt and custom metrics is a matter of the delivery mechanism. Custom and prebuilt metrics both leverage Monitoring built-in metrics. The exceptions include the following:

- The ability to create custom metrics in the GCP project.
- The naming convention to all the custom metric begins with custom.googleapis .com.
- The ability to delete custom metrics.

Among all the essential features of custom metrics, it is possible to write a time series dataset.

GCP allows you to create custom metrics in two ways: using the Stackdriver Monitoring API and leveraging OpenCensus, an open source monitoring library. OpenCensus can be accessed at http://www.opencensus.io. A cloud engineer would use OpenCensus over the Stackdriver Monitoring API because it offers a more granular, monitoring-rich API. Stackdriver provides a lower level of experience. To use the Monitoring API, you need to be familiar with utilizing the API Explorer and comfortable with one or more of these programming languages: C#, Go, Java, Node.js, PHP, Python, and Ruby on Rails. Similar to with a predefined metric, you must specify specific fields. With a custom metric, however, the details you can provide are much more granular. Items to specify include the following:

- Type name that is unique to a project
- Project name
- Display name and description
- Metric kind/measure (that is, gauge, delta, point in time)
- Label
- Monitored resource objects that include time series data points

For a cloud engineer to utilize a custom metric, a programming call to the Monitoring API or OpenCensus library is necessary. The process varies based on the programming language used. Each programming language has a specific approach to implementation. To review each strategy, go to https://cloud.google.com/monitoring/custom-metrics/creating-metrics.

Logging with Operations Suite

Logging is a service intended for the collection, storage, filtering, and viewing of logs and event data generated in a given Workspace. The Workspace source is likely either GCP or Amazon Web Services. Because logging is a managed service, there are limited configuration and deployment settings required to use the service. For the exam, you must be familiar with the following topics:

- Configuring log sinks
- Viewing and filtering logs
- Viewing log message details

The next few sections review each of these areas independently.

Configuring Log Sinks

With Google Cloud Platform, log data is retained for 30 calendar days. When your environment captures log data purely for operational purposes, seldom does the organization need to maintain logs for longer than a week or two.

However, for many organizations, the retention period is not enough. Most organizations must keep data for more extended periods due to government and regulatory compliance mandates. Organizations might like to keep a historical record of an application's performance. To address the post-30-day requirement, you need to export logging data into a long-term data storage facility. You can save your data to Cloud Storage, BigQuery, Cloud Pub/Sub, or a separate data storage facility outside of GCP.

When you copy data from Cloud Logging to a storage facility, you are exporting the data. The data sink occurs when you write the log data to a given location. The term *sink* refers to the actual storage facility destination. To create a log sink, locate Logging under the Operations menu in Cloud Console and then select the Logs Viewer. Upon opening the page, you will need to search for the log type desired. In Figure 11-11, an inquiry for all logs associated with VM instances that contain information over the past seven days is being evaluated.

Once the list is loaded, click the Create Sink button. A panel on the right side appears, where you are asked to supply the following information:

- Sink name
- Sink service
- Sink destination

The sink name is what you intend to call the export from Cloud Logging to the export location. The sink service is the storage type that log files are housed in once an export is complete. GCP allows for BigQuery, Cloud Storage, and Cloud Pub/Sub internally. Splunk or a third-party source can also be used. Depending on the sink service, the option in the Sink Destination field varies. In Figure 11-12, the sink service is BigQuery. The sink destination is elearningdata. If you have filled out all the required fields, you can create the export by clicking the Create Sink button. Depending on which option you choose, the export is saved differently.

Table 11-3 illustrates the differences between Cloud Storage, BigQuery, and Cloud Pub/Sub (the three GCP storage options) and a custom destination.

Once the sink is saved, a message box appears, as shown in Figure 11-13.

Figure 11-11 View of all logs associated with a VM instance

Figure 11-12
Creating a
sink form

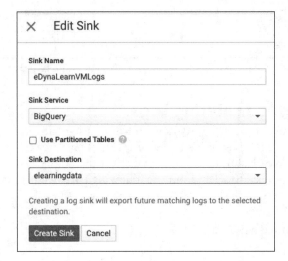

Storage Sink Option	Sink Service/Sink Destination Behaviors
Cloud Storage	Points to an existing bucket or requires a new bucket.
BigQuery	Points to an existing BigQuery dataset or requires a new dataset.
Cloud Pub/Sub	Choose between using an existing topic and creating a new one.
Custom destination	Assumes the creation of a new destination other than the existing project that is hosting the sink. Creating a custom destination also requires you to come up with a new sink name.

Table 11-3   Sink Service/Sink Destination Options

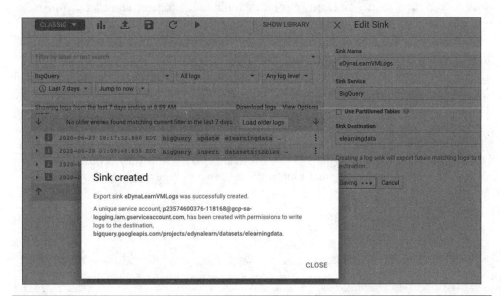

Figure 11-13   Confirmation of sink creation

Figure 11-14 Filtering of log data options with a log listing based on specific parameters

Viewing and Filtering Logs

Similar to exporting a log, to view and filter a log, all activities occur by accessing the log files using the Logs Viewer. To access the Logs Viewer, go to the Operations menu in Cloud Console, locate Logging, and select the Logs Viewer submenu option. To filter the logs, you need to select from the following parameters to get your desired log file:

- Label or text search
- Resource type
- Log type
- Log level
- Time

In Figure 11-14, the log data is being filtered to identify all BigQuery logs regardless of log level or log type, with no time limit.

Should you want to jump to the latest logs for a given resource, select the resource from the resource type drop-down menu and click the option Jump to Now. Each of these drop-downs has a range of options to narrow down the log files available to a user. The most important of all the drop-downs, however, is the audited resource. If there is no resource available, there will be no log file. The output of log files is also highly dependent on the time frame. You can select a prebuilt time range or enter a custom range using the calendaring function accessible from the drop-down menu.

Viewing Log Messages in Operations Suite

Assuming a set of logs entries is available as established in the previous section, you will notice that each log file is represented on a single line. You can expand a log entry by double-clicking its line or by clicking the triangle on the left side. By double-clicking the line, you only see the specific details for a single log entry, not an entire set. To view all details for all log entries, go to the right side of the Logs Viewer page and click View Options | Expand All (see Figure 11-15). Every log entry is now fully exposed for you to review. An example of an expanded log entry is shown in Figure 11-16.

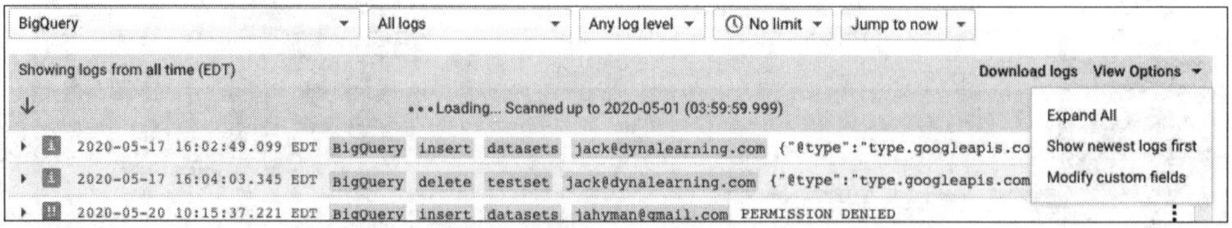

Figure 11-15 The Expand All option on the Logs Viewer page

Figure 11-16 An expanded log entry

Cloud Diagnostics

As a cloud engineer, when you are asked by a development or operations team what issues are triggering problems in Google Cloud Platform, a tool to turn to is Cloud Diagnostics. Within the Google Operations Suite, Cloud Diagnostics collects information such as performance data. Using the data collected, you or your development counterparts can better utilize Cloud Trace or Cloud Debugger to understand the data collection during execution.

Cloud Trace

There might be times you must identify why an application is behaving a certain way. For example, one measure often looked at is the time it takes to execute tasks in an application. This measure is known as performance degradation.

To review Cloud Trace data, go to the Operations menu under Cloud Console, locate the submenu option Trace, and select the menu option Overview. An overview page loads similar to Figure 11-17. The Overview page presented is the classic interface. An interface that integrates metrics is also available.

Within Cloud Trace, you can list traces tied to a running project. A trace is generated only when a developer requires Cloud Trace to run in their application. From the Overview menu, you may review all traces under Trace List and create reports to filter trace data under Analysis Reports. An example of an Analysis Reports page is shown in Figure 11-18.

EXAM TIP You should remember that Cloud Trace is a distributed tracing application. The sole purpose of Cloud Trace within the Google Operations Suite is to enable developers and their counterpart operations engineers to identify where performance issues exist—specifically code-based performance challenges.

Figure 11-17   Cloud Trace Overview page

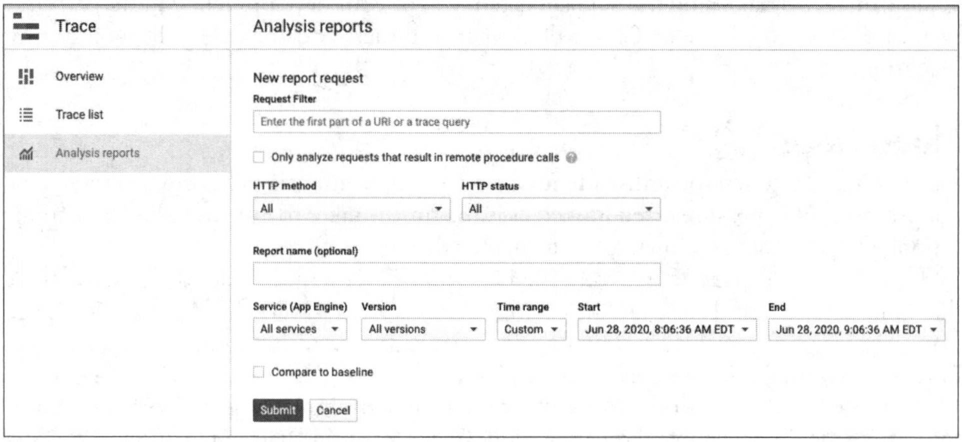

Figure 11-18   Cloud Trace Analysis Report page

Cloud Debugger

Developers and cloud engineers might need to evaluate the state of an application, trying to pinpoint performance issues within it. Often, Cloud Debugger is more helpful to developers than cloud engineers. The tool enables the insertion of log statements or can take a snapshot of an application to best identify issues. Cloud Debugger is enabled by default when you're creating an App Engine instance; it must be enabled for Compute and Kubernetes Engine.

TIP Debugging tools are quite useful; however, access should not limited to only the cloud engineer. The developer needs access as well in order to best diagnose and determine the root cause of technical issues. Without proper access using Cloud IAM, the value of the tool is significantly reduced.

To access Cloud Debugger, go to Cloud Console, locate Operations, and click the Debugger submenu option. A page such as the one presented in Figure 11-19 appears.

In order to review specific changes within an application, select one of the files in the left panel. On the right, the code for the application appears (see Figure 11-20).

Figure 11-19 Cloud Debugger overview page

```
 1  # Copyright 2016 Google Inc.
 2  #
 3  # Licensed under the Apache License, Version 2.0 (the "License");
 4  # you may not use this file except in compliance with the License.
 5  # You may obtain a copy of the License at
 6  #
 7  #      http://www.apache.org/licenses/LICENSE-2.0
 8  #
 9  # Unless required by applicable law or agreed to in writing, software
10  # distributed under the License is distributed on an "AS IS" BASIS,
11  # WITHOUT WARRANTIES OR CONDITIONS OF ANY KIND, either express or implied.
12  # See the License for the specific language governing permissions and
13  # limitations under the License.
14
15  import webapp2
16
17
18  class MainPage(webapp2.RequestHandler):
19      def get(self):
20          self.response.headers['Content-Type'] = 'text/plain'
21          self.response.write('Hello, World!')
22
23
    logpoint("This is an example of a GCP Logpoint")
24  app = webapp2.WSGIApplication([
25      ('/', MainPage),
26  ], debug=True)
27
```

Figure 11-20 Code displayed in Cloud Debugger

```
17
18   class MainPage(webapp2.RequestHandler):
19       def get(self):
20           self.response.headers['Content-Type'] = 'text/plain'
21           self.response.write('Hello, World!')
22
```

Figure 11-21   Example of a snapshot taken using Cloud Debugger

Figure 11-22
Example of
a logpoint
injection

```
22
23
     logpoint("This is an example of a GCP Logpoint")
24   app = webapp2.WSGIApplication([
25       ('/', MainPage),
26   ], debug=True)
27
```

If you are looking to test a few lines of code and create a snapshot of the intended behavior in question, highlight and then click the lines of code. On the left side, the lines selected have arrows associated with each respective snapshot (see Figure 11-21). The code debugger provides an issue report once the application runs.

The use of logpoints is also available. A logpoint is a log statement written to an application log upon the execution of a statement. To create a logpoint, go to the right panel next to the code and enter the required information in the fields. Then, place your cursor where the logpoint should appear. Once you are satisfied, click Apply. The logpoint is added, as shown in Figure 11-22.

EXAM TIP   While it is important for you to know how to configure both a snapshot and a logpoint, it is far more important for you to know the difference between the two. Snapshots allow a cloud engineer to evaluate the state of an application during execution. Logpoints allow for the insertion of log messages into the code, without any modification to source code.

Cloud Platform Status

A cloud engineer is also required to understand the state of the cloud environment itself, not just the specific application, projects, and services. For global services, go to the home page of Cloud Console and locate the Google Cloud Platform Status card on the dashboard (see Figure 11-23).

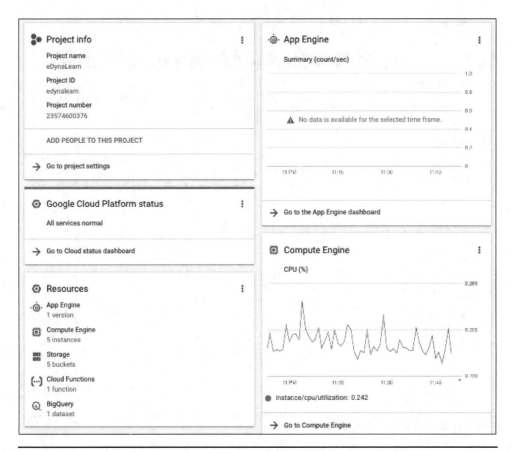

Figure 11-23 GCP Status card

Google also offers a dashboard outside of Cloud Console to show the status of all GCP-based applications in process. The dashboard can be reviewed at https://status .cloud.google.com/. The dashboard, shown in Figure 11-24, provides a list of all GCP services and their current health. A green check mark indicates the environment is up and running. An orange exclamation point indicates there has been some level of disruption, and a red X indicates a service outage.

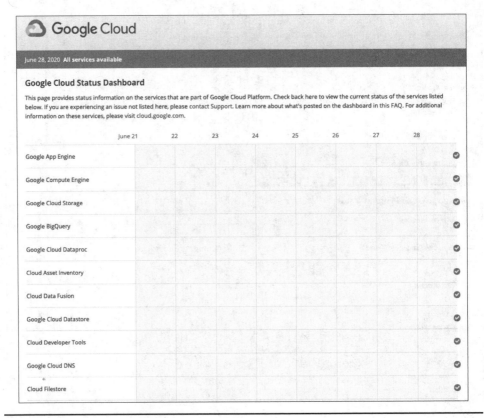

Figure 11-24 Google Cloud Status dashboard

Planning and Estimating with the Pricing Calculator

At the beginning of the book, you learned that a project must be associated with a billing account; otherwise, it will not run. Understanding just how much a resource costs to operate in the Google Cloud Platform environment is essential to many organizations. You may want to understand the value of running a few different database alternatives, for example. Another scenario is identifying the impact that adding clusters or nodes may have to a Google Kubernetes Engine instance. The Pricing Calculator, available at https://cloud.google.com/products/calculator/, provides a GCP user clearly defined pricing estimates when a service or configuration is utilized for a selected resource.

Figure 11-25 shows some services the Pricing Calculator can offer estimated quotations for in relation to GCP usage.

When you click a service, a form will appear asking you to provide specific data. Each service area has varying requirements. By filling in all the required fields and offering some insight into optional parameters, you can get the estimated pricing for a GCP service. In Figure 11-26, an example of creating a price estimate for Cloud SQL for MySQL is presented.

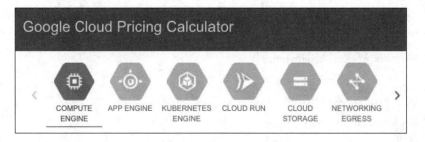

Figure 11-25   Example of a Pricing Calculator's services list

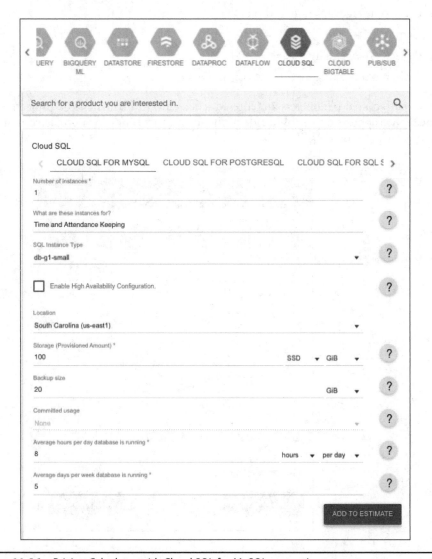

Figure 11-26   Pricing Calculator with Cloud SQL for MySQL cost estimate

The following are some of the required parameters for receiving an estimate for the specific resource:

- Number of database instances
- Name/purpose of the database
- SQL instance type (size)
- High availability requirements
- Data center location
- Primary storage requirements (amount and type)
- Backup storage (amount and type)
- Committed usage
- Projected usage daily
- Projected usage on a per-week basis in days

Once all required parameters are entered, click Add to Estimate. The projected cost for the service appears on the right side of the form. An example of a projected cost estimate appears in Figure 11-27.

Figure 11-27
Sample cost estimate from the Pricing Calculator

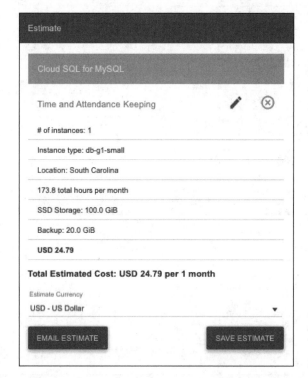

Estimate

Cloud SQL for MySQL

Time and Attendance Keeping

# of instances: 1

Instance type: db-g1-small

Location: South Carolina

173.8 total hours per month

SSD Storage: 100.0 GiB

Backup: 20.0 GiB

USD 24.79

Total Estimated Cost: USD 24.79 per 1 month

Estimate Currency

USD - US Dollar

EMAIL ESTIMATE   SAVE ESTIMATE

In summary, the Pricing Calculator is a tool to estimate the price of services available on the Google Cloud Platform. Using it, you can create a complete picture of the anticipated cost to run a project.

Chapter Review

As a cloud engineer, your responsibility does not end at establishing infrastructure services. You must ensure the health and well-being of the systems operating in your cloud environment. GCP offers a broad portfolio of monitoring, logging, debugging, tracing, error reporting, and profiling solutions as part of the Google Operations Suite, formerly referred to as Stackdriver. While Google has not changed the Stackdriver API names, the Operations Suite now integrates many advanced analytics features within the API collection to evaluate the performance of not just GCP data but also Amazon Web Services and on-premises solutions.

Monitoring allows a cloud engineer to create alerts, policies, and notifications on metrics. Assuming a metric is breached in the system, you and others on your team can be notified the infrastructure is not performing up to par. Logging collects, stores, and manages application and resource log entries. If your data must be stored for more than 30 days to meet organizational or government compliance, you can export it into one of four storage solutions: Cloud Storage, BigQuery, Cloud Pub/Sub, or a storage facility of your choosing. Cloud Diagnostics is just as necessary as monitoring and logging, as it helps your development and operations team understand where applications and resources are not performing as expected. Tools that help evaluate code-level behaviors include Cloud Trace and Cloud Debugging. Cloud Trace provides a distributed tracing service for the developer or cloud engineer to pinpoint what part of the code is running slow. Cloud Debugging provides the developer or cloud engineer running code the ability to identify issues using snapshots. The developer or cloud engineer can also inject log messages into the code execution without modifying the source code.

The chapter ends with a discussion on identifying not just project-based status, but global GCP performance. As a cloud engineer, you can review all systems' conditions at the Google Cloud Status dashboard. Finally, throughout the book, you have learned about numerous services offered by GCP. Google has created the Pricing Calculator to help you understand the cost of operating the services within your cloud environment.

Questions

1. Which Google Operations Suite service provides alerting policies, metrics, health check results, and uptime checks?

   A. Cloud Trace

   B. Cloud Logging

   C. Cloud Profiler

   D. Cloud Monitoring

2. A newly hired cloud engineer is trying to identify line-specific code issues because the DevOps team is complaining about application performance issues. What would you recommend the cloud engineer do in order to isolate the application performance issues using GCP best practices?

   A. Use Cloud Trace to evaluate the code, create reports, and filter trace data to better understand why performance degradation is occurring.

   B. Use Cloud Debugging to evaluate the code, create reports, and filter trace data to better understand why performance degradation is occurring.

   C. Set up a series of alerting policies using Cloud Monitoring to better understand the issues in the platform pertaining to application performance.

   D. Consider merging two host projects together to create a single Workspace.

3. After how many days does a cloud engineer need to plan for exporting log data within GCP due to the platform's threshold?

   A. 14 days

   B. 30 days

   C. 90 days

   D. 60 days

4. You are required to store log entries for three years to meet regulatory compliance control rules. Which sink methods could you use within GCP? (Choose two.)

   A. Cloud SQL

   B. BigQuery

   C. Datastore

   D. Cloud Pub/Sub

5. DynaLearning.com is experiencing performance issues with its recently upgraded learning management system solutions. Customers are complaining about ambiguous system errors they are receiving at certain points in the day. Assuming the solutions were deployed using a Linux virtual machine instance, what two filtering parameters would the cloud engineer or developer need to isolate to find the necessary log data?

   A. Resource Type

   B. Time

   C. Label/Name

   D. Log Level

6. A customer of Dynalearning.com has asked if they can create a dedicated hosting environment for some eDynaLearn system modules. The modules will require the use of two virtual machine instances, Cloud SQL for MySQL, and a mixture of VPC Networking services. How would DynaLearning.com help the customer configure and identify an estimated monthly project cost?

   A. Use Cloud Monitoring.

   B. Use Google Pricing Calculator.

   C. Use BigQuery to evaluate past billing trends to provide the customer an estimate for their service needs.

   D. Google pricing is not available without working with an Enterprise Customer Success Manager.

7. Your organization utilizes GCP to host its distributed intranet across three continents. The help desk is getting many calls about not being able to access certain GCP services. How would you go about identifying whether the performance issues are isolated to your team or a result of a global outage using free GCP resources and following best practices?

   A. Create new alerts that trigger alert notifications.

   B. Use the Google Cloud Platform Support.

   C. Validate the current status of all GCP systems at https://status.cloud.google.com.

   D. Shut down and restart your virtual machine instances.

8. The marketing team at DynaLearning.com wants to better understand technical operations performance, as they need to make sure that GCP performs on par with other cloud competitors. The team requires the use of custom metrics for corporate reporting. What is an alternative approach recommended by Google to gather Monitoring analytics?

   A. Google Analytics

   B. OpenCensus

   C. Amazon Web Service Analytics

   D. Google Profiler

9. Besides GCP, what other infrastructure offerings can utilize the Stackdriver API for monitoring resources? (Choose two.)

   A. Microsoft Azure

   B. Amazon Web Services

   C. On-premises applications

   D. Stackdriver only works with GCP.

10. A cloud engineer has been asked to merge two company projects: project_a and project_b. Both have existing Workspaces and maintain host status. What would the engineer need to do for the two projects to be merged into a single Workspace using project_a as the primary host?

   A. The cloud engineer should go to the first Workspace (project_a), locate Settings, click Merge, and then select project_b. To save the changes, click Merge again.

   B. The cloud engineer should go to the second Workspace (project_b), locate Settings, click Merge, and then select project_a. To save the changes, click Merge again.

   C. The cloud engineer should create a new project, go to Settings, click Merge, and then select both project_a and project_b. To save the changes, click Merge again.

   D. The cloud engineer cannot merge two host projects.

11. DynaLearn LMS recently deployed a new feature for its users. The help desk has received numerous phone calls about errors when users upload documents to the system. What debugging technique would a DevOps or cloud engineer use following Google best practices to isolate the issues during application execution?

   A. Logpoints

   B. Snapshots

   C. Monitoring

   D. Tracing

12. Which tool is required to install the Stackdriver API agents?

   A. Google Cloud Console

   B. Cloud SDK

   C. Cloud Shell

   D. SSH

Answers

1. **D.** Cloud Monitoring offers alerting metrics, health check results, and uptime checks. Cloud Logging is a comprehensive analysis tool that allows a cloud engineer to store, search, analyze, monitor, and establish alerts for logging data and events from Google Cloud. Cloud Profiler provides real-time profiling of resources in production, intending to identify and eliminate issues. Cloud Trace provides latency samples and reporting for App Engine usage only.

2. **A.** Because the DevOps team and cloud engineer are trying to identify line-specific application code issues, that should automatically trigger an evaluation of App Engine code. Isolating the code within the instance can easily be accomplished using Cloud Trace. Cloud Debugging is not ideal, as it is a testing tool for

inspecting the application state while it is still running. Answer C is incorrect because Cloud Monitoring will not contribute the best results to isolating the issue. It may provide insights using alerts, but it cannot solve the actual problem. Answer D is incorrect because the question does not indicate the need to merge two host projects or Workspaces.

3. **B.** Cloud Logging is limited to storing up to 30 days of log data. Cloud Logging can amply hold more than 14 days of data. However, after 30 days, a requirement to create an external sink is necessary to meet operational and regulatory norms. Therefore, both answers C and D are incorrect.

4. **B** and **D.** Google offers three ways to store external log data besides custom storage and the use of Splunk, a third-party tool. The methods are Cloud Storage, BigQuery, and Cloud Pub/Sub. Cloud SQL and Datastore are not standard approaches used by GCP to manage log entries.

5. **A** and **B.** While the name of the resource may be useful, assuming there is only one resource required, only Resource Type and Time are ideal for filtering the log data to isolate the technical anomalies. Log Level can help reduce the number of entries; however, it is impossible to know if the solution is throwing an error classified using a flag such as Warning, Info, or Critical. Using a label or name does not help filter log data for technical anomalies specifically; it helps to better qualify the result sets alone.

6. **B.** The easiest way to estimate pricing is to use Google Pricing Calculator with projected configuration data for each resource. Cloud Monitoring will not offer any value to identifying price estimates. BigQuery can help estimate certain usage requirements; however, it does not provide specific project costs across all resources. Answer D is not an actual method.

7. **C.** The status of all global operations can be viewed at http://status.cloud.google .com. Alerts and triggers do not provide any insight into the state of global operations. Reaching out to Google Cloud Platform Support can also provide you the answer, but it is not a free and easily accessible online method to identify global operations status. Shutting down and restarting a system provides no visibility to global operations indicators specific to a given environment.

8. **B.** OpenCensus, an open source project supported by GCP, provides extended analytics and metrics not offered by the Stackdriver Monitoring API. While not covered in this text, Google Analytics is another Google product that gathers data specific to public-facing websites outside of GCP. A user may integrate Google Analytics to better understand traffic activity to their public website for search engine optimization. Amazon Web Services offers many analytics solutions, but it does not integrate with the Stackdriver Monitoring API. Only the data ingested from AWS or an on-premises platform can help monitor visibility using monitoring features within Operations Suite. Google Profiler provides real-time profiling of resources in production to help a cloud engineer identify and eliminate performance issues; therefore, it is not a Monitoring tool for extending the features as described.

9. **B** and **C.** Stackdriver API also supports data ingest from Amazon Web Services and on-premises applications. At this time, there is no support for Microsoft Azure. Answer D is an inaccurate statement.

10. **A.** Since the primary project is project_a, the cloud engineer needs to merge the two projects from project_a's settings area. The initial clicking of the Merge button allows the cloud engineer to view all projects available. They need to select project_b and then merge the two projects. The combined Workspace will then contain project_a and project_b, where project_a is the primary host. Answer B has the opposite impact of what is desired. Answer C would create an unnecessary project, project_c. Answer D is incorrect because merging two project Workspaces is indeed feasible, as seen in answer A.

11. **B.** Isolating specific code lines while runtime execution occurs to observe unusual behavior can be accomplished using a snapshot. Snapshots allow a cloud engineer to evaluate the state of an application during execution. Logpoints allow for the insertion of log messages into the code, without any modification to the source code. Monitoring does not provide the execution of specific features to help mitigate code-based issues. It can only possibly alert the help desk of potential issues, assuming an alert or policy is defined. Cloud Trace only offers reporting outputs to assist in mitigating issues; tracing does not offer code-level-specific execution support.

12. **D.** You must use an SSH client, even if it is the web browser–based interface at cloud.google.com, to install an agent. You cannot install an agent using Cloud Console, Cloud Shell, or Cloud SDK, as these changes must be made local to the virtual machine instance.

Objective Map

Google Cloud Certified Associate Cloud Engineer

Official Exam Objective	Chapter
1.0 Setting up a cloud solution environment	
1.1 Setting up cloud projects and accounts. Activities include:	2
• Creating projects	2
• Assigning users to predefined IAM roles within a project	2, 10
• Managing users in Cloud Identity (manually and automated)	2, 10
• Enabling APIs within projects	2
• Provisioning one or more Stackdriver workspaces	2, 11
1.2 Managing billing configuration. Activities include:	2
• Creating one or more billing accounts	2
• Linking projects to a billing account	2
• Establishing billing budgets and alerts	2
• Setting up billing exports to estimate daily/monthly charge	2
1.3 Installing and configuring the command line interface (CLI), specifically the Cloud SDK (e.g., setting the default project)	1, 2
2.0 Planning and configuring a cloud solution	
2.1 Planning and estimating GCP product use using the Pricing Calculator	11
2.2 Planning and configuring compute resources. Considerations include:	1
• Selecting appropriate compute choices for a given workload (e.g., Compute Engine, Google Kubernetes Engine, App Engine, Cloud Run, Cloud Functions)	3, 4, 5, 6
• Using preemptible VMs and custom machine types as appropriate	3
2.3 Planning and configuring data storage options. Considerations include:	1, 7
• Product choice (e.g., Cloud SQL, BigQuery, Cloud Spanner, Cloud Bigtable)	1, 7
• Choosing storage options (e.g., Standard, Nearline, Coldline, Archive)	7

Official Exam Objective	Chapter
2.4 Planning and configuring network resources. Tasks include:	1, 8
• Differentiating load balancing options	8
• Identifying resource locations in a network for availability	8
• Configuring Cloud DNS	8

3.0 Deploying and implementing a cloud solution

3.1 Deploying and implementing Compute Engine resources. Tasks include:	3
• Launching a compute instance using Cloud Console and Cloud SDK (gcloud) (e.g., assign disks, availability policy, SSH keys)	3
• Creating an autoscaled managed instance group using an instance template	3
• Generating/uploading a custom SSH key for instances	3
• Configuring a VM for Stackdriver monitoring and logging	3, 11
• Assessing compute quotas and requesting increases	3
• Installing the Stackdriver Agent for monitoring and logging	3, 11
3.2 Deploying and implementing Google Kubernetes Engine resources. Tasks include:	4
• Deploying a Google Kubernetes Engine cluster	4
• Deploying a container application to Google Kubernetes Engine using pods	4
• Configuring Google Kubernetes Engine application monitoring and logging	4, 11
3.3 Deploying and implementing App Engine, Cloud Run, and Cloud Functions resources. Tasks include, where applicable:	5, 6
• Deploying an application, updating scaling configuration, versions, and traffic splitting	5, 6
• Deploying an application that receives Google Cloud events (e.g., Cloud Pub/Sub events, Cloud Storage object change notification events)	5, 6, 7
3.4 Deploying and implementing data solutions. Tasks include:	7
• Initializing data systems with products (e.g., Cloud SQL, Cloud Datastore, BigQuery, Cloud Spanner, Cloud Pub/Sub, Cloud Bigtable, Cloud Dataproc, Cloud Dataflow, Cloud Storage)	7
• Loading data (e.g., command line upload, API transfer, import/export, load data from Cloud Storage, streaming data to Cloud Pub/Sub)	7
3.5 Deploying and implementing networking resources. Tasks include:	1, 8
• Creating a VPC with subnets (e.g., custom-mode VPC, shared VPC)	8
• Launching a Compute Engine instance with custom network configuration (e.g., internal-only IP address, Google private access, static external and private IP address, network tags)	8
• Creating ingress and egress firewall rules for a VPC (e.g., IP subnets, tags, service accounts)	8

Official Exam Objective	Chapter
4.3 Managing App Engine and Cloud Run resources. Tasks include:	5, 6
• Adjusting application traffic splitting parameters	5, 6
• Setting scaling parameters for autoscaling instances	5, 6
• Working with management interfaces (e.g., Cloud Console, Cloud Shell, Cloud SDK)	5, 6
4.4 Managing storage and database solutions. Tasks include:	2, 7
• Moving objects between Cloud Storage buckets	7
• Converting Cloud Storage buckets between storage classes	7
• Setting object life cycle management policies for Cloud Storage buckets	7
• Executing queries to retrieve data from data instances (e.g., Cloud SQL, BigQuery, Cloud Spanner, Cloud Datastore, Cloud Bigtable)	7
• Estimating costs of a BigQuery query	7
• Backing up and restoring data instances (e.g., Cloud SQL, Cloud Datastore)	7
• Reviewing job status in Cloud Dataproc, Cloud Dataflow, or BigQuery	7
• Working with management interfaces (e.g., Cloud Console, Cloud Shell, Cloud SDK)	7
4.5 Managing networking resources. Tasks include:	8
• Adding a subnet to an existing VPC	8
• Expanding a subnet to have more IP addresses	8
• Reserving static external or internal IP addresses	8
• Working with management interfaces (e.g., Cloud Console, Cloud Shell, Cloud SDK)	8
4.6 Monitoring and logging. Tasks include:	11
• Creating Stackdriver alerts based on resource metrics	11
• Creating Stackdriver custom metrics	11
• Configuring log sinks to export logs to external systems (e.g., on-premises or BigQuery)	11
• Viewing and filtering logs in Stackdriver	11
• Viewing specific log message details in Stackdriver	11
• Using cloud diagnostics to research an application issue (e.g., viewing Cloud Trace data, using Cloud Debug to view an application point-in-time)	11
• Using cloud diagnostics to research an application issue (e.g., viewing Cloud Trace data, using Cloud Debug to view an application point-in-time)	11
• Viewing Google Cloud Platform status	11
• Working with management interfaces (e.g., Cloud Console, Cloud Shell, Cloud SDK)	11

Official Exam Objective	Chapter
5.0 Configuring access and security	
5.1 Managing identity and access management (IAM). Tasks include:	10
• Viewing IAM role assignments	2, 10
• Assigning IAM roles to accounts or Google Groups	2, 10
• Defining custom IAM roles	10
5.2 Managing service accounts. Tasks include:	2, 10
• Managing service accounts with limited privileges	10
• Assigning a service account to VM instances	10
• Granting access to a service account in another project	10
5.3 Viewing audit logs for project and managed services	10

About the Online Content

This book comes complete with TotalTester Online customizable practice exam software with 100 practice exam questions.

System Requirements

The current and previous major versions of the following desktop browsers are recommended and supported: Chrome, Microsoft Edge, Firefox, and Safari. These browsers update frequently, and sometimes an update may cause compatibility issues with the TotalTester Online or other content hosted on the Training Hub. If you run into a problem using one of these browsers, please try using another until the problem is resolved.

Your Total Seminars Training Hub Account

To get access to the online content you will need to create an account on the Total Seminars Training Hub. Registration is free, and you will be able to track all your online content using your account. You may also opt in if you wish to receive marketing information from McGraw Hill or Total Seminars, but this is not required for you to gain access to the online content.

Privacy Notice

McGraw Hill values your privacy. Please be sure to read the Privacy Notice available during registration to see how the information you have provided will be used. You may view our Corporate Customer Privacy Policy by visiting the McGraw Hill Privacy Center. Visit the **mheducation.com** site and click **Privacy** at the bottom of the page.

Single User License Terms and Conditions

Online access to the digital content included with this book is governed by the McGraw Hill License Agreement outlined next. By using this digital content you agree to the terms of that license.

Access   To register and activate your Total Seminars Training Hub account, simply follow these easy steps.

1. Go to this URL: **hub.totalsem.com/mheclaim**

2. To register and create a new Training Hub account, enter your e-mail address, name, and password on the **Register** tab. No further personal information (such as credit card number) is required to create an account.

   If you already have a Total Seminars Training Hub account, enter your email address and password on the **Log in** tab.

3. Enter your Product Key: `2xgn-743r-574x`

4. Click to accept the user license terms.

5. For new users, click the **Register and Claim** button to create your account. For existing users, click the **Log in and Claim** button.

   You will be taken to the Training Hub and have access to the content for this book.

Duration of License   Access to your online content through the Total Seminars Training Hub will expire one year from the date the publisher declares the book out of print. Your purchase of this McGraw Hill product, including its access code, through a retail store is subject to the refund policy of that store.

The Content is a copyrighted work of McGraw Hill, and McGraw Hill reserves all rights in and to the Content. The Work is © 2021 by McGraw Hill.

Restrictions on Transfer   The user is receiving only a limited right to use the Content for the user's own internal and personal use, dependent on purchase and continued ownership of this book. The user may not reproduce, forward, modify, create derivative works based upon, transmit, distribute, disseminate, sell, publish, or sublicense the Content or in any way commingle the Content with other third-party content without McGraw Hill's consent.

Limited Warranty   The McGraw Hill Content is provided on an "as is" basis. Neither McGraw Hill nor its licensors make any guarantees or warranties of any kind, either express or implied, including, but not limited to, implied warranties of merchantability or fitness for a particular purpose or use as to any McGraw Hill Content or the information therein or any warranties as to the accuracy, completeness, correctness, or results to be obtained from, accessing or using the McGraw Hill Content, or any material referenced in such Content or any information entered into licensee's product by users or other persons and/or any material available on or that can be accessed through the licensee's product (including via any hyperlink or otherwise) or as to non-infringement of third-party rights. Any warranties of any kind, whether express or implied, are disclaimed. Any material or data obtained through use of the McGraw Hill Content is at your own discretion and risk and user understands that it will be solely responsible for any resulting damage to its computer system or loss of data.

Neither McGraw Hill nor its licensors shall be liable to any subscriber or to any user or anyone else for any inaccuracy, delay, interruption in service, error or omission, regardless of cause, or for any damage resulting therefrom.

In no event will McGraw Hill or its licensors be liable for any indirect, special or consequential damages, including but not limited to, lost time, lost money, lost profits or good will, whether in contract, tort, strict liability or otherwise, and whether or not such damages are foreseen or unforeseen with respect to any use of the McGraw Hill Content.

TotalTester Online

TotalTester Online provides you with a simulation of the Google Cloud Certified Associate Cloud Engineer exam. Exams can be taken in Practice Mode or Exam Mode. Practice Mode provides an assistance window with hints, references to the book, explanations of the correct and incorrect answers, and the option to check your answer as you take the test. Exam Mode provides a simulation of the actual exam. The number of questions, the types of questions, and the time allowed are intended to be an accurate representation of the exam environment. The option to customize your quiz allows you to create custom exams from selected domains or chapters, and you can further customize the number of questions and time allowed.

To take a test, follow the instructions provided in the previous section to register and activate your Total Seminars Training Hub account. When you register you will be taken to the Total Seminars Training Hub. From the Training Hub Home page, select **Google Cloud Certified Associate Cloud Engineer TotalTester** from the Study drop-down menu at the top of the page, or from the list of Your Topics on the Home page. You can then select the option to customize your quiz and begin testing yourself in Practice Mode or Exam Mode. All exams provide an overall grade and a grade broken down by domain.

Technical Support

For questions regarding the TotalTester or operation of the Training Hub, visit **www.totalsem.com** or e-mail **support@totalsem.com**.

For questions regarding book content, visit **www.mheducation.com/customerservice**.

A record   Information stored in a DNS server recordset that associates a domain name to an IPv4 address.

AAAA record   Information stored in a DNS server recordset that associates a domain name to an IPv6 address.

action   Associated with a firewall rule. Actions indicate if a rule allows or denies either ingress or egress traffic.

aggregator   Describes the way to aggregate data points across a times series. By default, aggregation results in a single line so that the values are the result of applying the aggregators across a time series.

alerting policy   Notification method that determines if the performance of an instance within a cluster, an entire cluster, or a container breaches an expected performance threshold.

aligner   Allows for the data points within an individual time series to be brought together under an equal period of time. When aligned for each time series, data points are aggregated into a single point. The value of the single point is determined by the aligner option used.

alignment period   The period determining the time interval in which aggregation takes place.

Apache Hadoop   Available as a managed service with Cloud Dataproc, this open source platform is intended for processing large volumes of data over cluster servers.

Apache Spark   Available as a managed service with Cloud Dataproc, this open source platform is intended for performing analytic activities associated with large datasets over cluster servers.

application programming interface (API)   A software intermediary that allows two applications to talk to each other.

archival storage   Storage intended for infrequent access to files, usually greater than one year.

Associate Cloud Engineer   A technical professional, often referred to as a "cloud administrator," who deploys applications, monitors operations, and manages enterprise solutions.

audit logs   A record of all activities that occur in an information system. Often used to identify critical issues, warnings, and information details regarding configuration or access control issues.

auditing   Captures all activities for who you are and what you did through logging.

authentication   Determines who you are when accessing any project or resource in Google Cloud Platform (GCP).

authorization   Determines what you can do when accessing any project or resource in Google Cloud Platform (GCP).

autohealing   Enables the automatic restart of applications that are compromised. When this feature is enabled, a failed instance is automatically restarted. The instance is re-created so clients can be served again.

automatic scaling   Associated with App Engine, the creation of an instance is achieved under several conditions: request rate, response latencies, and specific application metrics. A minimum number of instances must be available to operate in App Engine.

automatic updating   The ability to deploy a new version of software to one or more instances in a managed instance group.

autoscaling   A method to add or remove instances from a managed instance group. Load capacity determines the use of autoscaling.

basic scaling   Concept associated with App Engine in which instances are created only when requests are received. Each instance shuts down when the application idles. Intended for intermittent or user-based activities.

BigQuery   Google-built relational database analytics solution intended for data warehousing and big analytics data appliances. The ingest rate tends to be tens of thousands to millions of rows per minute. Can hold petabytes of data, with the ability to hold the greatest number of columns and rows of all the Google-supported relational database products.

binding   Approach associated with identity and access management (IAM) data structures intended for linking user accounts, Google groups, Google domains, or service accounts to a defined role.

block storage   Storage approach that breaks up data into smaller increments, known as blocks. Each block has a unique reference identifier.

boot disk   A persistent disk that stores an operating system and other mission-critical software needed to start a Compute Engine virtual machine instance.

bq   The command-line operator used to execute BigQuery services.

bucket   A resource inside a project that maintains a global namespace, which means that when you call the resource, it can be unique across all projects, not just a single project.

budget alert   Method in Google Cloud Platform (GCP) intended to inform one or more users that a spending threshold has been reached or exceeded.

cache   In-memory data store that allows fast access to data. Cache access is measurable in submilliseconds. Any delays in access to data results in latency (that is, a reduction in transfer speed from one location to another).

capital expenditure   When an organization makes a lump-sum acquisition or agrees to a long-term lease to operate IT resources.

cbt   The command-line operator used to execute Bigtable services.

classless inter-domain routing (CIDR)   A type of IP addressing scheme that improves IP address allocation by extending the IPv4 range.

cloud architecture   Consists of eight components: applications, data, runtime, middleware, operating systems, virtualization, servers, and storage, part of which may be hosted by a third-party service provider.

Cloud Armor   GPC built-in load-balancing security service for HTTP-bound traffic. Restricts access based on IP address. Offers protection from SQL injection and scripting attacks. Can block activity using geolocation targets as well as rules at the network and application layers. Similar to a network WAF (web application firewall).

Cloud Bigtable   A wide-column NoSQL database where all rows do not need to map to a column to create a fixed schema. Storage capacity is designed for petabyte scale. Bigtable offers consistent sub-latency, replication, high availability, durability, and resilience in the event of any zonal failures.

Cloud Billing account   The central hub to associate payment information with one or more projects.

Cloud CDN   Google Cloud Platform (GCP) content delivery network solution. Cloud CDN enables users to request content from anywhere around the world and experience consistent performance at a given endpoint. Since the content is cached through a distributed global network, there is often a reduction in latency issues.

cloud computing   The consumption of IT resources in an on-demand capacity.

Cloud Console   An interactive web-based interface that allows users to deploy, scale, and diagnose production issues using a browser.

cloud dashboards   Leveraging the Dashboards API, cloud dashboards are standard and customizable dashboards integrated into Google Cloud Platform (GCP) as visualization tools to meet project needs for managing alerts, notifications, and logs and for monitoring data.

Cloud Dataflow   A managed service that works with Cloud Pub/Sub, BigQuery, Cloud Dataproc, and other Google Cloud Platform (GCP) services for processing streaming and batch datasets using Java and Python APIs. Also known as Apache Beam.

Cloud Dataproc   A managed Apache Spark and Hadoop data service designed for big data applications intended for analysis and machine learning.

Cloud Datastore   Nonrelational database that supports nonstructured datasets with nonanalytic, nonrelational storage requirements. The database is based on the document structure and does not have a fixed schema, although a pattern does exist to organize document data in a system.

Cloud Debugger   A testing tool that enables an engineer to inspect the state of an application, without reducing the application or having to stop it. The output produces logging statement entries, making it easier to diagnose issues.

Cloud DNS   The Domain Name Service enables the mapping of a domain name to an IP address.

Cloud Error Reporting   Analyzes and aggregates all errors in one or more cloud applications. When errors are detected, notifications are sent out based on set conditions.

Cloud Filestore   A fully managed no-operations service that mounts file shares on Google Compute Engine (GCE) instances as well as Google Kubernetes Engine (GKE) for containers to reference shared datasets.

Cloud Firestore   A managed NoSQL database that leverages a document data model similar to Cloud Datastore. Supports storing, synchronizing, and querying data in distributed applications at near-real-time capacity. Offers transactional and multiregional replication support.

Cloud Functions   Quickly scalable solutions that are event-driven and can easily extend to Google and third-party services.

Cloud Identity   Google's identity, access, app, and endpoint management (IAM/ EMM) platform enabling IT operations to protect data across various workspace types.

Cloud Identity and Access Management   Also referred to as Cloud IAM, this is Google's security offering that supports fine-grained access control and visibility for managing cloud resources in Google Cloud Platform (GCP).

Cloud Interconnect   Enables an organization to connect its networking infrastructure to the Google Cloud Platform (GCP) through extended reach via a private, dedicated network connection (not using the Internet).

Cloud Key Management Service   A cloud-hosted management key service that allows for the hosting of cryptographic keys for cloud, similar to on-premises.

Cloud Logging   A comprehensive analysis tool that allows a cloud engineer to store, search, analyze, monitor, and establish alerts for logging data and events from Google Cloud.

Cloud Marketplace   Website hosted by Google that offers commercial off-the-shelf products, predefined templates with Deployment Manager, virtual machines with open source applications, and readily available productivity solutions for user consumption.

Cloud Memorystore   A managed Redis service, Cloud Memorystore is an open source cache solution offering a fully managed in-memory data store with submillisecond data access, along with features such as scalability, a well-built security posture, and high availability—all managed by Google.

Cloud Monitoring   Provides alerting policies, metrics, health check results, and uptime check results based on criteria set by a cloud engineer.

Cloud Profiler   Provides real-time profiling of resources in production with the goal of identifying and eliminating issues.

cloud provider   Offers IT resources that an organization would typically need to purchase for the data center, but for cloud computing consumption.

Cloud Pub/Sub   An asynchronous messaging service that decouples services that produce events from services that process events. Three key elements to Pub/Sub are topics, subscriptions, and messages. Pub/Sub also offers durable message storage and real-time message delivery with high availability throughout Google Cloud Platform's worldwide footprint.

Cloud Router   Google-based software-defined router that manages routing traffic between Google Cloud Platform (GCP) virtual private clouds, alternative cloud provider virtual private clouds, and on-premises infrastructures with the support of a Border Gateway Protocol (BGP).

Cloud Run   A Google-managed serverless compute platform that requires an application run in stateless containers.

Cloud Run for Anthos   A Google Kubernetes Engine (GKE) serverless container option built on Knative, an open source platform. Anthos allows for mixed architecture support between on-premises and cloud consumption.

Cloud SDK   A collection of command-line tools that support development across the Google Cloud Platform.

Cloud Shell   A web-based interactive shell environment specific to the Google Cloud Platform. Users can manage projects and resources without having to install a software development kit (SDK) on their computers.

Cloud Spanner   Google-built relational database intended for large data ingest with global distribution. Often characterized by systems requiring consistency, transactional integrity, and redundancy at scale and speed.

Cloud SQL   A managed database service for relational usage, including MySQL, PostgreSQL, and SQL Server. Intended for databases that require minimum horizontal scaling. Architecture by design is for adding more memory and CPU capacity instead of adding additional servers to a cluster.

Cloud Status dashboard   Web page found on Google Cloud Platform that indicates the status of all global services. The site can be accessed at https://status.cloud.google.com/.

Cloud Storage A type of object storage used when there is a requirement for extensive storage capacity as well as the ability to share that capacity. Files are treated as atomic units.

Cloud Storage bucket An affordable cloud object storage solution. See *bucket* for a full definition.

Cloud Trace Specific to App Engine, this tool set provides latency samples and reporting for application performance.

cluster A collection of computing resources that are aggregated with the intent of coordinating compute capacity to address one or more tasks.

cluster master Acts as the single endpoint for a cluster.

CNAME A canonical name record stored in DNS that associates an alias name to the true host name for a given web-based system.

coldline storage Storage intended for infrequent access to files, usually around 90 days or more.

container An approach to packaging applications together with libraries and other dependencies that isolates an environment to run necessary software services.

Container Registry A single location to manage Docker images, perform vulnerability analysis, and decide who can access what with granular access controls.

custom image Instance type when there is a business need for a specific operating system and application that must run in a dedicated environment and be configured in a specific manner.

custom role User-defined and self-maintained permissions. Roles are bundled using existing predefined roles and can only be applied at the organization and project levels.

DaemonSet Ensures that nodes run a copy of a Pod. DaemonSet acts as both a counter for added nodes and garbage collection monitor for deleted nodes.

debug snapshots Method for capturing local variables and the call stack at specific points in source code. Allows for certain conditions and locations to return feedback from app data and view it in detail for debugging purposes.

Deployment Manager Provides an approach to deploy all resources needed for an application in a declarative format using YAML, in conjunction with Python or Jinja2 templates to parameterize the configuration.

Deployment A set of like-kind Pods managed by GKE. When an instance becomes unhealthy, a Deployment can run one or more replicas of an application to replace failed or unresponsive instances. Deployments ensure that application instances are available to serve user requests perpetually.

DNSSEC Domain Name Service Security Extensions (DNSSEC) offers authentication of DNS data as well as data integrity protection.

document database A class of NoSQL databases for storing semi-structured data not requiring a fixed schema. Cloud Datastore and Cloud Firebase are both document databases.

domain Virtual group of all the Google accounts that have been created in an organization's G Suite domain or Cloud Identity platform.

egress The flow of traffic sent from a target to a destination. Rules apply to packets for new sessions where the source of the packet is the target.

enforcement status Method to determine if a firewall rule is active. Often used to debug firewall rules exclusively.

ephemeral IP address An IP address that does not persist with a resource beyond its active state.

event Occurs when a particular action initiates within the Google Cloud Platform.

external IP Type of IP address used as a method to communicate over the Internet not reserved for private networks.

file storage Also called file-level or file-based storage, file storage organizes data inside structured folders. The folders may maintain a hierarchical design within the structure.

filestore High-performance file storage for Google Cloud users.

firewall rule Allows or denies traffic from the VM instance configured. Rules are defined by the network, while connections are managed at the instance level.

flexible environment Standalone serverless environment that requires supportable resources, including Docker containers, code libraries, operating systems, and third-party applications. Applications utilizing the flexible environment will often support backend and background processes.

folder A grouping of resources that share standard identity and access management (IAM) policies. May contain multiple subfolders or resources. Can only be part of a single parent relationship.

function A response to a trigger whereby a data argument is passed to a given event.

gcloud A cloud-based SDK component used with most Google Cloud Platform (GCP) services such as Compute Engine, Cloud SQL, and networking services.

Google App Engine (GAE) When an organization wants a hands-off approach to system administrative but wants to develop and deploy a custom application, Google App Engine is the method used. GAE is Google's Platform as a Service offering.

Google Compute Engine (GCE) The Google Infrastructure as a Service (IaaS) offering allows users to create virtualized environments, called a virtual machine (VM), instead of having to manage traditional hardware and software in a server environment.

Google Kubernetes Engine (GKE)   Google Kubernetes Engine (GKE) is a managed, production-ready environment for running containerized applications on Kubernetes, a portable, extensible, open source platform.

Google Operations Suite   Formerly referred to as Stackdriver, this service offering collects metrics, logs, and event data from Google Compute Engine (GCE), Google Kubernetes Engine (GKE), and Google App Engine (GAE) environments, depending on suite feature. Operations Suite also collects operational and access logs from across Google Cloud Platform (GCP), including BigQuery, Bigtable, and Firestore. Data ingestion is available from Amazon Web Services and on-premises data sources.

Google-managed service account   Runs internal Google processes on behalf of the user. This service account type is publicly viewable, although it is also viewable in IAM. All Google-managed accounts are granted Project Editor role by default. You cannot delete a service account unless its associated project is deleted as well.

graphical processor unit (GPU)   Processing unit that leverages non-CPU capabilities to off-load compute capacity when data ingest is intensive. GPU computing is often used with graphics management, machine learning, and other analytics-intensive operations.

group   Used to apply a policy to many like-kind users.

gsutil   A Cloud SDK utility for managing storage in Google Cloud Platform (GCP).

hard disk drive   A type of persistent storage available in Google Cloud Platform (GCP) that uses older technologies than flash-based SSD storage, resulting in lower operational cost and weaker system performance.

HBase   Apache-based database used with Cloud Dataproc for managing services.

health check   A method to determine if backend systems such as instance groups and zonal network endpoint groups will properly respond to traffic.

HTTP/HTTPS load balancing   Globally available load-balancing capability in Google Cloud Platform (GCP) that manages HTTP and HTTPS traffic. Features included with this load balancer are target proxies, forwarding rules, and backend services to handle received requests.

hybrid cloud   In a hybrid cloud, an organization might use certain commercially available applications that are only distributed via a public cloud but also require its sensitive data and custom applications be maintained in a dedicated hosting environment.

identity   The digital record of the user or account within Google Cloud Platform (GCP).

image   An instance that contains an operating system to create boot disks.

Infrastructure as a Service (IaaS)   Offers the deployment and management capacity of preconfigured and virtualized hardware to organizations that require compute power.

ingress   The incoming connections from a given source to a target instance within a Virtual Private Cloud (VPC) network.

input/output operations per second (IOPS)   A measurement methodology that provides performance data on solid-state drive (SSD) and hard disk drive (HDD) persistent storage.

instance   Another name for a virtual machine. Instances are associated with Google Compute Engine.

instance group   A collection of virtual machine instances that are available within a single unit. The instance either acts as a form of system redundancy or coexists with one or more virtual machines to support a complete enterprise system.

instance template   A global resource in Google Cloud Platform (GCP) that is appropriate if the goal is to standardize configuration settings such as the machine type, boot disk image or container image, labels, and other instance properties.

internal IP   A private IP address intended for handling traffic from a Virtual Private Cloud (VPC), shared VPCs, or peered VPCs.

internal TCP/UDP load balancing   Type of load balancer only available to internal Virtual Private Clouds (VPCs).

Internet Control Message Protocol (ICMP)   Protocol used for communicating operational data relating to the operational state of network devices.

invoiced billing accounts   Typically used by organizations that consume extensive Google Cloud Platform (GCP) resources or have multiple billing statements under one organizational or resource hierarchy. Payment is not automatically debited.

IPv4   Formally known as Internet Protocol version 4. The protocol uses 32 bits to represent an IP address whereby an address is written as four groups of digits ranging from 0 to 255.

IPv6   Formally known as Internet Protocol version 6. The protocol uses 128 bits to represent an IP address whereby an address is written as eight groups of four hexadecimal digits.

job   A controller object representing a finite task. Jobs run tasks until completion rather than until a desired state is reached.

kubectl   The command-line utility used to configure and manage Kubernetes clusters.

Kubernetes   A container orchestration system created by Google.

Kubernetes cluster   Consists of several machines accessible from Compute Engine that work together to form a cluster.

label   Using a key–value pair, a label (or tag) can be assigned to resources in Google Cloud Platform (GCP).

least privilege   A security best practice associated with granting only the permissions necessary for a user or service to complete a task successfully.

load balancing   Allows for the even distribution of workloads across an infrastructure.

local solid-state drive (SSD) storage   High-performance, transient, local block storage.

log sink   Approach to export logging data into a long-term data facility because Cloud Logging only has a 30-day retention policy.

logging   Approach used to gather and record information about events that occur during application or system processing.

logpoint   A log statement written to an application log upon the execution of a statement.

machine type   A virtual machine configuration that requires the identification of specific parameters, including CPU, storage, and memory capacity. There are two types of machine types: predefined and custom.

managed instance group   Also be referred to as a MIG, this instance type enables one or more virtual machines to operate at a given time concurrently. Workloads within a managed instance group support scalability, high availability, and autonomous services within Google Cloud Platform (GCP), including regional deployments, autoscaling, autohealing, and updating.

managed zone   A container that handles all DNS records in a given domain.

manual scaling   Associated with App Engine, this type of scaling supports operational continuity based on how many instances run regardless of load level. Intended for systems that run based on complex capacity needs.

Marketplace Deployment Manager   Solution that provides summary data about the current state of the deployment as well as how to access administrative control points once the process is complete.

memcached   An in-memory key–value store intended exclusively for caching data.

message   The combination of data and associative attributes that a publisher sends to a topic, which is then delivered to a subscriber.

message attribute   A key–value pair associated with Pub/Sub that the publisher can define for a message.

metrics   A measure used to evaluate performance of resources in Google Cloud Platform (GCP), with particular emphasis on compute, storage, and networking resources.

microservice architecture   A type of software development technique that allows for an application to be treated as a collection of lightweight, loosely coupled services.

monitoring   A method of collecting data from applications, virtual machines, and Google Cloud Platform (GCP) resources in the form of metrics, events, and metadata.

multiregional object storage   A type of object storage accessible across multiple regions, enabled by redundancy and disaster recovery options that are in place in case of failure at one or more zones.

nearline storage   Storage intended for infrequent access to files, usually around 30 days.

network endpoint group   A type of configuration object to specify a group of backend endpoints. Network endpoint groups, or NEGs, are commonly used with containers.

Network Peering   Allows the administrator to establish services across the Virtual Private Cloud (VPC) network by using internal IP addresses.

network TCP/UDP load balancing   Type of load balancer that supports regional, non-proxy load balancing. Can be utilized to balance UDP, TCP, and SSL traffic on ports not supported by other load-balancing alternatives.

node   One or more working instances that run a containerized applications and other workloads.

node pool   Node pool is a group of nodes within a cluster that all have the same configuration. Using a NodeConfig specification, a cluster can be deployed containing either a single node or many nodes.

nonrelational database (NoSQL)   Also referred to as a NoSQL database, this type of database is used in organizations looking for speed, flexibility, and scale in comparison to the traditional tabular relational database. The data structure in a NoSQL database may include a key–value, wide column, graph, or document-based design. Whereas a SQL database places constraints on data types and enforces consistency, a NoSQL database does away with most of these requirements to optimize performance.

notification channel   Used to send alerts produced by the Stackdriver Monitoring API to e-mail clients, mobile systems, or enterprise applications meant for alert distribution.

object life cycle management   Supports the configuration of rules to current and future objects in a bucket based on a criteria. When a rule is met, an action is taken on a specific object.

object storage   A storage approach that allows for items to be broken out into distinct units, or objects in isolation. Objects have relevant metadata and a custom identifier.

objects   Persistent entities within Google Kubernetes Engine that manage the operational state of a cluster.

on-premises computing   Also referred to as data center computing. With on-premises computing, an organization manages all IT operations on its own.

OpenCensus   An open source monitoring library.

operational expenditure   With respect to resource-based operational expenditure (OpEx), an organization is not engaged in purchasing or leasing the equipment. Instead, it expenses resources based on consumption and demand, as necessary.

orchestration   The automated configuration, coordination, and management computer systems and software. An example of orchestration is Google Kubernetes Engine, a container orchestration system.

organization   The root of the resource hierarchy in Google Cloud Platform.

permission   Allowable operations assigned to a user, role, or group.

persistent disk   Type of block storage that does not directly attach to a server. Rather, the disk type attaches to the server hosting the network-accessible virtual machine. Two types exist: solid-state disk (SSD) and hard drive disk (HDD).

Platform as a Service (PaaS)   Used to develop and deploy custom applications in the cloud without the need to manage the infrastructure.

Pod   A single instance in a Kubernetes cluster where a process is actively operating. At a minimum, there must be one container for a Pod to exist. Typically operating in a single container, Pods can be distributed when resources are shared. Pods share container resources, including networking and storage capacity.

predefined role   Approach to securing resources, as a predefined role follows the principle of least privilege. Only allows users to gain access to resources they require. Permissions set are updated by Google. Tied to Google-built resources found in Cloud Console.

preemptible instance   Allows for the creation of virtual machines that will terminate after 24 hours. Intended for application testing, quick batch jobs, and to support fault-tolerant applications.

Pricing Calculator   Online tool that offers clearly defined pricing estimates when a service or configuration is utilized for a resource within Google Cloud Platform (GCP).

primitive role   Offers a basic level of access: either owner, editor, or viewer. Can be applied to most Google Cloud Platform (GCP) resources. Grants more control to resources than users often require. Google no longer recommends the use of primitive roles. Supported mostly for backward compatibility reasons.

private cloud   In a private cloud, an organization has exclusive rights to the infrastructure capacity within a third-party hosting provider's domain. While the servers are not hosted in the organization's own data center, the third-party infrastructure that the organization is paying for is dedicated to a given businesses need and is not shared with anyone else.

private IP address   A reserved IP address intended for internal use behind a router or other networking device, not accessible to the public.

project   A project is a master organizer for all Google Cloud resources associated with a focal purpose. Projects contain resources, including APIs, billing information, authentication credentials, and monitoring settings, among other details.

public cloud   In a public cloud, data is stored in an infrastructure that is shared by many organizations. No single organization can take ownership of the infrastructure. Many organizations will share the computing resources offered by the cloud computing provider for security and operational reasons.

public image   Preconfigured image with an operating system that allows for the creation of a persistent boot disk for one or more instances.

Redis An in-memory data structure store that can be used as a database, cache, and message broker.

reducer Computational approach used by the Stackdriver Monitoring API with time-based metrics to calculate max, min, mean, sum, and other aggregate values.

region Geographic-specific target that houses the Google Cloud Platform (GCP) cloud infrastructure.

regional object storage A type of object storage that is location specific, which infers that multiple disks are housed in the same geography or data center. Note, however, that this does not constitute true redundancy or disaster recovery.

regional persistent disk Available as a hard disk drive (HDD) or solid-state drive (SSD), this storage type offers regional block storage replication in two zones.

relational databases Used as a tool to record transactions where data is clearly defined and stored in a series of tables.

Remote Desktop Platform (RDP) Allows for a user to connect to the remote desktops of a Windows Server instance.

ReplicaSet Ensures a stable set of Pods run perpetually. A ReplicaSet is associated with one or more fields, including a selector to set parameters such as the number of Pods that can be acquired, the number of replicas that can be maintained, and a template for establishing the creation of new replicas should new Pods be required.

resource Individualized components that make up all Google Cloud Platform services. Examples of a resource that could reside in a project within the organizational hierarchy might include a Compute Engine virtual machines (VMs) or App Engine instance.

resource hierarchy Method by which a cloud engineer structures an organization, its folders, and projects used to group Google Cloud Platform (GCP) resources.

RFC 1918 Outlines a standardized approach to handling the private assignment of a single IP address.

role Sets of responsibilities or tasks assigned to a given identity.

schema The organization of data within a database, often synonymous with a blueprint or data model.

scope Also referred to as access scope, this is a type of permission granted to the virtual machine instance when associated with API authorization.

Secure Shell (SSH) A software standard to support encrypted data transfer between two computers. For Google Cloud Platform (GCP), the use of Secure Shell is accessible using Cloud Console to the Compute Engine instance. SSH can be used to support secure logins, file transfers, or general-purpose connections.

Secure Socket Layer (SSL) Secure Sockets Layer, or SSL, is a secure protocol providing encryption and authentication to compute resources.

self-service billing account   Used when an organization sets up a form of payment with Google to be billed directly each month. This method requires the use of credit cards or direct ACH transfers for monthly payments to Google.

separation of duties   A security best practice that limits assigned roles to individuals in an organization, ensuring that limits are placed on performing sensitive tasks. Google Cloud Platform (GCP) requires the use of predefined roles that have limited privileges based on the assigned tasks.

serverless computing   Allows a developer to focus on development activities, such as writing code, instead of having to worry about infrastructure and system maintenance.

service account   A machine-based account assigned permissions to access only those resources required. The service account permissions also limit the resources that services control. Service accounts have a unique e-mail address; however, they do not constitute user accounts. Service accounts are similar to "programmatic users" in other environments.

Services (Kubernetes-based)   A Kubernetes Engine feature that enables many sets of Pod endpoints to become a single resource using configurable grouping options.

shared VPC   Also known as XPN in the API and command-line interface, shared VPC enables an administrator to export subnets from an existing Virtual Private Cloud (VPC) network to a host project or other service projects inside the same organization.

Shielded VM   A secure, 64-bit, hardened virtual machine available in Google Cloud Platform (GCP) that has protections against malicious attack vectors such as rootkits.

snapshot   A method to incrementally back up data from a persistent disk.

Software as a Service (SaaS)   Software that is made available exclusively through the Internet.

sole tenancy   An instance that does not share any physical hardware with another virtual machine project.

solid-state drive (SSD)   A type of persistent storage that uses flash memory, resulting in more reliable, consistent performance. SSD storage is more expensive than HDD storage.

splitting traffic   Allows for an organization to divide traffic capacity between one or more application versions. Can be accomplished by IP address, HTTP cookie, or random assignment.

SSL proxy   Type of load balancer that terminates SSL/TLS connections, in which SSL traffic can be decrypted before being forwarding to an VM instance on a load-balanced cluster.

Stackdriver   A series of service-based APIs within the Google Operations Suite that helps monitor, log, trace, and debug applications or resources.

standard environment   Google App Engine approach to establishing a sandbox environment supported by a standalone programming language–based application without a need for an operating system or any third-party software.

standard storage   Storage intended for frequent file access, usually less than 30 days in duration.

stateful workload   Allows for saving data to a persistent disk for its use with a service.

StatefulSet   A set of Pods that maintains unique, persistent identities as well as stable hostnames across Kubernetes Engine that can support regardless of schedule.

static IP address   An IP address that maintains an association to a project unless released.

subnet   A type of regional resource associated with an IP address range.

subscription   A named resource within Cloud Pub/Sub that represents the stream of messages from a single, specific topic to be delivered to a subscribing application.

target   The internal destination or external source system of a packet associated with firewall activity.

TCP   Formally known as Transmission Control Protocol, TCP is an Internet protocol that provides consistent, structured delivery of network data packets.

TCP proxy   A global load balancer offering by Google Cloud Platform (GCP) that requires Premium tier service, as it uses a static, single IP address. This proxy type distributes traffic based on geographic context for optimal compute engine resource performance.

topic   A named resource associated with Cloud Pub/Sub to which messages are sent by a publisher.

tracing   Method for collecting a variety of data points, including latency measures from Google Compute Engine (GCE) and Google App Engine (GAE) resources using Google Operations Suite APIs.

trigger   The result of an event response.

unmanaged instance group   A collection of virtual machines that are self-maintained and contain heterogeneous instances you can arbitrarily add and remove from the group. Unmanaged instance groups do not offer any automation capabilities.

uptime check   An alerting policy that ensures a system properly utilizes a default configuration.

user   Single person who is responsible for executing actions. Can be associated with one or more roles and identities.

User Datagram Protocol (UDP) An Internet protocol offering connectionless communication but lacking the same reliability and guarantees as TCP-based communication.

user-managed service account A type of service account used by an application or virtual machine (VM) instance, not a person, to make authorized API calls for the purpose of creating, reading, updating, or deleting (CRUD) cloud resources.

versioning Approach to keeping a historical record of all objects without risking the accidental deletion of changes.

virtual machine Virtual machine (VM), also referred to as an instance, is an operating system–based environment installed on a hosted environment that imitates dedicated hardware. The virtual machine often has specific end-user applications installed within the virtualized environment.

Virtual Private Cloud (VPC) Allows for the isolation of cloud resources to a specific organization. Public Internet is not required so long as the organization's internal network is connected to the Google Cloud Platform (GCP) platform.

virtual private network (VPN) Commonly referred to as a VPN, a virtual private network allows a user to send traffic from a cloud environment to a defined network. Traffic can be routed dynamically, be route-based, or be supported using policy-based management. Data travelling the network is encrypted within a virtual tunnel between both endpoints.

workload Packaging of containerized, hardware-independent, isolated applications.

Workspace A tool for monitoring resources contained in one or more Google Cloud projects or third-party accounts, including Amazon Web Services (AWS) and on-premises applications.

YAML file A script to create configurations and settings, often used with Google Kubernetes Engine and Google App Engine. YAML is short for "YAML Ain't Markup Language."

zonal persistent disk Available as both standard and SSD persistent disk, this storage approach offers efficient, reliable block storage.

zone Zones are data center–specific resource targets that share specific configuration attributes. A zone is located within a region.

INDEX

A

A resource records, 230
AAAA resource records, 230
access management, 255
    App Engine, Cloud Functions, and Cloud Run, 138
    IAM. *See* identity and access management (IAM)
    questions, 273–277
    review, 273
    service accounts, 266–272
accounts
    billing, 18, 28–29
    organization hierarchy, 20
    projects, 23
    service. *See* service accounts
actions in firewall rules, 216
add command, 95
add-access-config command, 56
add-iam-policy-binding command, 56
add-labels command, 56
add-metadata command, 56
add-tags command, 56
add Workspace approach, 283
Admin role in Compute Engine, 40
agents package repository, 285
aggregators for alert policies, 289
alerts
    budget, 30–31
    Kubernetes Engine policies, 86–87
    Monitoring service, 288–289
    Stackdriver, 284
aligners for alert policies, 289
alignment periods for alert policies, 289
alpha services in billing, 28–29
Analysis Reports for Cloud Trace, 295–296
Anthos, Cloud Run for, 131
Apache Spark service, 185
App Engine, 7, 8, 107
    application deployment, 111–115
    application scaling, 115–117
    vs. Cloud Functions and Cloud Run, 125, 138–140
    components, 110
    vs. Compute Engine and Kubernetes Engine, 108–109
    delivery environment, 107–109
    questions, 120–124
    review, 119–120
    traffic handling, 118–119

app.yaml file, 112–113
application pods in Kubernetes Engine, 82–84
application programming interfaces (APIs)
    defined, 17
    functions, 31–33
applications
    App Engine. *See* App Engine
    Cloud Run deployment of, 129–131
architectures
    cloud, 2–3
    Kubernetes Engine, 74–75
archive storage, 155–156
assigning
    IAM roles, 26, 261
    service accounts to instances, 269–272
attach-disk command, 56
audit logs, 272
autohealing virtual machine instances, 45
automatic scaling
    applications, 115–117
    virtual machine instances, 45
automatic updating for virtual machine instances, 45
Autoscale interface in Kubernetes Engine Pods, 92
availability requirements as pricing factor, 302

B

backend-buckets command, 229
backend-services command, 229
background threads for applications, 116
backups
    Cloud Datastore databases, 181
    Cloud SQL databases, 172–173
basic scaling in applications, 115–117
beta services in billing, 28–29
BGP (Border Gateway Protocol), 220
BigQuery databases
    billing data, 30
    configuring, 164–165
    deploying and managing, 177–180
    description, 162
    importing and exporting data, 192–194
    logging data, 292–293
Bigtable databases
    configuring, 169
    deploying and managing, 181–182
    description, 166
    importing and exporting data, 195

335